The Story of a
Christian Motorcycle Gang

UNIVERSITY OF ILLINOIS PRESS

Urbana and Chicago

RIDERS FOR GOD

RICH REMSBERG

Afterword by Colleen McDannell

Library of Congress Cataloging-in-Publication Data
Remsberg, Rich, 1965–
Riders for God : the story of a Christian motorcycle
gang / Rich Remsberg ; afterword by Colleen
McDannell.
p.   cm.
ISBN 0-252-02521-0 (alk. paper)
ISBN 0-252-06943-9 (pbk.: alk. paper)
1. Unchained Gang. 2. Motorcycle gangs—Indi-
ana—Case studies. 3. Motorcycle gangs—Indiana—
Pictorial works. 4. Gang members—Indiana—Reli-
gious life—Case studies. 5. Witness bearing
(Christianity)—Case studies. I. Title.
HV6489.I38R45   2000
277.3'0829—dc21   99-050473

C 5 4 3 2 1

For Lisa,

who had faith in this

when I did not

*In living
one swims through seas
strewn with wrecks.*
                    —*Emerson*

CONTENTS

ACKNOWLEDGMENTS

During the evolution of this project I enjoyed the company and assistance of a tremendous combination of colleagues, friends, and friendly strangers. The list of people to thank is long, and I suppose it is simplest and most appropriate to start with the Indiana University School of Journalism.

I am grateful to Dean Trevor Brown for keeping me gainfully employed throughout this project and for providing me with darkroom facilities. Several members of the J-school faculty offered their much needed expertise. Many thanks to Claude Cookman, Jon Dilts, Carol Polsgrove, Steve Raymer, and Paul Voakes for sharing their knowledge so graciously. Thanks also to Carol Rhodes, Ken Rider, Michael Valliant, and Eric Wacker, who kept my computer running despite my best efforts to misuse it.

Will and Vivian Counts and John and Lois Ahlhauser have always been an inspiration to me. They continued to be that through my questions and doubts surrounding this project. More than that, they went far above and beyond the call in putting me in touch with people interested in this story. They are the most thoughtful and generous people I know.

I hired Mark Murrmann for a four-hour-a-week job as a photo lab monitor because he had a funny picture on his student ID card. He turned out to be a priceless darkroom assistant and grew to be a good friend.

Across campus, the Department of Religious Studies expressed its interest in the photographs by hosting a small exhibition half-way through the project. The response from the students and faculty of the department meant a lot to me, and I thank them for that.

A number of individuals and institutions offered their thoughts and introduced me to people who proved helpful in moving the project forward. I am grateful to all of them, especially Judy Cebula, the alumni of the Collins Living-Learning Center, Su Fidler Cowling, Joe "Ghost Rider" Edington, Michael Farabaugh, Larry Fink, Robyn Holtzman, George Juergens, Brian Kearney, David Kimbrough, Susan Meiselas, Beth Millett, Wilbur Montgomery, John Morris, Marvin Smith, and Joe Vondersaar.

I was pleased to discover a terrific group of photographers who congregate in Daytona every year for Bike Week. I benefited from their warm welcome and constructive criticism, especially from Eric Breitenbach, Keith McManus, Alison Nordstrom, and Jim Stone.

And, of course, my regular photo pals, John Bragg, Cindy Brown, Yara Cluver, Kim Ferrill, Stephen Fletcher, Robb Hill, Kent Phillips, Gary Reyes, Sam Riche, Dan Schlapbach, Ruth Witmer, and the rest, provided good feedback and encouragement.

My inquiry into the religious world was a journey to a foreign country. Without several ambassadors to answer my questions, I would have stayed hopelessly lost. I have never met Harvey Cox, but his excellent book on Pentecostalism, *Fire from Heaven: The Rise of Spirituality and the Reshaping of Religion in the Twenty-first Century* served as my roadmap through a sometimes very confusing landscape. David Greeley and Dawn Hewitt were also helpful in sharing experiences from their Christian pasts.

Over the years, a number of people have had an influence on my aesthetic growth, most significantly, Pepi Benge, Fred Campeau, Chris Cherry, Peter Holquist, Dot McCullough, Rick Miller, Bruce Phillips, Bonnie Remsberg, Chuck Remsberg, Scott Southwick, Pete Sutherland, Art Thieme, and Bob Wagner, as well as a number of the people mentioned elsewhere in these acknowledgments.

A tip of the hat and a deep bow to a number of people at the University of Illinois Press: Peter Bacon Hales and Bruce Jackson both diligently read the manuscript and their suggestions for improvement made it a much better work. Mary Giles is as good a copy editor as Cope Cumpston is a designer. The vision and careful attention both women brought to this book has strengthened it through greater clarity and elegance.

A friend of mine once commented that there are no good writers, only good editors. Maybe so. I had been told that Judy McCulloh was the best editor in the business. I never found any reason to doubt that.

In addition to Judy, there are five individuals I must single out for special thanks.

Few people have shared and shaped my view of the world as much as Eric Rensberger, my close friend and distant relative. His insights into religion, language, and the human condition have enriched this book along with the rest of my life.

I once heard Kurt Vonnegut give a lecture where he said that the reason for living was to have the opportunity to know the people he called "the saints": those who behave humanely in an inhumane world. I can't think of anyone who represents that idea in my life better than Bob Orsi. His interest in this story had meaningful effects professionally, and his overwhelming approval and confidence fueled me through the second half of the project. I relied on him heavily for advice and knowledge, and through the course of that we have become friends. He is one of the truly decent people in this world.

While I received a lot of feedback and suggestions on these images, the most and best of that came from two photographers.

Costa Manos gave me such honest and piercing criticism that I could not hide from it. Any passion that comes through in these images is the result of his sensibilities, and any lack of passion is the result of my not following or understanding his suggestions well enough.

I hardly know where to begin recognizing Tyagan Miller's contributions to these photographs. He was there when I just had to show someone successful shots before the film was even dry; he walked me through the difficult edits; and he found good shots on my contact sheets when I couldn't bear to look at them. About a third of the good ideas in this book grew from discussions with him.

I always thought it was sentiment or obligation that compelled an author to identify his or her spouse as the most important person in the acknowledgments. Now that I am married and have completed a book, I realize how wrong that notion was. Lisa Nilsson is amazing in many ways, one of the strongest being her visual sophistication. Living together with a shared vision and no competition gives both the life and the vision a profound depth.

Finally, words fail to express how grateful I am to the members of the Unchained Gang and the congregation at the Ellettsville House of Prayer who so graciously allowed me into their lives, even though that often meant probing questions and an obtrusive camera. If I have a regret about the final edit of pictures, it is that I never really show the bikers' tremendous sense of humor. I have never been very good at photographing that, but it is a large part of what made my experience with the gang so enjoyable.

In the Christian world, the word *blessing* gets used a lot. Not that it isn't sincere, but it does become a little diluted. I mean it in the most potent sense when I say that they have been a blessing.

RIDERS FOR GOD

INTRODUCTION

The question everyone asks is if I ride a motorcycle. No one asks if I am a Christian. The answer to both is no. My interest in this story was journalistic.

I had been peripherally aware of the Unchained Gang for a few years, noticing the patches on their vests at concerts, in traffic, and among the protesters at Planned Parenthood. Like many people in town, I became more aware of the gang in the summer of 1995 when they stepped into the heart of a controversy.

People's Park is on Kirkwood Avenue, the main drag through Bloomington, Indiana. It is a block west of the campus of Indiana University and one of the few places for teenagers to hang out in a town that revolves around college students. In the past few years there have been more homeless people, more drugs, and, if you believe the police, an explosion of gang activity.

The police maintained a presence, parking a squad car in the alley, sometimes stationing officers in the park. The park denizens didn't like it, although there was not much they could do about it. And there was some concern in the community about what was happening to downtown at night.

It was a manageable tension until the night of March 24, when the police came into the park, lined the approximately thirty people present against a wall, and conducted a pat-down search. The town quickly became polarized. Accusations were hurled in both directions, lawsuits were filed, and the letters to the editor column became a fire storm of emotion and constitutional principals.

That summer, as the town grew farther from any kind of reconciliation, the members of the Unchained Gang rode their motorcycles to the park. It was a Friday night, and they talked to the kids; more important, they were the first adults to listen to them.

"When we first got there, they thought that we were narcs and that we were there to rat them out," said Larry Mitchell, president of the Unchained Gang. "Then they thought that we were there to fight the police and that we were on their side. Then they thought that we were there to stamp out the wannabe gang members, that we were gonna come down there and bust some heads. Then they just decided that, well, they really are Jesus freaks!"

Made up primarily of former bikers and drug dealers, ex-convicts and recovering addicts, the Unchained Gang is an outreach ministry, going into Indiana prisons and jails, biker rallies, and other places where people on the fringe are ignored by other churches and the rest of society. Although they have given up alcohol, drugs, tobacco, and violence, they have kept their motorcycles and use them as a tool in the witness of the word of God.

I talked with Larry Mitchell on the telephone about taking photographs at the Ellettsville House of Prayer, a church affiliated with the Unchained Gang, where he is the pastor. He gave me directions, and when I asked what was appropriate dress he told me, "Come as you are."

———

When I began this project, I had a limited knowledge of bikers and their world. Growing up in the 1970s, I was aware of the usual mythology surrounding outlaw bikers. They were figures admired as the last true American rebels exiled on the literal and symbolic highways and feared as legions of savage animals fueled by violence, racism, and misogyny.

The legends were made up, I am sure, of a combination of truth, half-truths, exaggerations, generalizations, and lies. There were stories of initiation ceremonies where inductees were doused in buckets of urine and feces, as well as accounts of bar fights, gang rapes, white slavery, and fierce patriotism. Bikers were said to line their jeans with fishhooks in anticipation of police patdowns, and they wore motorcycle drive-chains for belts. Doing so was consistent with their unbathed aesthetic; more important, the chains could quickly be unhooked and used as weapons. A strict code of behavior required unquestioning loyalty among their own, politeness and helpfulness to stranded motorists, and unspeakable retaliation to outsiders who deigned to offend bikers' sensibilities, especially by insulting a club's patch or "colors."

I remember a tavern in Virginia that had barred windows and a crudely hand-lettered cardboard sign on the door that read

No colors
No foul language
Limit two rings
on each hand.

Had I gone in, it probably would have been a disappointment. But I never did, and my imagination reeled. The Wagnerian possibilities that lay on the other side of that door grew in my mind over the years. "Heard melodies are sweet," the poet says. "Those unheard are sweeter still."

When I began hitchhiking around the country I encountered some real bikers, and I learned more about that world from two important books: Danny Lyon's *The Bikeriders* and Hunter S. Thompson's *Hell's Angels.*

Photographing this relatively new phenomenon, Lyon sought to make a "personal record" of motorcycle riders he knew. He also was interested in the power and freedom central to the tragic-biker image. "If anything has guided this work beyond the facts of the worlds presented," he wrote in the introduction to his 1968 book, "it is what I have come to believe is the spirit of the bikeriders: the spirit of the hand that twists open the throttle on the crackling engines of the big bikes and rides them on racetracks or through traffic or, on occasion, into oblivion."

In *Hell's Angels,* Hunter Thompson confirms many of the widely held beliefs and fears about bikers and distinguishes them from paranoia. He describes that particular club as riding "with a fine unwashed arrogance, secure in their reputation as the rottenest motorcycle gang in the whole history of Christendom." He also clarifies some important distinctions in the biker world, such as the differences among the archetypal Hell's Angels, the more law-abiding and sportsmanlike American Motorcycle Association, other one-percenters (the baddest of the bad, the "1 percent" of motorcyclists shunned by the AMA), some less menacing outlaw clubs, and plain old biker trash.

When I began this project, I knew even less about Christianity than I did about bikers. When I was a child, my family was not observant of any faith. The bulk of my minimal religious experience came through my extended family—Jewish on my mother's side, Methodist and Presbyterian on my father's—and television evangelists in whom I found a horrid and immature fascination in high school. In college, and again through hitchhiking, I met a number of born-again Christians, but my interactions with them did not add up to much more than a vague notion of what being born again meant.

More than anything, what attracted me to this topic was Russell Lee's Farm Security Administration photograph of three hymn-singing women in Pie Town, New Mexico. It is one of the better known photos from that era, and it has always affected me emotionally and deeply. Perhaps it is because I could not explain why the image moved me so strongly that I set out to do a project on Christianity.

————

The fundamental purpose of social-documentary photography, since its beginnings, has been to bear witness to what is otherwise inaccessible. Entering the domain of the Unchained Gang, I found two such hidden worlds, that of outlaw bikers and Spirit-filled Christianity.

Gaining entree to the Unchained Gang's world was occasionally difficult; for the most part, it required patience and respect and sometimes a shared sense of humor.

Much of the first three months of the project was spent getting used to each other. These are people who believe that actions are caused either by God or by the devil, and they needed time to discern which was responsible for my presence.

I took relatively few pictures during this time, although I always carried my camera to be honest about my reasons for being there. When I did take pictures, I tried to learn where the boundaries were. How close could I photograph someone while he or she was praying at the altar? How close when people were "slain in the Spirit"? Who was more uncomfortable being photographed and why? On the several occasions that I was asked to stop photographing—before they knew me or when there were guests at the church—I complied.

The bikers and others in the church had a lot of questions for me. Most had to do with my spiritual beliefs and religious background, and I was often asked what I thought of the church. The resulting discussions ranged from brief pleasantries in church to deeper and more intimate late-night conversations around the campfire when we were on the road.

Although my salvation was, and remains, a serious concern for all of them, they were seldom heavy-handed or belligerent about the matter the way evangelizing Christians can often be. There were exceptions to be sure, and awkward ones at that, but these people remember where they came from and know what it's like to be on the other end of the witnessing. "Our job isn't to clean the fish," Paul told me over a cup of coffee. "Our job is to catch the fish. God can take care of the rest."

Another important means of gaining their trust was conducting interviews. This provided me with a better understanding of the bikers' lives as well as an opportunity for them to see that I was not there to ridicule them and that I was genuinely interested in what they had to say.

Most of the text that appears in this book is taken from transcriptions of these taped interviews. While I have removed most of my questions for literary impact, the bikers' words are direct quotes, although they have been edited for length. The interviews were conducted in their homes, at restaurants, at the church, and while driving. I usually tried to speak only when necessary and asked questions that grew from my curiosity or from questions that others had asked me about the gang. When a comment was made that I thought to be incredible, I sometimes challenged it; at other times I let it pass, feeling the statement reflected a worldview or an idea more important than factual accuracy.

A number of interviewees made serious accusations, including parental negligence and being raped by another member of the gang. Some implicated others in criminal situations that were impossible to verify. In many of these cases, some statements have been excluded, as have identifying characteristics, and sometimes names have been changed.

After the first few months, the Unchained Gang and the congregation at the House of Prayer grew more comfortable with me, I with them, and the photographing moved with greater facility. Still, there were always obstacles: new people joining the group, the presence of people outside the group (especially bikers who might have pretty good reason for not wanting to have their pictures taken), the legalities of photographing at a prison, and so forth.

I found photographing their worship to be extremely difficult, particularly at the altar. Even when I was filled with energy, concentration, and purpose, I almost always felt clumsy and intrusive, although the worshippers had a variety of reactions to my presence. Some, after particularly powerful prayer, asked me for photos of the experience. Others disliked being photographed but felt it was important to allow God to be glorified in that way. A few asked me, sometimes through tears, to stop photographing and said that I had gone too far, gotten too close. The very hardest aspect of this project was to face someone whose worship I had interrupted after the service, apologize, and return to the same situation the following Sunday.

I am sometimes asked if there were circumstances when I felt it was more appropriate to put my camera away and not take pictures. Such occasions do occur, but I didn't experience them during this project, which is not to say I didn't sometimes go too far. In a difficult situation it is a great temptation to *not* take a photograph, and although I always tried to be sensitive to potential delicacy, I made a tremendous effort not to fall back on this as an excuse.

There were other instances that were tough to shoot. Certainly one of them was photographing Paul visiting the shell of his father in the nursing home. Another time, the gang met and talked for a while with a woman in a restaurant parking lot who sobbed uncontrollably as she explained, essentially, how God had told her to kill her dogs. It was obviously a very serious and personal matter for this woman. I thought she was crazy and vulnerable, and she recognized me as a foreigner. I wasn't sure I had any place there at all, let alone walking around the circle of Christians and getting shots from different angles, however respectful I might have been.

At Bike Week in Daytona, Chris and Sparky got into a number of verbal fights, the most explosive of which was several yards away from me. When Chris asked me afterward if I had photographed the altercation, I acknowledged that I had. He seemed upset for only a moment. Then, I believe, he understood what has guided me through this story all along.

The bikers place a tremendous importance on their "witness." The notion of a witness resonates beautifully for photography, and, like that of the Christians, it is a matter of telling the truth as one sees it. Truth is truth, even when it is difficult or not immediately understood. Perhaps I should say *especially* when it is difficult or not immediately understood. It should never be necessary to misrepresent or pull back, only to give consideration to how and when and where to tell an important story.

The structure of this book reflects the structure of my getting to know the group. At first I saw only the ironic juxtaposition of outlaw bikers and Christianity and their startlingly dramatic worship. To my eyes, it was strange and without context.

Every foreign world has its own depth and integrity. But where does one start to understand the unfamiliar? In this case I started with curiosity and showing up. After spending time with the group and the individuals in it, and by observing and asking questions, I learned more about the bikers' pasts, recognized the importance of the group dynamic, and saw how they incorporated their beliefs into the world outside the church. In short, I grew to understand their world and started to make connections that the people had made and integrated in their lives.

WORSHIP

Most of the Unchained Gang attends church at the Ellettsville House of Prayer a few miles outside of Bloomington. It is a nondenominational, Spirit-filled church. Many would recognize it as Pentecostal, although Pastor Larry is careful to avoid referring to it that way without qualifiers lest it be confused with snake handling or the more "legalistic" Pentecostal churches.

The House of Prayer has the hallmarks of a Pentecostal church. They anoint with oil and recognize gifts of the Spirit (speaking in tongues, prophecy and interpretation, and the laying on of hands). There is an emphasis on spiritual experience over religious dogma, and the services have good music.

As with most churches, the people are friendly to a first-time visitor. Bikers make up only a portion of the congregation, which numbers two to three hundred for Sunday morning services. Saturday and Wednesday evenings attract a little over a hundred. The content and tone, though, cater to the biker aesthetic. "Raise your hands in surrender," said Pastor Larry, leading the congregation in praise and worship. "Many of you, the police was getting you ready for this moment."

Looking over this room of leather, beards, and tattoos juxtaposed with the icons of Christianity, I can't help but think of Latin American Catholics, where the distinctive details and mood of their native religions have blended with the official Catholicism of Rome.

Still, this is unmistakably American. I remember Hunter Thompson describing the concept of an outlaw biker as "American as jazz." Surely that description is only more apt when born-again Christianity is incorporated.

Many of the similarities between outlaw biker clubs and a Spirit-filled church stand out: the fulfillment of a lifetime longing to belong and the surrender of individual self to the group; the conservative politics that are sometimes surprising in a group rejected by conventional society; and the fact that being accepted by the group is in many respects contingent on displays of vulnerability. Too, both groups provide an arena where men can be affectionate with other men, both physically and verbally, without being labeled homosexual.

Early in the service, members of the congregation stand to issue both praise reports and prayer requests for themselves, others in the church, and family members. I am struck by how many have to do with serious illness or money: cancer, heart disease, diabetes, troubles with bills, jobs, and day care. Those who stand offer not only their problems but also how God has answered their prayers with miracle cures or by helping them cope with their situations.

The Ellettsville House of Prayer.

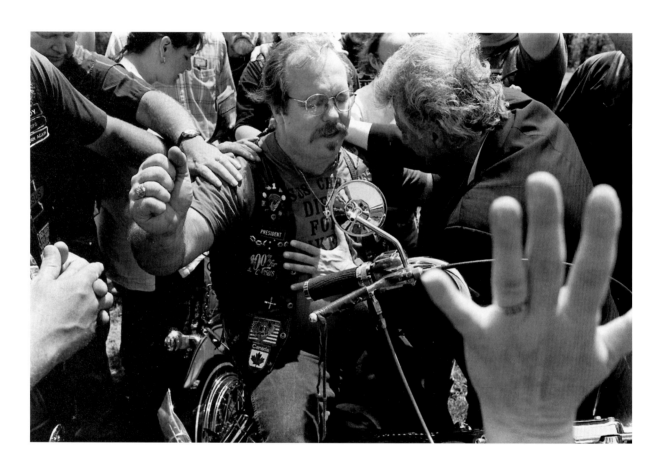

Traveling evangelist Irv Goldman leads a prayer over Pastor Larry during the annual blessing of the bikes.

The blessing of the bikes.

The blessing of the bikes.

Altar call at the House of Prayer.

Praying at the altar.

Mary, speaking in tongues during praise and worship.

Laying on of hands.

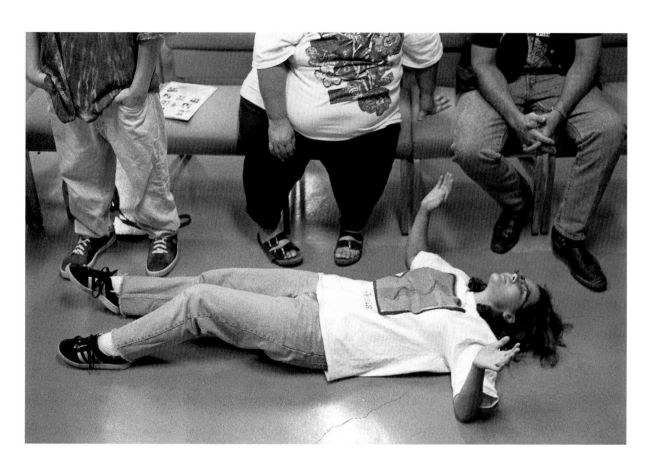

Slain in the Spirit.

Laying on of hands.

Altar call.

Altar call.

Chris and his daughter, Jennie.

Harley.

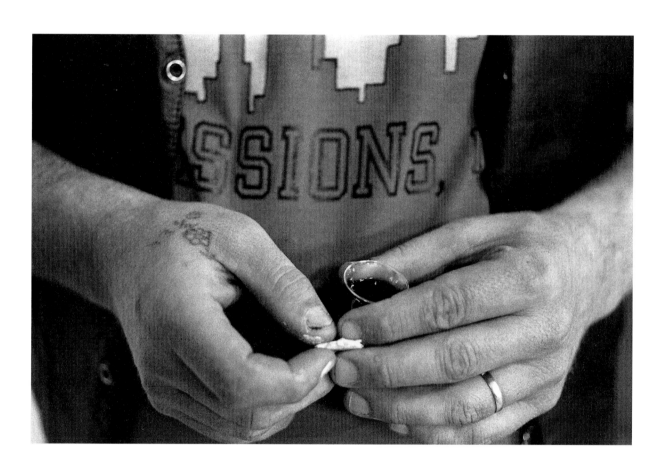

Communion.

PASTOR LARRY

*For six years he has been the president of the Un-
chained Gang. He is also the pastor at the House of
Prayer, where most of the Unchained Gang attends
church. Now an ordained minister, his background
was not at seminary but as a member and president
of several outlaw motorcycle clubs. "We always used
to carry a pocket full of spark plugs, and we'd throw
'em through people's windshields if they did anything stupid on the road to us," he recalls. "We'd
just come up around a car and kick their car doors
in, throw spark plugs through their windows."*

I was born in Bloomington in 1949, and I went
to Ellettsville schools all twelve years. I graduated from Edgewood High School in '67. Played
football, was on the wrestling team.

I got throwed in jail when I was fifteen, fourteen
or fifteen years old. I's drunk, with a bunch of
buddies of mine. I was a rebel. My hair was always the longest of anybody in school. I was always into a lot of stuff, nothing real serious. I
was put in jail down in Bloomfield, Greene
County.

It seemed like I was kind of being pulled a lot at
that time. I just felt rejected a lot, growing up,
and I used to get beat up a lot in school. Kids
was always picking on me because I never would
defend myself. Just had a lot of low self-esteem. I
didn't like to fight. So by the time I got to be in
the eighth grade, I was just—I'd had it. I'd really
had it. So I started working out real hard. I
mean I drove myself. It was just like every free
moment that I had, I just drove myself to pump
iron. Just keep workin' out and workin' out and
workin' out. I just made myself a promise that
nobody was going to touch me or I was going to
take their head off.

And I was going to get even. I was going to look
up all the people that ever tracked me down, that
ever hurt me, and I was going to get even with
them. I was just really mad. I had finally got just
really angry.

It was just the accumulation of everything. I was
just at a place where depression could have really
took over or I had to come out of that rejection,
and I used rebellion to do it. I was just determined that it wasn't going to get me, that I was
going to shove my way out of this thing. And I
wanted to be accepted real bad.

My mom always went to church. She grew up in
church. It was a legalistic church. That means
the preachers, they were clothesline preachers.
They taught you how to dress. They taught you
not to cut your hair. They taught you all those
things, but they never really taught a hands-on—
the word, apply it to your heart, and to become
overcomers in your everyday life. That's what I
really go after here. I want people to be able to
grab a hold of the word like it's a screwdriver or
a wrench or whatever and be able to know how
to apply it to their life.

Since Dad wasn't in church—Mom was—but
there never was a lot of conversation about God
in our home, even though my mom was faithful.
We were there every time the lights was on.

By the time we were teenagers we just decided
we didn't want to go anymore. And we didn't.

We were in the Boy Scouts, growing up. That
was a great time of my life. There was a lot of
good things there. It was just within me, I guess.
I don't know where all this rejection that I was
feeling was coming from.

My brother, man, I just thought the sun rose
and set on him. It seemed like he could always
do everything real good. And I just idolized my
brother.

He'd fight a buzz saw. He'd wade through Hell to fight a buzz saw. He just had this boldness, this bravery about him. He wasn't afraid of anything. Why am I afraid? It was like I had this spirit of fear on me all the time. I was afraid of things, afraid to try things. And I hated that about myself, so maybe it was coming from within more than from everybody else.

But all that really changed by the time I hit high school. I remember the first couple of fights I got into I about killed the guys. And that scared me 'cause I didn't want to do that. And I hurt 'em so bad, and that really freaked me out. I was really determining then that I really didn't want to hurt anybody. I guess I thought, Well maybe if I punch a few people out, then people will just leave me alone. And it didn't work.

I saw guys in the school that were popular, that were rough. And it seemed like since they got drunk on the weekend and since they were tough, nobody bothered them, that made them popular, that made them accepted. So I thought, Well if I do that, then maybe I can be accepted. Then maybe I can not feel the way that I feel all the time. It seemed like I was wrestling with that.

That made all the rough guys want to see how bad I was. It was just fighting all the time then. Even though I had this sense of not wanting to fight, if there was a way that I could deter that, I'd always talk first. And I'd always make the other guy swing on me first, before I ripped his head off. 'Cause then I felt like it justified me tearing him apart.

I had an experience whenever I was a teenager. This was before the jail experience. It didn't last very long, but I do remember the old church was having a revival, and I just really felt God touch my life. And I went to the altar one night, and I was baptized in the Holy Ghost, and I re-

member I spoke in tongues for a half an hour I bet. And the evangelist was interpreting everything that I was saying. I was prophesying in tongues is what I was doing. And I went on. I remember I'd speak a while, and then they'd interpret what I was saying. I'd speak a while, and they'd interpret what I was saying. This went on a while.

When I got up—I was maybe fourteen—and I remember when I got up from the altar, I was just, WOW! I just felt like a zillion-watt lightbulb. I never forgot that. Never ever forgot that. And it seemed like no matter where I was at, there was this keeping power. I really did want peace. And even though here I ended up in a motorcycle gang. Gosh.

I got my first Harley when I was seventeen. My dad was always a mechanic. My brother, he was a mechanic. He had some real nice cars, and he'd a '57 Chevy and a '63 Chevy and a '58 Chevy, and he had a '48 Chevy coupe. I had a few nice ones: a '55 Chevy and a '48 Plymouth coupe. So we was into cars a lot. He'd take them out on the weekends, drag race 'em, rip the transmissions out of them. He'd have the transmission back in, ready to go by Monday, when school was coming around.

When I got my first Harley at seventeen, this thing was a mess. Fifty-one Flathead, forty-five-cubic-inch. Just immediately I wanted to take this thing apart and rework the whole thing. And I did. That began my motorcycle mechanic thing, and I just started working on that.

I had it for a year or two, and then all of sudden there were some guys that came up from Texas. They rode with the Bandidos, which is one of the big clubs in America. They came up here, and they started a club up here called Cain's Children. They already had a couple sets of patches made up. I was riding around town then with a guy on a '49 Panhead. Me and him was riding around and just, you know, not really into anything a whole lot except our bikes, just messing with them. So these guys, they pulled up alongside of us uptown, in Bloomington. This was in 1969.

They wanted to know if we was interested in riding with a motorcycle club. And of course we didn't call them gangs back then. Of course, that's what they are, but we didn't call 'em that. We said, "Yeah, we're interested." We just laughed, you know. It was all a joke. So they really did have a meeting, and we went to it. There was ten of us. And we formed Cain's Children, and I was the youngest of all of 'em, all ten of 'em. I wasn't even old enough to go in bars yet. But I did. I been going in bars since I was eighteen.

That's when the motorcycle clubs started. So that's when I was really introduced to drugs. When I was in high school, the heaviest thing you had was all the alcohol, which was easy to get. And diet pills, back then. You could pop the capsules open, take the little yellow thing out of the middle of it, and get high on that if you take enough of 'em. [Laughs.] That was about the extent of it. There really wasn't any weed or nothing back then. Until '69, and that's when I was really introduced to everything. It was just there in mass quantities.

'Course, when we started from the ground up, that made all of us full members. They said they wanted to start their own thing. 'Course there was everybody. That's the reason you got ten thousand different motorcycles gangs. That's the reason you got ten thousand different kinds of denominations of churches. Everybody wants to do their own thing. I think these guys just wanted to head up their own thing.

We got in as full members, and there was ten of us, and we drew up bylaws. But after that, anybody coming in, you had to go through a prospect period and a probation period. Mainly, that meant you was a gopher. It was just like going to boot camp. When the motorcycle gangs started, all these guys like the Hell's Angels and the Booze Fighters, these guys were out of the military. And so really they put you through boot camp—they knew it all—before you were able to fly full-patch.

It got so bad, some of the guys—there were several of us who were in it for the camaraderie and the motorcycles and all that, but then there was a lot of people that was in it for the image. They just wanted the patch. They just wanted the glory of it. A lot of them was just alcoholics, wanting to join, and never did keep their bikes together. That was always real upsetting to me.

What was your attraction to it?

Just belonging to something. I liked the motorcycles and that part of it. I really got into working on bikes. And those was my early years of training, 'cause everybody was always letting me work on their bikes, which I really enjoyed. They'd give me a bag of weed or a case of beer, and I'd go rewire their bike or overhaul something on it. So I didn't have to spend a lot of money on alcohol or drugs. [Laughs.] I'd just work on their bikes.

So it was just a sense of belonging, really. Maybe, subconsciously, it was, too, if I belonged to something that looked bad, then here again, everybody would just leave me alone. That didn't work. [Laughs.] It still didn't work!

We'd get into it with other clubs. It'd go beyond fists then. We were into automatic weapons and knives and chain belts and baseball bats.

There was a lot of bigger clubs that came into being. So Cain's Children from Bloomington, we formed a three-way alliance with the Cloven Hooves from Terre Haute and the Grim Reapers from Indianapolis. We were all independent clubs and young clubs, so we formed an alliance so that some of the bigger clubs around here would leave us alone.

Actually, there wasn't any really bigger clubs in southern Indiana until the Outlaws came into being sometime in the early '70s up in Indianapolis. And, of course, when they barnstormed into town they put a lot of clubs out of business and told the other clubs, If you want to fly your patch, you will pay tribute to us. I don't know how much a month, but they had to pay the Outlaws so much a month for the Outlaws to leave them alone, to let them fly their patch.

Actually, these clubs became farm clubs. They would come over and see the members that they really liked, and they would draft them into the Outlaws. There's still a lot of clubs that the big clubs use for that.

Was there anything at stake other than image and reputation? Were you controlling drug traffic?

Yeah, there was infringing on each other's territory and things like that. Making money and the glory, too, saying this is our territory. So all that was going on. Plus fighting. We got into fights all the time around here with all the rednecks.

There was a lot of rednecks that hung together. It seemed like that was a never-ending battle. 'Cause we was going to their bars. We'd go to any bar we wanted to.

A biker's kind of a cross between a hippie and a redneck. This is a drug-using redneck. Long-haired redneck, I guess. We just didn't fit in.

Didn't fit in with the hippies and didn't fit in with the rednecks. It was just a whole different thing, but it was stuck right in the middle there somewhere.

But we had friends. We had a lot of friends. We was country people around here. We had a lot of hippie friends, we had a lot of redneck friends. We was trying to control making sales and dealing.

Who would you sell to?

Anybody.

Mostly hippies? Mostly rednecks?

Just anybody and everybody. It was nuts.

We'd get into a bar and, of course, everybody, if you're on whiskey or alcohol of some sort, you feel like you're Superman. We either instigated something or somebody would instigate something with us and then first thing you know . . .

They could just look at you wrong, and then the beer bottles would start flying. We was literally in fights in bars where I mean there wasn't nothing left. Literally, just nothing left. Everything was smashed, and we just tore the place apart.

I lived in an old farmhouse. My house was the party pad so to speak. It was our clubhouse, so everybody knew where I lived. So I got a call about three o'clock in the morning one night, and a friend of mine at one of the bars in town said that there was a club in town that was asking questions where I lived. Somebody told 'em.

And so I got up. I had a semiautomatic. I sat there and loaded it up, and I just sat there in front of my front door, and sure enough a van pulled up. I counted them. There was thirteen guys got out of the van, and they started walking around the house and started beating on the doors and windows.

I remember thinking, Well, my clip held fourteen shots. I could miss once.

I didn't even answer the door, 'cause I's by myself. Me and my old lady back then, my wife. And they left. They didn't do anything. I was really surprised when I got up the next day. They took duct tape, and this club was called the New Breed, and they wrote "New Breed" in the barbed-wire fence at the bottom of my driveway. And it was funny.

So we paid them a visit. We went to Indianapolis. They lived in Talbot Village. Even though they were nice and didn't do anything to my place, we found their place and found their president. He was the only Harley rider of the bunch. All the rest of 'em was pretty much kids.

We found out where the president lived, and we kicked his front door open. We all went running in there, and we just kinda, just told him the way it was if he ever should—we laid down the rules and said this is what's going to happen if we ever see you again. We never saw 'em again after that.

It was just always retaliation. And that gets real old, year after year after year. You're fighting these people. I couldn't get to sleep till the bars closed. 'Cause I knew some of the guys would be uptown, and there'd always be a fight, and I'd always get a phone call: "Come on up. We got a thing going." And that got real old. And here, basically, I didn't want to fight.

I was just tired of it, really sick and tired of it. Oh, there was a few times. I'm not going to say that I never enjoyed it. 'Cause there was still this anger part within me. And if somebody'd really push me and I'd get mad. But it seemed like I had a long fuse, normally. I was president of the club for a long time, and I think maybe that's why. I was always a mediator.

It's kind of funny, because most of the presidents that I ever found of clubs, I liked 'em all. They were usually mediators. I think about that now as a Christian, looking back, and I'm thinking, basically, all these guys that were nuts, although there were some Geronimos every once in a while. They wanted to be a boss, but they never was a leader.

I was so drugged up back then it was really hard for me to care about anything anymore. There was always this struggle going on within me. And it was probably that experience I had growing up. I grew up in church, then all of a sudden it was like, right before I really rebelled, God just zapped me, and I never could quite fit in to the whole scene that I was a part of. The anger and the violence and all the lifestyle that went with being part of a motorcycle gang.

I remember I got in a fight one night, and this guy had ahold of my hair, and I was mad. I wanted him out of my hair. I had an opportunity. I stuck my fingers in his eye sockets, and I told him I was gonna rip his eyeballs out if he didn't get his hands out of my hair. And he still wouldn't do it. This guy was so drunk. I knew he was wiped out. And I didn't do it, 'cause I didn't really want to do that. But I could've. I coulda just popped his eyeballs right out. And I didn't do it.

So then I thought I'm gonna strangle this guy till he passes out. 'Cause he was a redneck and he didn't have no hair, so I couldn't pull his hair back. I just, I beat this guy. He was just gone. He was out of it. The guy was nuts.

And I remember having ahold of his Adam's apple until I could almost touch my forefinger and my thumb. I mean I was ripping his Adam's apple out. But I remember thinking, I don't want to kill this guy. I just want him to get out of my hair. I just want him to leave me alone. I kept thinking that.

So then I was faced with some situations, just like those guys showing up, where I coulda killed somebody. I remember thinking, Man, this is getting out of hand. My whole life was getting out of hand. It seemed like it was always just "grrr." It was always with somebody, all the time.

My wife was real unhappy. She was sick and tired of it. She never really did fit in. She was a good girl and had a good family. We were high school sweethearts and all this. We ended up getting married. She proposed to me. I just married her 'cause there wasn't nothing else to do. That's what I told her. I don't know. I wasn't ready for marriage. I wasn't ready for none of that. Most guys aren't.

We never did have any kids in my first marriage. It was ironic that I ended up leaving her. I ended up with some other gal at a party, and so I just left. 'Cause there was a lot of turmoil at our house, and I was sick and tired of that, sick and tired of her trying to tell me what to do.

Here again, I couldn't, I couldn't, I couldn't care. I couldn't keep a job. Longest job I'd had was about a year and a half, and I thought I was making a career out of that. I could've got sent up a couple times because of drugs and stolen stuff. I got involved in a lot of stolen stuff.

I was thrown in jail a few times but always out the next day, but the things they could have really nailed me on, it just seemed like I was always, just, I don't know. Things would happen.

I finally got a job at the Harley shop here in town. I worked up there for four years. I liked that job real well, but still, my drug habit. I missed at least one day a week, maybe two, because I was riding with the gang. We was partying all the time and going on runs all the time.

If I took a notion I was going to stay at a bar all day and get drunk, that's what I'd do instead of going to work.

Who were the customers in the Harley shop? Was it bikers or cops or both?

Everybody.

What was the status of Harleys back then?

They've always been number one ever since I've been riding motorcycles. Triumphs was a good second. Anything Japanese was out. We would have bike shows and swap meets and things like that. We'd always go get a Honda or Suzuki or Yamaha or something like that, and we would always auction off the first swing of a sledge hammer. We'd bid that off, and the first guy'd get to take the first three whacks at this thing. After that it was like a dollar a whack. And we'd make a lot of money. They'd pulverize this Japanese motorcycle.

I've let go of all that. In fact, I had a Honda once. When I ride with the Unchained Gang, one of the guys, Forrest, the bottom end went out so I was overhauling it. He picked up this 750 Honda at a car dealership for three hundred bucks. We took a paint brush and painted on the gas tank, "It's not what you ride, it's who you serve."

Tell me about when you were saved.

It was in 1978. But leading up to that, I was really running. God had started really dealing with me in '75. Had a son that was born in 1974. That was the beginning, because of this gal that I'd ended up leaving my wife for, I was shacking with. We were living at the clubhouse most of the time. She got pregnant right off the bat. I welcomed that. I remember that feeling, you know, Hey! This is gonna be cool. I'm gonna have a kid.

We found out it was going to be a boy, and I was just even more, you know, I was just really happy about it. 'Course at the same time I was riding with a club out of Chicago called Hell's Henchmen. And this was a big city club. These boys was bad boys, real bad boys.

I was getting sick and tired of some of the stuff that was going on with this group. And to make a long story short, we wanted out. And some clubs you don't get out. You go out feet first.

What sort of things did you have to do to get in?

Muff diving after two hundred guys had gang-banged her, you know. Sticking your face in it. I did all that stuff. We's prospects then. We wasn't full members. We were prospective members, so anything they told you to do, you did it if you wanted in.

Anyway, we was gonna get out. So they came from Chicago one night in a big old Lincoln Continental, and they found me and some of the guys I was running with from another club down here then, the Cloven Hooves. So that night they was gonna blow my brains out.

And they could've. They could've blowed my brains out, and nobody would have cared. They could have all gone back to Chicago, and it would have all been forgotten about. They tried to talk me into staying. They wanted us to stay. They didn't want us out. There was five of us that they wanted to stay in.

And here this woman was pregnant with my son. I just told 'em that. I said, "Hey, I'm real happy right where I'm at. I don't want to go to Chicago. I don't want to be a part of you anymore." And they started teasing me real bad that night,

but I didn't care. It didn't phase me at all. I remember this is something that I wanted.

There was a bunch of us in a trailer court, visiting at this guys's house, and they come kicking the doors in and had us at gunpoint. Some of the other gals was there. So they was kicking everybody and stompin' 'em. They took me and another guy, and we went to my house, my place, where I had all of their patches and everything that belonged to them in a sack, which they took and all of our money and stole everything else we had that they could carry back.

I remember them saying that they didn't want to do what they came to do, 'cause they came to kill us. Finally, they drug me outside the trailer, took me outside, and they stuck a .45 to my head. They was all high on LSD. One guy was slobbering, frothing at the mouth. I remember him telling me, he said, "I've come to do this. I come to kill you. I can't do it. I don't know why, and this really makes me mad."

I'm thinking, I don't care why you can't do it. I'm just really thrilled you're not going to do it! But I never forgot that. I look back and I know that was God. Man, that was God that just kept that guy—'cause I knew, that's just exactly what they were gonna do.

They left that night. They went over and took the keys out of my motorcycle and said they'd be back to get it. Of course, the next day that motorcycle got a whole new paint job. It got a whole completely different face-lift. Didn't even look like the same bike after that.

They never came back. Never did, really. I'd never seen them again until I became a Christian, riding with the Unchained Gang. I've seen a lot of those [Hell's Henchmen], but I've never seen any of the old faces. I'd look at 'em from a distance.

That was quite a religious experience for me. 'Cause I remember really thinking about God. That was something that stayed with me two or three days. Now some people, that would have been a life-changing thing, but it wasn't. I was just so far out. Couldn't care. So I did think about it for two or three days, but shoot, I was right back doing the same thing again.

The drugs and the alcohol was really wearing me down. I was becoming more paranoid, becoming more confused. God was speaking to me. I wasn't having fun anymore. I's getting mad at the guys that I rode with. This kept going for like three years.

I went to bed one night, and that was one of the first times I could remember that I'd drank no alcohol. I didn't smoke any weed. I took no drugs. In fact, the last beer that I drank was October of 1977, and it made me so sick. I was sick for three days. I thought I was going to die. And I never had another beer after that. And I got saved January of '78, just a few months later.

But all these things was happening. It was just driving me nuts. I was ODing a lot. Even when I was smoking weed. I grew it, smoked it, sold it, ate it, drank it. Marijuana had really become my life. But I remember I couldn't even smoke the bottom leaves of a plant. It seemed like I had this rubber band in my head that was being pulled and stretched.

It was a short time after that, a buddy of mine died of a stroke from using too much marijuana. They said it was from the marijuana use. I believe that's probably what was about to happen to me. I don't know, that was just speculation, but a lot of crazy things was happening. My health was really going bad. I was getting pneumonia all the time. Couldn't fight off a cold in

the middle of the summer. My immune system was so far out.

On the night of January 28, I went to bed. It was two-thirty in the morning. I couldn't sleep 'cause usually I'd have to get tanked up, doped up, drunked up, or something to be able to sleep. I remember wallowing around there. All of a sudden—I was in there on my back—and I had a vision. God gave me this vision.

Now, I've hallucinated many times in my life, but I'm thinking, This is not a hallucination. I was completely conscious. I saw a giant set of scales, a huge set of scales. On the left side of the scale I saw God. I didn't see God, but I knew it was God. I don't know how I knew that, but I knew it.

He was putting in my drugs, the alcohol. I saw the motorcycle gang, the patch that I was riding with then. I saw him put my '72 Harley in there. And I knew all these things that were going on the left side of the scale were things that had priority in my life, that my life was given to. These were gods that I had in my life.

These were things that I didn't think I could turn loose of to serve God. I didn't know that. At that time I knew that those were things that my life revolved around.

The scale dropped. And when the scale dropped, I heard God's voice. I don't know if it was audible or if it was just so impressionable. I don't know if anybody else could have heard it if they'd been in the room. But God said, "Larry, you are choosing death." He says, "Larry, if you'll serve me I'll give you life, but you are choosing death."

And, wow! That had such an impact on me, because I knew that where I was at, I didn't get there overnight. And it was all a series of choices that I had made, from the time that I started working out to get even with all these guys who ever beat me up. I was still rebelling. I was going to be my own boss. Wasn't nobody going to tell me what to do anymore.

I was sick and tired, I want everybody to leave me alone. I want everybody to leave me alone, and yet here I am a people person. I like being around people. I just hated all the violence, and I hated all the tempers. I hated all the garbage, but here I was. I was just right in the middle of all of it.

Then the Lord spoke that, and on the right side of the scale, I don't even know how I saw what I saw, except in the Spirit, but I saw him putting on the right side of the scale peace and real joy. Eternal life. "I'll be with you when the clip runs out. I'll be there." All these promises.

The scale dropped, and when the scale dropped it was like all of a sudden my whole thinking was different. It was like everything that had ahold of me for years of my life had to turn loose for a while. And I'm laying there, and I knew that I had to make a decision. I felt like everything that had been happening to me had been leading up to a crossroads in my life and what God was asking me was, "Do you want to live or do you want to die?"

And he was giving me an opportunity to make a choice again. I think about the mercies of God. He didn't have to do that. I was so rebellious, he could have squashed me like a bug, took me right out. But he said, "Hey, do you want to live or do you want to die?"

'Course I wanted to live, but I didn't know how to live. I was trying to find life in all the wrong places. Boy, that was scary. That was real scary to me. It was like God was asking me to take a

jump across Grand Canyon. That's how mammoth it seemed like it was.

But I knew the weight. I kept thinking, God reminded me, "Hey, you said you'd try anything once." 'Course I did try him once at fourteen years old, and that weighed against me, too. I thought, Well, I didn't make it then. I didn't live for God. I had such a wonderful experience. Why didn't I stick with it? If I couldn't do it then, I couldn't do it now. Of course, that was the devil telling me that. But I had try to it again. And I said yes, and it was just like when I said yes that night, the vision was gone.

I had such a peace in my life. I slept like a baby. I mean slept like I never slept before. Woke up the next day, I had such a desire. I thought, Man, I've got to have a Bible here somewhere. Whenever I was a kid, I won this Bible in a Sunday school contest, and I'd been dragging this thing around in a cardboard box from place to place where I was moving. And I looked and I looked and I found that old Bible that I'd had since I was a kid. And I started reading it.

I never read. I graduated from school and I could read. I couldn't sit still long enough to read. I didn't like to read. But that first year after I gave my life to the Lord, I read the entire Bible all the way through and fifteen other books besides that. All I'd ever read for years was *Easyrider* magazine and that was it.

I was just so hungry. It was like I'd been in a desert for years. When I woke up the next morning, snow was piled up to the bottoms of my windows. I realized that a blizzard had hit that night. It was pretty wild.

I've never had a moment since then to ever turn back. I've had a lot of bad situations hit, some real doozies. It was like a few months later, I realized, God showed me, 'cause my health was so bad by then. I remember going to church and I was so nauseated. I just felt like I was gonna die.

I remember I came home one night, I remember feeling real bad. 'Course the devil was always telling me, "You're gonna die. Too bad. God came too late" and this and that. And I remember going to bed that night with the devil setting on my brain, telling me that stuff.

And I'd went to sleep, I don't know for how long. I woke up. When I woke up—God's allowed me to see a lot in the Spirit—when I woke up, I saw these two death angels standing at the foot of my bed. How'd I know they was death angels? All I'd ever seen was a tattoo or a picture. These dudes was huge.

Death Angels is not a gang? These were death angels?

These was real death angels. Their heads was bumped up against the ceiling. They had hoods. I couldn't see no faces. They were standing at the foot of my bed like they were talking to one another. I couldn't hear 'em saying anything. I'm laying there like, Am I really seeing this? [Laughs.] I mean I really remember thinking that.

I'm thinking, Gosh, I'm awake. It was like whenever I was awake, they knew I was awake. They both turned and was looking at me. I still couldn't see their faces. And it was like I knew that they were death angels. All of a sudden I realized that they were there to get me. So I got to thinking, Man, I must have been really close to death, through all of this, for these creeps to show up.

When they turned to look at me, and all of a sudden the realization hit me that they were there to get me, whew! I mean I just felt God

well up inside of me, the Holy Ghost is really what happened. And the Bible says that when Satan would come in like a flood, the Holy Ghost would raise up a standard against him.

And I just felt this confidence inside of me. And of course I didn't have a great—my prayers, I didn't have no fancy words. I still don't. I just try to pray out of my heart. I just told these, I said, "Hey!" I was speaking out loud to them, and I said, "God didn't save me just for you bums to think you can come here and haul me out of here, and I rebuke both of you'ns in the name of Jesus Christ!"

And the church I was going to didn't even teach me that. That just came out of me. And I'm rebuking both of 'em in the name of Jesus and they're just, they're gone. They disappeared. And I'm laying there, I'm pinching myself. Did this really happen?

It was from that day forward that I started being healed, that my health was getting better. It got better and better and better after that. And that was pretty wild.

I went to the very last. I's president of the club at that time. I'd got out of the Henchmen 'cause they left, and I rode with the Cloven Hooves for years after that. And a bunch of the guys that was in the Cloven Hooves were around in Cain's Children. They were a part of that club. They were riding with the Hooves now. And I just thought these are people that I rode with and I'm gonna tell 'em. I just felt compelled to go to this last meeting to tell them what I decided, what had happened in my life.

[Laughs.] They thought I was nuts. They thought I'd completely flipped out. Sure, give Modo* a couple weeks. He'll be back. And of

---

* The name he went by in the biker world.

course it didn't happen. Give him a couple months, give him a couple years, and it just never did happen. And finally I sold my motorcycle and they knew that I meant it.

Since I gave my life to the Lord, nineteen guys have given their hearts to God. Out of this one club, not counting their wives and children. Nineteen men. And almost all of them, to this day, are still serving God.

I know now that God was always there, always dealing with me. Always. And he kept me. I did a lot of terrible, terrible things. But I realize now that he kept me, he kept me from—I coulda killed somebody. I coulda done even worse things that he kept me from doing. He really did.

And he kept me, period. I mean I coulda got my brains blowed out several times. I walked away from motorcycle wrecks a lot of normal people died in. And I just walked away from it. Overdoses. I got overdoses so bad, I felt like a mummy. I'd get to the place, as long as I could move my finger, then I'd think I'm okay. [Laughs.] It was nuts. It was really crazy.

CHICO

His arms are covered with tattoos, although he won't get any more because of his interpretation of Leviticus 19:28: "You shall not make any cuttings in your flesh on account of the dead, nor tattoo any marks upon you."

I've lived here all my life. I was born and raised here. Only time I was gone from here was a hitch I done in the army. I got married half-way through my junior year of high school. Finished out my junior year going to school days and working two jobs nights, and my senior year I worked two jobs days and went to school nights.

And then I went in the military. I spent two tours of Vietnam. Come back home and just worked.

I was married four times by the time I was twenty-seven and divorced four times by the time I was twenty-nine. All I ever done was run to bars, fight, do everything you're not supposed to do. Years later I got into dealing drugs. I done that for quite a while. And then I met Becky and things started changing.

I was forty years old, five years ago. I was dealing. Becky didn't know it. I tried to hide it from her, because by that time I had people that was working for me. Finally I had to make a choice: either Becky or the drugs. So it was time I settled down and quit all the junk. Even after that we had a lot of problems. We were on our way to getting a divorce when I started going to church.

My son, he'd been in a lot of trouble, and he'd run away from his mother, my youngest boy. He come and stayed here for a while, and I mean he had things in a turmoil. Larry Dyer, works out at Otis with me. Larry got to witnessing to me at work.

At first I would just cuss and go on. I didn't want to hear it. But Larry didn't give up on me. Larry kept talking to me, and it got to one day I could feel the tears welling up when he was talking to me. I told him about Josh and everything. He told me, "Maybe we just need to take Josh to church." Maybe he needed the Lord in his life the same as I did.

One night I took Josh and went over to the House of Prayer, walked in the double doors and there's a guy standing there, long grey hair, beard, had this shirt on that had writing on the back of it, and I could read part of it but not all of it. Then he moved his head, and it said, "Jesus

Christ died for bikers too." It was just like he knew that I was reading it, 'cause soon as I finished reading it, he turned around, he put his arms around me, and he told me that he loved me. That was my turning point right there. It didn't get my son, but it sure got me.

I'd been going to church just a short time and some old buddies got to calling me, wanting to know if I wanted to make a run, make some money. And I almost did. Larry Dyer had a motorcycle for sale. And I'd quit riding years ago and decided, Well, I'll start riding again, 'cause they were riding for the Lord. I thought maybe I would too. It was just kind of like on my mind. It wasn't anything I'd made my mind up about. Larry had the bike for sale. I told him I'd think about it.

Well, these used-to-be friends of mine called, wanted to know if I wanted to make some money. Well, it was gonna take an investment to make this money. I thought, Man, I can take the thousands of dollars I was gonna buy this motorcycle with, and I could invest this and more than quadruple my money. And I got to thinking about, Well, if I do this, I go back to where I came from. I'm stuck. So I took every dime I had and I bought that bike. I made the choice. Because I knew if I invested the money in the cocaine that I'd be right back on the road to Hell again. It was just like the Lord told me, "Here's your choice: Buy the bike, ride for me; go back where you came from." And I bought the bike. And I've been riding for the Lord ever since.

There for a long time, guys that I used to run with, from Chicago and down to Florida, they've called, and they know what I'm doing. I had one call—oh, it's been some months back now—wanted to know if I was still doing that Jesus thing. I said, "Yep." I said, "I sure am." He told me, "I might come up and see you." I said, "I

tell you what, you're more than welcome to come on up, see what's going on. Take you to church with me."

He kind of laughed. He said, "Boy, wouldn't that be a sight?" I said, "Don't you think it was a sight the first time anybody saw me walking into church that ever knew me?" I said, "It's been great. I don't have material things. I can't get the material things like I used to, but I got something a whole lot better. I got the Lord."

I can sleep nights. I don't look over my shoulder, don't worry about who's looking for me. I don't worry about somebody out of my past coming around any more.

People that I used to mess with, deal with, they know what I'm doing. I've even seen some of the guys from around this area that I used to know come to church now, too. It's moving, it's moving fast, the Lord is.

As far as getting out of it, when I made the choice I had some people that didn't like it, but they knew it wasn't going to do 'em any good because I wasn't going to go back to doing what I was doing.

You were dealing mostly in cocaine?

When I first started out I collected money that was owed from other people. And then I got into dealing myself. I got to where I had enough capital. I got into dealing. I had people I knew up in Chicago, different parts of Illinois. I had acquaintances I got to know in Florida. I even made a trip to Peru once. One trip to Peru for me was enough. It was scary.

What happened there?

Let's just say it wasn't a trip I'd ever want to make again. I tell you what, being in Peru, parts of it was like being back in 'Nam. It was like being back in 'Nam again. It's that bad. Because of the people you had to work with, because life meant nothing to them. I wouldn't go back, 'cause I wouldn't trust a soul there for nothing.

I went down with another associate. We flew down there, and he had his own pilot and everything. We went down. It was to make a deal. Like I said, it was a one-time thing and I'd never do it again. 'Course I'd never do it again now, anyway.

It's not worth it. I never knew just how dirty and nasty anything could be until you see the people that really hurt for it, like there in Peru. Them people don't make nothing. I mean poverty-stricken. We don't know what poverty is. They're working for nothing. People back here's the ones making all the money. It's something I wouldn't wish on anybody.

What were some of the similarities between that and Vietnam?

The killing. Like I said, life meant nothing. Just a word just out of the way said, somebody's done. It was crazy. And the jungle and stuff you walk through and go through to get to some of these places. Its like something out of a nightmare.

So you were down there for a while?

No, just a few days. Just a few days. Flying over it looks like a beautiful country. When you hit the ground it's all together different.

Let's go back and talk about when you received that gift, at the House of Prayer, when that guy turned around and hugged you.

That's when I felt that love.

Is that when you accepted Christ?

No. I'd gone there for a while. Like I said, my wife and I were already on our way to a divorce

when I started going. She started seeing the change in me, and she's walked with the Lord before.

We started going to church together there. One night I was standing there. They give an altar call, and I wanted to go. It was like my feet were tied to the floor. They wouldn't move. I begin to weep, and I looked at Becky, and Becky just gave me a nudge, with her arm. Told me, she said, "Go on." When she nudged me with her arm, it was like she threw me out there in the aisle.

I headed for the altar, dropped to my knees, asked the Lord to forgive me for my sins. I got numb from the top of my head to the bottom of my feet. It was like I got a numb feeling all over. I went to get up. I got about half-way up, and it was like He threw me back down again, like, I'm not done with you. And that time, everything just started getting hot. By the time I got up from that altar, my shirt and my pants were wringing wet from sweat. It was a feeling, oh, it was great. I'll never forget that.

Becky, she's helped me a lot. She knows so much about the Bible, Scripture. I got saved December 4, 1994, and Becky rededicated her life, I think it was Christmas night, there at the House of Prayer.

RANDY

He is a deacon at the House of Prayer and plays electric bass for their services.

I remember going to jail the first time at eleven, and it was like, Great! It was like breaking free. I remember we was in there when they gave us these tin cups, you know what I'm saying? Just taking these tin cups and rattling them on the bars, like we was big criminals. That was the start of it, man. That was the start of going to jail.

I went to reform school. They sent me to three different foster homes. This was very unusual in my family, 'cause wasn't nobody else did—you know, I got two brothers and two sisters and that stuff never happened to them. We had a tight family. Dad was an alcoholic. We still, we always had a roof over our head and always had food. And discipline. [Laughs.]

So they sent me to a foster home in Chicago. I'm from Illinois, from Danville. And they sent me to a foster home in Chicago and a foster home in Champaign. I left both of them and did various illegal acts and then finally got sent up. Stealing stuff, breaking into houses. At that time there wasn't any street drugs, so my first drug was glue. I sniffed a lot of glue at that time. Drank a lot of wine and sniffed a lot of glue.

And then your dad struck a deal with the reform school?

They was gonna keep me until I was of age. I was pretty hard-headed. And what I'd heard, they was gonna keep me till I was of age and either send me to some other place or, I don't know, let me out maybe—I don't know—which would have been seventeen.

My mom went and seen my probation officer one day, and she was talking about she wanted to get me out. He made some suggestions to her on, If she would do this or that or whatever it would be much easier for me to get out. She left out of there. 'Course Dad come up and—I don't know if it was that day or the next day or whenever, but—saying that he was going do something to him or he was gonna get me out there. So I was out of there not long after that.

That's what I was talking about, the Establishment. I've just seen 'em burn and burn and burn and burn people. I don't have a whole lot of respect for them. I know under the word of the Lord it says that we are to respect them, respect the laws of the land. But as you watch people get burnt, their lives get just turned around because of somebody in a power position that is abusing it. I just got real tired of it. And I still am.

There was always this act that was put on. They wanted us, when, like, say, we had open house or whatever at the reformatory, we had it all cleaned up, everything was looking good, we were all spiffed up. We put on this big act that everything was all hunky-dory, when actually behind the scenes it was just, it wasn't that.

There was molestation going on, to some of the younger kids by one—I remember, the youngest kids we had, they were called the Indians because, I don't know, they were small. And one guy, I come to find out later on, this was a couple years after I'd got out of there, that he'd been molesting these kids for quite a while.

Now, I'm not saying that there weren't some good people up there. There was. There was. I remember one guy, one probation officer that I can think of, that I would have stood behind him on anything because he was right up-front. He was for you, he tried to do good for you, treat you right. That's few and far and in-between, man.

It was a different world when I got out. To me, anyway. I really felt alienated. I felt I didn't fit in anywhere. I tried different groups to run around with. Didn't work. So I just resorted to more drugs and alcohol, more illegal acts. Got on the road. I just got on the road at about seventeen. Hitchhiking and living on the streets. I lived in about every, about every skid row as I can call it now because of AA—that's what they'd call it.

Living on the streets, living back down in there. Sleeping under bridges and about wherever you can, abandoned buildings. Stealing, selling drugs that weren't really drugs. Doing a lot of scamming, basically just making it on the streets. Lot of jails. Couldn't tell you, probably I know it's at least two hundred, if not more, times I been arrested.

Petty things. It always was. They got me once down in the Keys for breaking and entering. Oh, you know, doing this job on a grocery store. They let us out. They just got us out of the Keys. They said, "You guys just leave."

I thought it was dropped, and I got arrested a couple years later in St. Augustine. Found out it wasn't dropped, 'cause they shipped me down there. I paid 'em, I think it was three hundred and fifty dollars, and they let me go. It was crazy.

I remember I started getting a lot of death in my head. I remember I was just getting so tired of people. I had suicide thoughts a long time ago, but it was really fleeting. It wasn't nothing that I'd cut my wrists or none of this crap. But then I started thinking about really just opening up on people. Cops or somebody. I don't know really how to explain it. I was just tired. I was tired, and I was thinking about—probably, that was a death wish, too. 'Cause I knew it would just end in death.

Opening up, you mean with a gun?

Yeah. Yeah, like totally becoming—I don't know how you'd say it. Crazy, ridiculous. Never was able to do it though. Never was. I beat up on a few people. I mugged a few people. But I never liked hurting people. Never did. I just never

did. So it started just coming back, back around on me.

And this is so true. I tried to lose everything 'cause I was brought up with some hypocrisy—I think everybody is as far as I know. At least I was—about do this and do that but don't do as I do, do as I say. And that was pretty confusing.

I wanted to go out, and I wanted to lose everything that had been put inside of me. But I couldn't lose this one thing. I didn't know what it was then. Now I know it was God. God, he didn't leave me. Never did. Never did, man.

I did a lot of tripping and this and that and everything, too. And some of that was the spiritual seek. [Laughs.] This is gonna sound, you know [laughs], but there was this one time when I thought I was a resurrected Jesus. I was so blown. Doing so much cocaine and stuff. I had a few people believing me, too!

I don't know, looking for something better, definitely. Knowing there was something better but not knowing how to find it, not knowing where to look. You know, trusting some of the wrong people.

Lot of gommin'. Lot of messing around. Lot of being here, lot of being there.

I remember going through Kingman, Arizona, and walking through the desert. Getting out there, coming to Kingman, got a ride with this old Hell's Angels president. He took us home with him and got us loaded. Took us home, and we were drinking and getting high and reading the word! It was pretty weird.

It's pretty wild how I started getting into a relationship with the Lord with bikers and street people. You know, when we's on the streets we had a creed, kind of. It was like we pretty much did stick together. Now I'm not saying that there weren't those that turned on you. But when I became a Christian, I's looking for that. I was looking for that togetherness. And it's still hard to find amongst us. I just really think that Satan just has a heyday with people. He uses us and abuses us and gets us against each other. I don't know. It's crazy. Totally crazy.

I think there's various bottoms that you hit. We was coming up out of Florida. Got a ride with this guy, me and this guy named Peyote. And we got a ride with this guy, and we was going over to Alabama. Got a ride with this guy, and he had this van. We's drinking with him. We's getting high and everything. He flashed all this money out. He had all this money. And I was gonna kill this guy for his money, for his van and stuff.

It was totally ridiculous, but this was part of reaching that bottom. We didn't kill him. We did steal his money, but we didn't kill him.

After we left Birmingham—we stayed at this cat house in Birmingham, and we made some money there, ripping off people—when we left there I split up from Peyote. I said, "Man, I'm gonna go on my own." So I split. And that always happened with me. I'd always end up going off on my own. And I got to thinking about killing, wanting to kill that guy, thinking about killing that guy, for his money and for his van. I figured, I thought, Man, I've just about sunk as low as I can go, you know, wanting to start doing that. Praise God that that didn't happen. Not saying the thoughts weren't there.

So that was really a kind of a turning around, too, of me really looking at what I was doing, where I had let myself go.

Then we did a job, a pretty heavy legal job in this area at one time, and then left out of here and shot up through Canada. Went up through Canada, and all through that, you know, I started hitting these spiritual lows. It's like, Man, this ain't working. Things ain't right. 'Course doing all this wrong sure wasn't helping your spiritual attitude. [Laughs.] You know what I'm saying?

But before, in my younger days, stuff didn't bother me as much as when you start getting a little tired, a little older. Stuff starts compounding and building up.

So anyway, we got on through Canada and come on down through Vancouver, coming down through Washington. Sold my truck. I had a truck at that time. We sold it in Washington. And me and this guy—he's dead now, he got killed on a motorcycle down in Florida—but me and this guy, we got a ride with this trucker.

I'm gonna tell you what: this is how God works. I about opened up—we had an M-16, and I about opened up in a bar up in Edmonton, Alberta, on some people that was messing with us, you know? But I didn't. He got me out of there, and we didn't do that. Praise God, he was watching out for me.

So we got down in there, and this trucker picked us up. Glen, he's from Ohio, I remember, a little-bitty guy. Started talking, preaching the word to me. Man, it was like soothing to me. It just felt so good. I could feel the warmth, feeling so good. And my partner, Bob, he thought it was a joke. We spent the night in his [Glen's] truck. The next morning, he had to go unload. Then he was gonna come back. This was in Bend, Oregon. Then he was gonna come back through there.

I split up with Bob right there. "You go your way, I'm going mine." I said, "I ain't gonna play your game no more. You don't have to play mine." I went in and out of Bend, Oregon, three or four times that day. I'd go in, get me a bottle of wine, get a ride back out, maybe ten miles or so. Sitting along the highway there. Finally, here come Glen. I seen that truck coming.

He picked me up, and we started praising God all the way to Little Rock, Arkansas. It was great. This was '76, '77. It was all fine. I think I was wearing him out. I think I was asking him too many questions, and he—I don't know if he had the ability to answer, or if there was any answer even, to these questions.

Come round Little Rock. We went in, took showers and stuff, and I come out to the truck and there was a twenty-dollar bill stuck in my pack. So it was kind of like, You know, you gotta go your way, I'm going mine. All right, that's cool. 'Cause he did me good.

So I got on the highway. The first ride I got, we got high. We smoked some herb. I was watching my inside, seeing if it was gonna break anything. Everything was fine. I got to my brother's place in Virginia. He was living out in Virginia. We got drunk, and I'm telling you what, it was just like I left. I walked away from that high that I had.

From that time on, like I said, that was about '77, it was just like everything was just miserable. Everything was miserable. My drinking got worse, I shot a lot. I shot so much dope, man. It's just totally ridiculous. I showed Outlaws how to shoot dope.

So I come back through here and met this German lady, and we got married. And that was totally a disaster. I's just using and abusing her and drinking. I quit shooting up so much but still did. Then I remember, the last time living with her I was on a two-week drunk. I mean I was just wasted. I was waking up in the morning, and she was gone, the boy was gone. Her boy. She had a boy. They were gone. I thought, Well, he's at school and she's at work.

So this went on. Then I'd go and get drunk, come back and pass out. That went on for about two weeks. One morning I woke up, and I said, "Maybe she's gone." [Laughs.] I mean, you know, this is the intelligence that went along with this lifestyle.

She was gone. [Laughs.] So we split up. I finally did get ahold of her and gave her back the apartment, and I went into detox. That was 1980.

I didn't stay sober then. So we got a divorce through all of this, then I met my wife now. I met her in an AA room.

You were in AA before you got saved?

Oh yeah. Before I got saved I had like three and a half, three years of sobriety.

So AA really changed your life?

Well, first off it helped me get sober. [Laughs.] It talks about it in the AA Big Book. It talks about how wide was the hoop you had jump through to get into AA. It was very, very wide. Because if it wouldn't have been very, very wide I wouldn't have did it. You know what I'm saying? The only requirement to be in AA is to have a desire to stop drinking. That's the only thing.

I stayed sober then for about four months. And that was quite a bit. That was a lot. And man, I started having this physical pain. And I drank again and I started getting high again. Just the pot, not a lot of other drugs. Maybe a little here and there.

Me and my wife now, Gracie, moved in together. Went through about ten more years of not-so-bad drinking, but still. I had the DTs and I had being sick, man, I'd just be sick. More treatments, more jails, all this stuff. Finally we got married. I think it was '87 when her and I got married. Then I got sober in '89.

Right after we got married, I put on one heck of a drunk. But in '89, through another couple DUIs and another couple thises and thats, she took me to a treatment center in Terre Haute. I didn't know it, but she was done. That was it. My spirit must have knew that or something, because everybody was done with me. I tell you, nobody would drink with me. There was one guy, a friend of mine, he was the last guy that drank, that would go to bars and drink with me. And at the end of that he would start taking me to bars and dropping me off. "I'll be right back," you know? [Laughs.]

I'd get totally ridiculous. So I got up there. I remember things started changing, started changing. Went in to talk to this one lady one time. She was called a spiritual advisor. She was a Christian. They called her a spiritual advisor. She said, "Well, what seems to be your main problem?" And this is weird because I had probably been asked this a lot of times in my life. But this time I had, I think, the right answer. I told her it was a lack of faith. I didn't have no faith or nothing.

This is so weird. My eyes started opening up. She said, "Where are you looking for this faith?" I said, "Well, I've got it—I know it's down in me some—I've had it before, down, you know." She told me to reach out to God for it, that it was a gift. And I had never looked at it like that. You know what I'm saying?

So I did, and, man, it started happening. It started coming. I started doing things. I didn't know why I was doing them. For my own good and stuff, you know what I'm saying? When I come up out of that treatment, I really worked that program that time. I really worked it. I didn't before. Before I was always trying to get through it, scamming. Even though I might have believed I was trying to do good, I was running a scam. But this time I wasn't, man.

When I come out of there I could have went home, but I didn't. I went to a half-way house for a while.

There's a saying in AA: God does for us what we couldn't do for ourselves. From the get-go of me getting sober, that's what happened. He was doing for me what I couldn't. 'Cause I didn't know how.

SHALOM

She has been a counselor for fourteen years and a Christian for seven. Her practice is primarily intensive out-patient and level three, counseling for those just beginning to experience problems with alcohol or other drugs. It is sometimes voluntary for the clients and sometimes court-ordered. Occasionally, for the right person, she will use a Christian-based curriculum, but it is not a Christian counseling service.

"I can go back to my AA upbringing, so to speak. A lot of people say that AA talks about God a lot, and it does. But I know that AA is for the whole world. AA is all around the world. And I know that Christianity is not in every spot that AA is. The people who are in those places where Christianity isn't have just as much right to be clean and sober as I do. I just go back to that. We talk a lot. For those who absolutely will bolt on me, I work with God. I just tell 'em to put another 'o' in. Let's go with 'good' for a while. I was unsaved a lot longer than I've been saved."

I started using when I was twelve, which is not totally unusual. Alcohol.

I'm from Spencer. I was raised there in a twenty-two-room house. My mother was the first woman coroner in the United States. My dad had been coroner prior to that. He was killed in an ambulance accident. So my mom inherited his position and then was voted in for two terms. It was quite the little deal. She was invited to be on *What's My Line?* and all that kind of stuff.

And I know you asked about addictions, but to me this is a part of it, because a lot of people think addictions happens to poor folks or people who are less privileged. And that wasn't the case.

I'm told that my dad drank until I was born, never to drink again. I know that's not true, because I remember seeing him drink twice. But I didn't see him drunk. However, my belief is that if you are an alcoholic you shouldn't drink at all.

My mom, after my dad's death, she went back to embalming college and all that. I lived in a funeral home. She started drinking, too. And I don't know but what she always had, but it had never looked to me like it had got out of control at all. But she did go a through a time when it was out of control.

My mom was in school a lot in Indianapolis. I don't know, it's hard for me to say if I was like a normal kid with maybe not quite enough supervision or if I was wild from the beginning. I don't know. But I know that Spencer had sort of a social separate system. You know, it was like you were only supposed to hang with your economic level or whatever. I know I never was very interested in that. I think it was because of the rule, of the unspoken rule. It always looked to me like the kids on the other side of the track or whatever were having more fun. [Laughs.] So I went there.

I drank. I drank a lot. Kind of funny in a way, because by the time most of the girls my age were involved in sexual sorts of things, I really wasn't. Because I was drinking. [Laughs.] It would take too much time out of drinking, I

guess. It was normal heavy drinking for teenagers. Nothing eventful happened, really.

When I was sixteen I got married. And even though that sounds pretty amazing today, then it wasn't all that terribly unusual. People in Owen County got married early. Very isolated. Owen County was very isolated when I grew up there. They called people from Indianapolis or Bloomington "foreigners," and they meant it. They were not interested in new money. New money could stay away. The old money was all that counted.

So I got married when I was sixteen. We stayed married three years. Neither one of us was old enough to be married, nor did we have a hint. A child was born to that marriage. That's my Gina, who's in New York. And I left. I went to the big city. Got in my girlfriend's car, and we both went. I wanted to be a dancer, and I was. A club dancer.

I can remember my folks telling me, Go to the city and somebody's gonna stick a needle in your arm. You know, almost like no control over that. I was always so afraid of needles.

I got to the place where I was sticking a needle in my arm every three hours, all day long, everyday.

How did that start?

I don't know. It's kind of like everybody around me was doing it, and I knew I would never do it. And then I did it. No preparation or forethought. It just kind of—I drank, never did any other drugs. One day, they gave me I think two bennies. Two Benzedrine. And I smoked part of a joint, which I'd never done before. And then they sent me to the store with a grocery list. And that was sort of my initiation. I can remember walking to the store and feeling like I was Boing! Boing! Boing! off of curbs. And I felt like I was gone for hours.

But I didn't have any fear. I hadn't been loaded enough. The horror that I experienced in later years—and I know other people do too—comes with experiences being loaded. That first high was just fun. I wasn't paranoid, I wasn't afraid of the police, I wasn't afraid of, you know, anything. It was just like I got to get this done and get back. It seemed like it took all day.

I was with a nationally well-recognized motorcycle gang who I ran into in Indianapolis, and they were to be my family for many years.

How did you meet them?

In a bar.

And they said, "Come riding with us"?

Well, pretty much. They kind of liked me. I'm really not sure what it was about me in particular that they liked, because they don't like everybody. But we just really had a good time together. I felt safe with them. I felt a family.

I never had felt like a little family thing in my life, 'cause my dad left me, through death. My mom immediately went to school and was working.

Anyway, I was always kind of envious of the kids that were my friends that had big families and mommy and daddy and the supper table and all that kind of stuff. I never had that. I would wake up at two in the morning with a house full of state police and detectives and all that kind of stuff. It just didn't seem familified. And I was in search of a family and found one.

So I started being more at ease with drugs I think, with the Benzedrine and the marijuana, although I hated marijuana soon. It did me no good at all. I didn't like it. But I sure liked the speed. I never liked sleep much. I felt cheated by sleep. Speed allowed me to pass through that. [Laughs.]

I don't know, I found myself wanting to please my family, my new family. Had a lot of violence in me. Lots and lots of violence.

Where was that coming from?

I really don't know.

Where was it going?

Anybody who was unfortunate enough to be in front of me. Part of it, I know, was that's what they were about. A lot of it was about violence. Not toward each other but outside of that. So I know part of it was that. Part of it was to please them, but it came a little too easy for that to be the whole reason. I was just a violent person.

Today I still don't know why I was so violent, what I was so angry about. I can go into "therapese" [laughs] and talk about, my dad left me and all that. I think I was searching for my dad for a long time, but . . .

I think it hurts when we start out kids by saying, "Here comes trouble." I always heard stories that my dad had been a really violent person, and my dad was my extreme hero. If I would do something—this is as a kid—if I would do something like, oh, I don't know, be clumsy or just go off in a little kid fashion or whatever, they'd say, "Oh you're just like your dad." All that kind of blended in, but today it'd be real hard for me to tell you whether or not that was the reason or whether because of my education in therapy I know those key things to look for, so I've put that neat little picture together for myself.

[Laughs.] I really don't know. It would be hard for me to separate that.

I got a real rush from violence. I was truly violent. Which again in therapy I see those who are truly violent and those who pretend to be violent. Some examples of that are a truly violent person won't warn you ahead of time.

I really hurt people. I seemed to get some sort of rush out of that, some sort of high out of that. Like a drug high. Pounding heart, sped up.

And you'd be beating the hell out of somebody in a bar?

Mostly, yes, because I lived in bars.

This was a 1 percent motorcycle gang. We spent all the time in the street scene. It was like bars, clubs. We, of course, had our own bar. At that time there were thirteen chapters in each city. Where there was a chapter, they had their own bar. So that was a start for the day.

So yeah, a lot of the violence as well as just interaction with other people, period, was done in bars or on the streets.

I enjoyed that we would ride motorcycles across country and that the police, the state police, would be there to greet us, and it was not to arrest us but to escort us through. They didn't want trouble. We'd sometimes be escorted halfway across the United States. I don't mean they came with us, but every time we'd come through their town. That kind of thing.

Were you with one guy? Were you an old lady or what?

Well, for the most part, one guy. I mean, I was with them like twelve years. So, yeah, I started out with one guy. He and I broke up at one point.

And was that like all the stories you hear about being a woman in a biker gang? What was it really like?

It was really like I was treated differently. There were women like that, but the thing is, those women were not in relationships with any of the men. Those women were women who would just sort of come in and say, you know, "Here I am!" sort of thing. I want to be a groupie or I want to hang out or whatever. Then the stories that you've heard about trains et cetera were very true.

What about being property and that sort of thing?

Property, very definitely. And that's why our patches today say "Property of Jesus Christ." Because as we interact with the worldly gangs we want our patches to draw their attention through familiar sorts of things. In the 1 percent world, women most assuredly are not entities in and of themselves. They are butt property of the man.

Did you mind that at the time?

No.

What about in retrospect?

I have to chew on my feminism, but in retrospect I see that it was a protection in one way. That's the good side of it: It was a protection. No other person would mess with property of one of the—my guy was a president, and for sure nobody was gonna mess with me as long as I was with him in the second part of my tenure with them. The first part I was indeed messed with, so to speak. I was raped by a person who was left there when the gang went away.

So he was not in the gang?

He was in the gang. But everybody else was gone.

You weren't speaking metaphorically. I thought you meant they killed him.

They didn't do him much good when they came back. They held what they called a kangaroo court in which he had the right to discuss his side of the story. But the executioner had been left behind, not for any particular reason other than he just didn't go on that run. And he just loved me to pieces, and he knew exactly what had happened. So he testified on my behalf, and the guy was really badly beaten. That was their way of not taking it to legal court. They had their own court. They had their own world. Violence was a way of life.

It gave reputation and a feeling of strength, I think, to the whole gang. You know about 1 percent gangs, about Angels and Outlaws and Bandidos and that kind of thing. Your view of it might be clearer than my view of it. My view came from living inside of it. I don't know. But I would say it was an identity. People were afraid.

The two worst parts for me, one of them is when we had a national run at one time and there were 750 motorcycles there. And of course many of those motorcycles had women on them, behind the man or whatever. A few women riders. One or two women riders, period. But there were at least 750 there. And a woman came into camp and said she wanted to be a mama.

Separate the folklore from what that really means.

It's not very separate. It's a sexual receptacle. Certainly no intimacy or anything like that. I don't know why anyone would want to do that. I don't know. I don't know. Don't understand why. I saw it happen on a few occasions with women coming into like a chapter or a clubhouse. This was 750. I don't understand a woman who would come in to twelve or thirteen or fourteen. But 750?

And they'd just line up and gang-bang her?

Yeah. And that was horrid. We sat out by the campfire, and we knew what was going on. Eventually we would hear her scream. There really was nothing that I could do. There was not a thing I could do. It got to not be part of the good old gang syndrome anymore. It got to be pretty messed up. Twenty-seven hours.

So that's a horrid memory for me. A horrid memory. I've dissected that one so many times since I've been clean and sober and then so many times again since I've been saved. What could I have done? What could I have done? What could I have done? And ultimately I keep coming up with there wasn't anything I could have done other than replace her. And I wasn't going to do that.

And of course the second thing is that I was arrested for first-degree murder and eleven other felony charges at one time and spent a little over three years locked up.

It was a tavern fight. Everything was a tavern fight. We were going to look for a car. A woman down on the south side of Indy had a car for sale. We were in Indianapolis at this time, and we were pretty straight because we were going out of our territory. South side of Indy at that point was definitely not where we hung. So we were pretty clean. And three folks took exception to our appearances.

They were redneck, glow-in-the-dark, big old folks at the bar. They came at us with their chairs up over their heads, cussing and saying how they were going to kill us and all that type of stuff. I had been given the guns when we went into the tavern. Because at that time, the police were not as quick to search women, 'cause there weren't as many women police.

And I had gotten rid of them. I had hidden them inside the bar so they weren't on me, but then when the fight broke out I went and got them.

From that stemmed the murder charge. Today I know that I did not shoot the person. I'm just pretty sure I didn't shoot the person. Alcoholics have blackouts. It's a little too dramatic to say I blacked out at that very second. I do remember putting the pistol in the person's throat, and they were shooting at my old man who was down the street. I remember him hollering at me to bring him the guns, but then we all got away, and the next thing I knew I came back and the person was actually shot right where I had held the gun. I really don't think I did it. I just don't think I did it. But I don't know. Maybe I did.

But anyway, they reduced the murder charge to involuntary manslaughter. I had a '35 and '38* weapons charge. Then they caught up with me on these other charges, counterfeited a construction company's checks and all that kind of stuff that I had been involved in before, but when I got arrested for this it was like it all came down.

I didn't go to prison; I never got out of county jail. It was like all these other charges just kept coming in, kept coming in, kept coming in. So every time I would like to be ready to go out—actually, one day I had my stuff together and was out of the building and they got me again. I mean, they were just screwing with me bad, really, really bad. Because they knew I had information.

The older 1 percent motorcycle gangs were not mean little rich kids, rich kids running rampant. They were well thought out, adult, intelligent yet devious, powerful people, and the police wanted all the information they could possibly gather on them, and I would not give 'em that information. And therefore, every time I would almost be out they'd whip another charge on me. They thought eventually I would break and do that.

I would just love to tell you that my extreme loyal being is what kept me from doing that. Part of it was loyalty. Part of it was the knowledge that anything the police could to do to me, they could do a thousand times worse to me if I gave up any information.

And when you got out, did you go back to the gang?

I did, but it was a little different. They tend to change and move, change and move, change and move. I was certainly not in any way opposed to them, afraid of them. They treated me well, all that, but I wasn't in the same way that I had been.

I ended up going back to them again years later. We were friends, but, no, I wasn't that high anymore.

What about the guy that you'd been involved with?

He went to the penitentiary also. Or, I mean, he went to jail also. Like I said, we were still friends. We were not together.

See, the actual murder was never solved. So we sort of changed our relationship. Prior to that time we were seen together a lot, then not so much anymore. If we were in the same bar or whatever we were very friendly and everything and quite comfortable.

I didn't even really leave. We just changed. There was never any kind of "Oh God, they'll kill me if I leave" kind of crap.

---

* The years the legislation was passed.

What do think brought most people to the gang?

I don't really know. Searching. Searching. You know, they talk in addiction about how there's an emptiness inside that you're just trying to fill, trying to fill, trying to fill. And people do that with alcohol and they do that with other drugs and they do it with violence and they do it with gambling and they do it with sex, food. There's all kinds of ways to do it. I believe that there is perhaps—I think the more intelligent a person is—just plain IQ-wise. I'm not going anyplace else, just there—possibly the higher their threshold for excitement or whatever. Perhaps the search carries them further. This is just completely I'm guessing, but it seems to hold true that out of all two hundred of those guys that I knew really well, there was only one who I would judge didn't have an exceptional IQ. So I don't know if that's true or not, but that's at least what I would romantically like to think, that their search took them further than just drugs or just alcohol.

I think alcohol and drugs had a big play in it. Didn't know any of them that didn't use. There seemed to not be a connection between military history and membership in that organization. Today, in therapy, when I encounter people with real violent problems, one of the first things I look for is a military background. And it seemed like with the gang, gosh, as many did as didn't. As many of 'em were avoidant of military involvement whatsoever as were those who had the background.

I know that the search was always on, the search for excitement. I know addicts have a real high excitement level. Almost an unquenchable excitement level. Even after we're clean and sober. You'll find that most addicts need to do things like ride motorcycles or snow ski or parachute. [Laughs.] Maybe not most, but you'll find a lot.

So a lot of those personality things are going on in all addicts. And I think the intellect part has play in it, and there's an unknown part. I just can't guess what would make people turn, for example, into 1 percent motorcycle gangs. If we're looking at excitement, control, gunplay, and authority, what would be the splitting point that would turn them into a 1 percent motorcycle gang instead of a cop? I don't know. Extra Y chromosome I guess.

Along those lines . . .

Chromosomes? Please!

No, no, no, that extreme behavior. Do you think there's a correlation between that and Christianity?

Sure! The search. The search. We've found what that emptiness is inside, what it's for. I think we're born with an emptiness inside, to find Jesus Christ. That's what the search is really for. It's just that not all people find the opportunity to discover the ultimate end. It's like they're searching for that fulfillment that knowing Christ can give you. I still think there's a correlation between the extremeness of folks. I think maybe those that were extremely on the dark side [laughs], I think that we have this glorious excitement and the extremeness. We are extremely saved!

We're very radical, very excited about it. I've never been mediocre about anything in my whole life. And I see that in the other Christian gang members. Everything is extreme it seems like. But the Bible says, "He'll spew out the lukewarm." I don't think many of us need to worry too much about that.

THE WORD

Drawing more than eight thousand people from around the world, Indiana's Bean Blossom Boogie is the largest biker gathering in the Midwest.

The temperature is in the nineties, maybe a little hotter because of the lack of shade and the exhaust from the constant belching of straight pipes.

At the end of the weekend, the scene will look like a Mathew Brady photograph of the aftermath of a Civil War battle, with people asleep on the backs of their bikes or dropped where they were. One man, sleeping on the ground just outside the main tent, holds a beer can in his hand, like a fallen soldier still clutching his rifle. Nearby there is a bumper sticker that reads, "This country was made great by white guys with guns," and a T-shirt, "If you don't limp, you ain't shit."

There is one main path that goes through the campgrounds. Most of the weekend revolves around standing on its edges and hoping one's cries of "Titties!" and "Let 'em blossom!" yield results. There is too much repetition, urgency, and recognition to bother with the full phrase of "Show us your tits!" although some of the more clever and industrious have posted signs advertising "Free Breast Exam," "OB-GYN Office: The Doctor is In," or "Lick Your Ass for a Dollar."

Those who are not on the sidelines are riding their bikes through this gantlet, providing the other half of a balanced equation.

A woman walking through the crowd stops for photographs. She hikes her leg and pulls back her shorts enough to expose her labia, and a swarm of cameras goes down on her. Two guys look at each other with enormous eyes. "Fuck! You can't get any closer than that without licking it!" "Ain't nothing wrong with that!" "You got that right!" And they exchange high fives.

Every year at the Boogie, the Unchained Gang sets up a hospitality area along the main road where bikers can come for coffee, water, shade, rest, or quiet—at least as quiet as it gets. Most get a drink and move on. Usually people are courteous to the Christians. Few are overtly rude, they just don't offer the courtesy of modifying their language and behavior for the brief time they are at the tent. Some stay to chat, and some are ex-cons who know the gang from its prison ministry. A few come in to talk about God and spirituality or to be prayed for.

The Unchained Gang, for the most part, sticks to the area around the tent. When they go into the thick of the Boogie to get more ice, to eat, or to look at the T-shirts, patches, and other biker paraphernalia, they go in pairs. They might go to the nighttime concerts but most certainly not to the wet T-shirt contest (which distinguishes itself by having no T-shirts).

Going into these situations is often difficult for them. It represents a past that is hard to face, it is loaded with temptations to which they are particularly vulnerable, and they often recognize in the non-Christian bikers a pain and emptiness they once knew. "This is Hell right here, brother," Gabby said to me as we walked around at the Boogie. "This is pure Hell."

Delivering the word in such an environment requires fortification by reading the word. They also speak of "being prayed up" and of "feeding on the word," refamiliarizing themselves with scriptural passages that they find strengthening and that reset their moral compasses.

Non-Christian bikers at the Bean Blossom Boogie.

Non-Christian bikers at the Bean Blossom Boogie.

Non-Christian bikers at the Bean Blossom Boogie.

Non-Christian bikers at the Bean Blossom Boogie.

*Randy, carrying a cross through the Boogie to
remind people of Jesus' sacrifice.*

The Unchained Gang's hospitality tent at the Boogie.

Chico offers counseling at the Boogie.

A drunken man named Tim wandered into the gang's camp during the Boogie. He said that his mother had died of brain cancer when he was six, and throughout his life he could never understand why God would do that. He asked questions about God and whether it was possible to be saved while drunk. Chico and Larry prayed with him.

"THE VALLEY OF DECISION"
Sermon by Pastor Larry, June 23, 1996

I love Jesus Christ. I thank you, Lord, because you went to the cross willingly. He wasn't made to, but it was love that held him there to that cross. I thank you, Lord, for every individual, every soul that's represented here this morning, Lord God, because I know that you, you have a hold of 'em, Lord, and they have felt your power, your love.

Lord God, we just, we just want to be challenged this morning. We want to challenge each other. We want to exhort each other. We want to keep on keeping on. Lord, we know that it's going to be the word that's gonna take us, that takes us through. Lord God, so through your word here this morning, I ask you, Lord, to help me to teach boldly and correctly that which you've given me, Lord God, so that your body, that your church, that your bride might be edified in the word, Lord that we might be challenged, Lord that we might be filled up with power from on high. And not being afraid, Lord, because we've not been given the spirit of fear but of power and of love and of a sound mind.

Lord God, we know that we're just a small part of your church, a small part of that army that's going out into the last days, Lord, repossessing lives and souls that's been stolen by Satan. Lord, we're claiming back ground, hallelujah. Lord God, we're claiming victory over the gates of the enemy this morning. Lord, we just thank you, and we praise you, Lord God. I thank you, Lord God, for victory in the camp. Hallelujah, hallelujah, in Jesus' name. And all of God's people said . . .

Congregation: Amen!

Larry: Praise the Lord God. Hallelujah. We are on the dawning of something fantastic. How many feels it? How many feels like God is just about ready to do something? But you know who he's waiting on? Us. Waiting on us. Praise God. Amen.

Some friends of mine wrote a song several years ago: "I'd Rather Be a Fool for Christ Than a Genius Any Day." You know, a lot of times we're held back because we don't want to appear to be a fool. Boy, I tell you what, I did a lot of things in my lifetime, very, very foolish, and appeared to be the fool. And I was the fool, so I'm not gonna let that stop me now. If I can be a fool for Christ, that'll be fine. Praise God. Thank you Jesus.

I don't care what the world calls me as long as I can just keep on pointing people to Calvary, just keep on pointing people to the cross of Jesus Christ. Hallelujah.

Turn in your Bibles to the Book of Joel, chapter 3, verse 9, beginning at verse 9. Like I said earlier, we're gonna be teaching on the power of the Holy Spirit this evening's service at six o'clock. We're going to have a time of intense praise and worship. If God allows me to. The last two services, he's just said, "Time out. This is mine." [Laughs.] Praise God.

It's always his, and we want it to be that way.

Joel 3, beginning at verse 9: "Proclaim ye, this among the Gentiles." Now when you see that word *Gentiles* here, that means heathen or pagans. Says, "Prepare for war. Wake up the mighty men. Let all the men of war draw near. Let them come up." Now he's addressing the heathens, the armies of this world. "Beat your plowshares into swords and your pruning hooks into spears. Let the weak say I am strong. Assemble yourselves and come all ye heathen and gather yourselves together round about."

Then I see Joel taking a little bit of a breather here, and he's saying, "And then Lord, cause your mighty warriors to come down, O Lord. Let the heathen be awakened and come up to the Valley of Jehoshaphat, for there will I sit to judge all the nations round about. Put in the sickle, for the harvest is ripe. Come on down for the press is full. The vats are overflowing with the wickedness of these men. Multitudes, multitudes are in the valley of decision, for the day of the Lord is near."

This message this morning is entitled "The Valley of Decision." Multitudes, multitudes are in the valley of decision, for the day of the Lord is near, in the valley of decision. Praise God, praise God.

This passage of Scripture is also confirmed in Revelations 19:19 when the nations of the earth will be gathered in the Valley of Jehoshaphat. We know that there is going to be one final battle, one decisive war that's going to be fought. This is going to be called the Battle of Armageddon. Now I believe it's called the Armageddon because the field or the plain or the valley of this place is called not only the Valley of Jezrahiah but also the Valley of Megiddo. So if you kind of look at that, it says Arm-mageddon or Armegiddo. And it's going to be a great and decisive battle.

When I used to put these Scriptures together, I see this. You know, many years ago, the great general Napoleon stood, looking out over this vast plain there. He made a prophesy and didn't even realize it. He says, "One of these," he says, "this place is so vast that all of the armies of the world could gather themselves, could assemble themselves together on this battlefield." And that's exactly what's going to happen. They're going to assemble themselves together, but coming out of this Valley of Jezreel, if you follow this down on a geographical map, this turns also into the Valley of Jehoshaphat, which is outside of Jerusalem. And I believe that that's where the heat of the battle is going to be fought. 'Cause they're gonna come down, they're gonna try to, they're gonna try to overrun, overtake Jerusalem. And there's gonna be a lot of blood spilled there.

John the Revelator saw this valley as the place where God would pour out his wrath in one final judgment upon the earth against kings and armies who were so proud and so defiant against God they thought they could actually make war with God and defy his power and judgment.

I tell you what, I'm reminded of that, that great ship the *Titanic*, and that word *titanic* actually means "in defiance of God." We saw how that one ended up.

Revelations 19:11 and 21 says, "And I saw Heaven open, and behold a white horse. And he that sat upon him was called faithful and true and in righteousness. He does judge and make war." John is describing our lord and savior Jesus Christ here. "His eyes were as a flame of fire, and on his head were many crowns. And he had a name written that no man knew but he himself. And he was clothed with a vesture dipped in blood, and his name is called the word of God."

Boy, I tell you what, this is a whole different description of Jesus than the way we see him now, because Jesus came into this world as our savior. As our savior. To whosoever will. To whosoever would believe on him should not perish but should have everlasting life.

I want to tell you folks, real soon he's coming back as our judge. And he's called the word of God.

Says, "His vesture was dipped in blood." That shows that he's coming back in judgment. Coming back to judge the world according to his word. John continues here, he says, "And the armies which were in Heaven"—this is us, praise

God. I'm gonna be there, and I'm gonna be riding a white horse—"followed him. His armies which were in Heaven followed him upon white horses, clothed in fine linen, white and clean." No more black leather. [Congregation laughs.] This'll be alright. We'll be with Jesus.

Says, "And out of his mouth went a sharp sword that with he should smite the nations. And he shall rule them with a rod of iron, and he treads the wine press with the fierceness and wrath of almighty God. And he has on his vesture and on his thigh written 'King of kings and Lord of lords.'" Praise God. This won't be the same Jesus that they spit upon. This won't be the same Jesus that they drove the nails through his hands, that they drove the crown of thorns over his head, that they mocked him and they spit upon him and then they slapped him and said, "Now prophesy to us who slapped ya" and all the terrible things they did to him. That's over. That's finished. That was done, once and for all. Praise God. And it was love, it was love that took him through all of that, but he's coming back, as a judge.

John said, "And I saw an angel standing in the sun and he cried with a loud voice, saying to all the fowls that fly in the midst of Heaven, 'Come and gather yourselves together unto the supper of the great God.'" Now, I know every once in a while we'll see some road-kill out here on the road, and you'll see a buzzard fly in. And that dude sets by the side of the road. Lot of times you see these hawks or buzzards, and you can drive by and they won't budge. I mean, their eye is on the carcass out there in the middle of the road. And as soon as your car goes by, they're out there.

Well, I've heard reports that these buzzards or vultures over in around Jerusalem like usually only lay one egg, and they're laying like two or three eggs now, getting ready to clean up the mess. I mean this is God's Rumpke service.* [Congregation laughs.]

And we're gonna see why. I mean there's gonna be, there's gonna be blood and dead bodies stacked up to the bridle of a horse. I don't know how high that'd be. Probably at least five feet tall, maybe. Five feet high.

Says that, "You may eat the flesh of kings and the flesh of captains and the flesh of mighty men and the flesh of horses and of them that set on them and the flesh of all men, both free and bond, both small and great." I mean there's gonna be dead flesh out there everywhere. And the vultures and all these birds, the fowls of the air, are gonna be coming in and eating the carcasses of men, both small and great. Not gonna be too much pride left after all this.

"And I saw the beast taken, and with him the false prophet that wrought miracles before him, with which he deceived them that he had received the mark of the beast, and them that worshipped his image. These both were cast alive into a lake of fire, burning with brimstone. And the remnant were slain with the sword of him that sat upon the horse."

Now see, we see this picture in the garden where Peter hacked off the ear of one of the soldiers when they tried to take Jesus captive, and I mean Jesus just flat got on Peter about that and put the ear back on and healed him and everything.

Now Jesus has got a sword.

Praise God, he said, "All the fowls were filled with their flesh." Church, we're looking right into the mouth of this thing. We really are. Revelation 14:20 says, "And the wine press was trodden without the city, and blood came out of the

---

* A trash collection company.

wine press even unto the horses' bridles, by the space of a thousand and six furlongs." Now, a furlong is an eighth of a mile. So you figure up a thousand and six furlongs, that equals out to a hundred and twenty-five and three-quarter miles. A hundred and twenty-five and three-quarter miles that the blood is gonna be up to the horse's bridle, in the Valley of Jehoshaphat. That's a lot of blood.

You know, it's amazing to me at this point that mankind could actually be made by God, created by God, and then to deny his very existence. Can you just get a scenario of this? Here is a gentle, loving God. You know, many of you in here have made things with your hands, and you do it very meticulously and very gentle, and you make things or you draw things and you take great care in it because you're hand-crafting something, and you want it to just really look good and be made right. And you can just see God doing that with mankind. You know, just takes a big hunk of dirt, big ball of clay, and then all of a sudden he's molding man and all of a sudden shaping and everything. And then he blows the breath into his nostrils, into man's nostrils, and all of a sudden—man, just all of a sudden—man is just up on his feet.

That's man. Whew! Whew! Here we are, at the end of the age, standing at the threshold of the tribulation period, and many, many people are still standing in the valley of decision, not able to make up their minds. Not able to make up their minds. How many has known people like that? Just can't seem to make up their mind.

In Matthew 24:37, it says, "But as the days of Noah were, so shalt also the coming of the Son of Man be, for as in the days that were before the flood, they were eating and drinking and marrying and giving in marriage until the day that Noah entered into the ark and knew not

until the Flood came and took them all away, so shall also the coming of the Son of Man be."

People is not gonna even know what hit 'em. Ain't even gonna have a clue until it's too late. Can you imagine when the door was closed on the ark? It was shut, and Noah and his family was inside that ark, and they could hear screams out there, and people beating on the side of that ark. "Let me in! Let me in!" And it's gonna be the same way, only it's gonna be too late. And it's not gonna be by water.

God promised that he'd never destroy this earth again with water or a flood. It's gonna be the same way as it was in the days of Noah.

You know, even though I've been able to reach many, many people with the gospel of Jesus Christ, it's those that came so close to making a right decision, but still they went out into eternity never quite making up their minds, never accepting the knowledge of the saving grace of the Lord Jesus Christ into their hearts.

You know, it's all of these people that urge me on the more, harder and harder, to witness Jesus to all of those people that are in the valley of decision. Makes me just want to try that much harder to get to these people. We met one guy up there on Friday night, and this guy had some word in his life. He'd grew up, somewhere along the line, and he had some word there. You know, when I heard that word, praise God, I wanted to water it. I wanted to put some water on it. And I believe we did. I believe we got some water on that word. 'Cause sometimes it gets perverted. You know, the devil will try to pervert the word in your heart and in your life. Sometimes he'll just try to throw a wet blanket over it or something. Or he'll try to make you forget about it. But I tell you what, the word will never return void.

And so we just gotta, we just gotta water that word. I said, "Where's you at last year when we's down here?" He said, "I's in jail." I said, "Well, you're out now, and you're not gonna go back. You don't ever have to go back, except to minister," praise God.

In the Book of Acts, the twenty-fourth chapter, the Apostle Paul had the opportunity to witness Jesus to King Agrippa. To a king! And after he had given much time to giving his testimony of how Jesus had struck him down on the road to Damascus, and how he came to believe in his heart that this Jesus was real, and how he had completely surrendered his heart and his life to the Lord Jesus Christ, here, in verse twenty-eight, King Agrippa told Paul, "Almost thou hast persuaded me to be a Christian." Almost. Almost.

You know, and I think it goes on to say, Paul says, "Not almost but I wish that thou would have completely accepted Jesus into your heart." You know, and it's still the same way today. All of those people that have come so close but still couldn't quite make the decision. Blinded by the darkness of this world, lied to by Satan into believing that they couldn't do it. You can't do it, you can't do it. You can't be good.

You know, there's gonna be a lot of people that's gonna miss Heaven by eighteen inches. How many times have you heard somebody say, "Well, I believe in God. I believe in God." It's in their head but it never got to their heart. They never made the surrender. And they're gonna miss Heaven by eighteen inches.

In the many years that I had my shop open, I's working on bikes and stuff, I remember a young man by the name of Jeff Jarrells. I don't know if anybody in here remembers Jeffrey or not, but his grandfather was a really good friend of mine. We used to go to church together, and I knew that Jeff meant a lot to his grandfather, and I felt that kind of love every time I talk to his grandfather about Jeff. Jeff had a Sportster, and he'd come into my garage, and I tell you what, I never let Jeff come and go without telling him about Jesus. And he knew everything that I was telling him. He was raised in church.

And I'd tell Jeff, I said, "Man, Jeff, Jesus is coming back." And I'd get to witness to him maybe fifteen minutes, a half an hour, whatever, however long he was there. And he would always listen to me, and he'd always say, every time, the same answer. He'd say, "Larry, I know that you're telling me the truth. I know that what you're saying is right, but I'm not ready."

And what he was telling me was that he wasn't ready to surrender yet. He still had things that he wanted to do. And I know that in Jeff's mind, he really, whenever he made that decision, he wanted to go all the way. He wanted to do it right. And I knew that about Jeff. But he didn't understand. He just didn't understand.

You know, whenever I fell away from God as a teenager, I thought, Man, there's a lot going on in this world that I'm missing out on, and I didn't want to miss out on anything, but I tell you what, the devil was trying to kill me while I was out there, trying to take me out before I could ever surrender my heart to the Lord.

And that's exactly what happened to Jeff. When I got the news that he'd been killed in a truck accident in Greene County my heart sank, because Jeff never took the time, he never got around to accepting Jesus Christ into his heart, into his life.

There is a lot of people out there that's in the valley of decision. Multitudes, multitudes. I was in my garage working late one night when a couple of guys pulled in. Porky Martin and Randy Tannahill. Porky had been a friend of mine. We used to party together before he got sent to the prison. He did eight years for murder. And he got out, and my house is the first house he came to when he got released, when he came down from Michigan City. He came out to the garage, and I remember it was getting late. He saw me, and he knew something was different. He didn't know about my, about my experience with Jesus Christ, and he started asking me questions.

I said, "Porky," I said, "I'm another person now." And I started telling him about what Jesus had done in my life. And Porky was standing there, and this guy was hard. I started telling him about what Jesus Christ had done, and all of a sudden the tears started running down his face. And he took his glasses off and kept turning around. He wouldn't look at me. And I kept talking. Finally he started looking, and he said, "What are you doing to me? What are you doing to me?"

I said, "What do you mean, what am I doing to you, Porky? I'm not doing anything. I'm telling you what Jesus had done in my life."

"What are you doing to me?"

I said. "That's not me, Porky." I said, "That's Jesus." I said, "That's the spirit of God, working on your heart. And you know what I'm telling you is the truth.

And we stood there for a long time, and he'd get mad at me because I'd still tell him about Jesus. He'd walk out in the drive, and he'd be walking out. He didn't want me to see him crying. And he'd walk out around there.

I finally told both of 'em, I said, "Hey," I said, "I'm gonna be going to church here in a little while." I said, "Why don't you come and go with us?"

And the other guy, Tannahill, spoke up and said—he was making a big joke out of it—and he said, "Yeah, Porky!" He said, "Why don't we just go with him?" He said, "We'll just call our wives and tell 'em we're going and why don't we just go to church with him, Porky?" He didn't think Porky'd say yes, and Porky said okay. [Congregation laughs.]

Randy was on his bike, and he was out of there. He was down the road real quick. Porky went to church with me that night. It was like a fellowship service was going on, and we got there late, and we had to sit way off over to the left side of the church. We's behind the piano. We couldn't hardly see the preacher that night, but I remember something amazing happened. They had a choir, a children's choir, get up from another church, and they sang, and they all, when they got done singing, all the children started to go back to their parents.

Porky didn't know anybody in that place except me. And this little boy—I don't know how old, maybe eight years old—started to walk down the aisle, then all of a sudden he just kind of made a right turn, and he walked over there and just walked right up, I mean just right up against Porky, and put his arms around him and said, "I love you."

And I'm setting there watching this and I mean . . .

Porky just cried and cried. I saw God going to great lengths, great lengths, trying to reach Porky's heart. Porky went to church with me several times after that. One evening he came by and said that he'd made a deal with the devil.

And I said, "Porky, you don't make deals with the devil." I said, "He's a liar." I said, "He don't follow through with any bargains or any deals."

And it wasn't too long after that I was working on Porky's bike in my shop and he came by. It was like about five-thirty. It was after closing. And I remember we stood down there in the door of my garage, probably for an hour and a half that night, and I spoke to him once again about the love of God and about what Jesus would do for him and what he wanted to do and what he did.

And we spoke, and Porky would always stand there and listen to me. And little did I know that was the last time that I'd ever talk to Porky Martin. Because that same night he went out and he got drunk. A hundred and twenty mile an hour made gravel out of his body, into a big roadside sign. I ended up going to his funeral.

In the valley of decision, never could quite make the decision. But he would listen. Many years later—I don't know how many, four or five years later—Randy Tannahill went out the same way. I witnessed to him so many times about Jesus.

You know what got me? Randy had called me after he got the news. And he called me up and he said, he said, "Larry, Porky got killed last night." I said, "Well, I'd heard the news." He said, "Man, we got to pray for him." I said, "Do what?" He said, "We need to pray for Porky." I said, "Randy, the praying is over now for Porky." He said, "What do you mean?" I said, "Porky has went out into eternity."

You know, a lot of people believe that there's an in-between place, that there's this place called Purgatory. You'll not find it in your Bible. But they believe that it's a place where you're not good enough to go to Heaven but you're not bad enough to go to Hell, so they just kind of stick you in this slot until people can pray you out of there. But the Bible says, in Ecclesiastes eleven and three, it says, "And if the tree falls

towards the south or towards the north, in the place where the tree falls, there shall it be."

The Greek word for "fall" here means "to cease, to die or to perish." We have a time to make a decision. I don't know how long, because you can go to cemeteries and you'll find that death is also not a respecter of persons. There's ages there on tombstones from babies all the way up to old age. And we're given a time-slot in there. This life here is only a dressing room, a dressing ground, for where we're gonna spend eternity. The decisions that we make now, the decisions who we're gonna live for, who we're gonna serve, who we're gonna follow.

And I told Randy that evening, I said, "Porky already made his decision. And he made his decision by not accepting Jesus Christ into his heart and into his life."

Matthew 3:10 says, "Therefore every tree which doesn't bring forth good fruit is hewn down and cast into the fire." You know, so many people get stuck in the valley of decision simply because they don't want to surrender. They don't want to change their way of thinking, they don't want to admit their way is wrong. They still want to hang on to their past, they still want to hang on to the pleasures of this life.

It's amazing. You know, I look back at the things that I held onto for so many years that I thought were so much of a priority in my life, and I look back at those things that I held onto for so long, and it wasn't nothing! They was not anything compared to what I have found in Jesus Christ. The peace that he has given me.

And you know, all those things that I turned loose of for the Lord, a lot of those things he gave back to me, only now they're a different perspective in my life. And I realize that any talent, anything that God had given, that God had given me—not anybody else. You know, there's a lot of musicians in this world, and they're playing tunes to the devil. Devil doesn't give them nothing but a hard time. He didn't give them that talent. He didn't give them all the talent that they have, the gifts that they have. God is the giver of gifts. He's the giver of everything that is good. And those things was given to us to use to his glory. Praise God.

In the Book of Luke, the eighteenth chapter beginning at the eighteenth verse, Jesus tells a story about a rich young ruler who was also faced with a decision. And this ruler asked him, saying, "Good master, what shall I do to inherit eternal life?" Jesus said unto him, "Why do you call me good? None is good except one, and that is God," implying, "Are you saying that I'm God?" I think that's what he was saying.

Jesus said unto him, "Why do you call me good? None is good except one that is God." He said, "Thou knowest the commandments, Do not commit adultery, Do not kill, Do not steal, Do not bear false witness, Honor thy father and thy mother." And he said, the young ruler said, "All these I have, all these things I've done, I've kept from my youth up." Now when Jesus heard these things, he said unto him, "You lack one thing."

He knew this rich, young ruler, riches meant a lot to him. "You lack one thing." He said, "Sell all that you have and distribute unto the poor and you shall have treasure in Heaven, then come and follow me."

And we know that it was a sorrowful decision this rich young ruler made, because it saddened him and he turned and he walked away. He walked away.

You know, I'm reminded of what Solomon asked. He didn't ask for riches, did he? He asked for wisdom. But he got everything. He wanted wisdom. He said, "God, I need wisdom to lead these people. I need understanding to lead these people," and God just heaped it on him, everything that he had need of. God was trying to show forth his glory in the riches of Solomon and in the wisdom of Solomon.

You know, I've met so many people that I used to ride with. Louie was such a good friend of mine, and he was one of the guys that I rode with for so long. And I'd witness to him in my shop, and he'd come over and I'd tell him about Jesus. He never talked back to me too much, but he would listen a little while and then he'd leave. After a couple of years Louie was killed in a bike wreck.

And I had another young man that came in. His name's Rusty Crowe, and he's a very good friend of mine. He started working for me, and then he started wanting to ride with the same club that I had rode with, and I said, "You don't want to do that." I said, "Rusty, you're a good guy, but I tell you what, when you start running with the devil, you start compromising your life. And you'll wind up doing things that you never thought you'd do."

And he'd tell me, Well, I'm just gonna do this and this. I'm not gonna do the rest of this stuff, and I'd just smile at him. I said, "You ain't even gonna know who you are a couple years from now when you get involved." I said, "You will end up doing things you thought you'd never do." And that's exactly what happened to him.

He ended up doing time in prison. Then his brother came along. His brother would come out. And his brother saw the things that happened to Rusty, and he said that he didn't want to have no part of that. But then later on, here come his brother and said, "Yeah, I think I'll join." And I told him the same story. I said, "You're gonna end up doing the same things that your brother did."

"Naw, I'm just gonna do this and I'll just do this. I'll just." What he was saying, "I'm just gonna sin a little bit. I'll just sin a little bit."

Did you ever say that? Just gonna do it a little bit. There ain't no sinnin' a little bit. You just, you end up, you get in the sinning business, and you just go on and you go on and you go on. And you end up doing things you never thought you'd ever do. And that's exactly what happened to his brother, Rod.

And because of reasons that I'm not even gonna say, Rod ended up in a fire that burned over 40 percent of his body because of sin in his life. The devil doesn't make deals.

Hebrews 11:25 says, "It's better to suffer affliction with the people of God than to enjoy the pleasures of sin for a season." I'm giving you actual true accounts of close friends of mine that I used to ride with and work with. A guy that I used to go to school with, we went through school together, we played football, we wrestled together. His name was Mike Perry. We called him "the Bee," Honeybee. Real good friend of mine. And after I got saved in 1978, man I worked on this guy. I loved him. And I'd tell him about what Jesus was doing. And he knew that there had to be a miracle involved here for my life to change the way that it did, but he called it "the big accident."

He referred to my getting saved as "the big accident." He didn't want to talk much farther beyond that, but that's what he called it. I remember, Mike ended up in Madison State Hospital because of drugs in his life, and he had to do some time down there for rehabilitation. And he wrote me a letter, and I still have that letter. He

referred to the big accident again once in my life and started talking about God. And he said, "Who knows? I may just have a Big Accident myself."

And I kept that letter for a long time. I don't know where Mike was, but I ended up preaching his funeral a few years ago. But I did see the devastating effects that drugs and alcohol had on his life, that just deteriorated his body, that just took him out. And I hope that he made his peace with God. I hope he called on the name of the Lord before it was too late. I don't know. I don't have a clue. But I tell you what, Satan doesn't make deals. Time is running out. Time is running out. And there's people that's in the valley of decision.

Isaiah 66:3 and 5 says, "Yea, they have chosen their own way and their soul delighted in their abomination. I also will choose their delusions and will bring their fears upon them, because when I called they didn't answer, and when I spoke they didn't hear."

Matthew 25:31 and 34, in closing, Jesus said, "When the Son of man shall come in his glory and all the holy angels with him, then shall he sit on the throne of his glory. And before him shall be gathered all nations, and he shall separate them one from another as a shepherd divides his sheep from his goats. And he shall set the sheep on his right hand but the goats on his left. And then shall the King say unto them on his right hand, 'Come, ye blessed of my Father, inherit the kingdom that was prepared for you from the foundation of the world.'" Praise the living God.

But verse forty-one says, "Then shall he say also unto them on the left hand, 'Depart from me, ye cursed, into everlasting fire, prepared for the devil and his angels.'"

[Music fades in.]

I want to tell you this morning that Hell was not created for mankind, that it was created for the devil and his followers. And I could have very easily have been there right now. My life was over eighteen years ago, and I recognized that because of the sin in my life, because of the per-version that was in my life. Oh, I thought I would sin just a little bit. But I tell you what, my sins kept getting bigger, and they kept getting bigger, and they kept getting bigger until they finally, I knew that my life was being destroyed. And it seemed like that I was on the highway to Hell, on a pathway to destruction. My accelera-tor was stuck. There was no brakes in the vehicle and seemed like that I just couldn't stop. I was out of control. But I thank God for his mercy, that he got me stopped. He got me stopped. Praise the living God. Hallelujah. Thank you, Lord Jesus. Thank you, Lord Jesus. Praise God. Joe's ready to make a decision. Praise the Lord. Thank you, Lord Jesus. Praise God. Hallelujah. Let's bow our heads and close our eyes.

[Singing fades up.]

There are people in this place this morning that are hanging in the balance. They've been in the valley of decision. You have been in the valley of decision for quite some time. God has been speaking to you this morning. It's time. It's time, my child! It's time. Come. Come! Come into my house. Come to my table. A place has been set for you. Hallelujah. Hallelujah. Thank you, Lord Jesus. Praise the living God.

If you need Jesus Christ into your heart and into your life, Jesus is bidding you to come this morning. You've been wavering too long. Too long. He wants you to come. Come. And say yes, God. Yes, Lord. Lord, take me, Lord. I sur-render to you. Thank you, Jesus. Thank you, Jesus.

Harley.

Harley and Chico follow a sermon.

PASTOR LARRY

Do you still have an interest in secular music or secular literature? I've heard you quote Aristotle and Jimi Hendrix.

John and I used to travel a lot, and we did seminars in high schools and a lot of churches on satanism and rock and roll music, complete with slides and videos. We gave a two-night presentation on all this stuff. It was pretty powerful. So my years of playing in rock and roll bands, I'd do a kind of connect the dots. I started in the 1950s with Alan Freed, and I'd work my way all the way up to where we're at today.

It was pretty powerful. I'd hit all the messages that's in rock and roll music. Of course it started with sex. It's rebellion. It started with sex in the 1950s. Rock and roll. Gonna rock you all night long. You know, rocking the car in the back seat then rolling on down the road. That's what rock and roll came from.

And then in the '60s, 'course there was drugs when the Beatles hit, and they introduced drugs into music and to a lot of kids. I was an avid Beatle fan, played all their music. Then in the '70s it was homosexuality and sexual perversion, and all this was displayed in the music and in the songs and the lifestyles.

And then the '80s it was satanism. Black metal music, heavy metal, speed metal, trash metal. We've got several boards—they're like four feet wide—with displays of all kinds of albums and paraphernalia. We'd set up a whole satanic altar. We got the chalices and the knives and skulls. We reached a lot of people.

Then right at the end of my program, I'd always talk about the Scripture out of Jeremiah. God would say to the effect of, How can I pardon you, for even your children have turned away

and worshipped gods that are not gods at all? And I took a picture, I've got a slide of a metal magazine that's got a couple of guitar players and lead players, and it says "Guitar Gods." And I'd show that big slide.

And that's what basically a lot of kids get into, worshipping these groups as gods. It was really effective. And I'd come off with a quote from Jimi Hendrix and Aristotle. I was really into that.

Tell me again your stance on Christmas.

My stance on Christmas? Well, taking it from the beginning, when the Roman emperor, Constantine, claimed Christianity, he was just—you know, I didn't know him personally, but [laughs]—he seemed like, he seemed like maybe one of the good ol' boys. Maybe he meant well. Maybe he wanted people to get along. They found out that he couldn't wipe out Christianity because there was such a persecution going on, but every time they'd kill two Christians, ten would come to take each one of them's place. There was such faith.

So, finally, this was the beginning of Roman Catholicism. He grabbed up a cross and danced through the street and claimed Christianity and all that, but this was just the beginning of a merge between Christianity and paganism. And he merged all of the holidays. I mean he took, he just, he brought 'em together.

I'm trying to think of the, I think it was the Nicaea Council—but there was no, there was no Jewish leaders there whatsoever, to talk about the Holy Days that God had ordained, that the Jewish people would celebrate.

So what they did was merges like Christmas, the birth of Jesus, which, you know, there is nothing in the Bible that tells us when he was born. Except we can only guess at the time of the year, which would have put it around October because of the climate and everything. The shepherds would not have been tending their sheep in the fields on December 25. No way. They would have already had their sheep out of the fields.

But there is a pagan festival called Saturnalia. A lot of these pagan festivals stem from around, there was a guy by the name of Nimrod, and he's the guy that—he was the great, great grandson of Cush, which was from Noah's line. He's the one that tried to build the Tower of Babel. He was gonna reach the heavens.

Anyway, he was a very, very evil man. He was the one that began astrology. They called him the child-destroyer because he would sacrifice children, throw 'em into the fire. He was so evil he ended up marrying his own mother. They had a son by the name of Tammuz, which that name is very popular among pagan, in pagan circles. Tammuz was believed to have been born December 25.

I don't know, the whole thing of Christmas, I just believe it's the same thing as what happened on the front porch of the temple that made Jesus so mad. People profiting, profiting from Christmas. Then it wasn't that long ago they took Christ out of Christmas, was calling it Xmas, under the disguise, well, the word was too long and so we want to shorten it up. And that's a bunch of baloney. They just want to take Jesus plumb out of it if they could.

Because people don't want to be convicted. We want to be able to, our flesh wants to do what we want to do. I believe that it was a bunch of blasphemy. I believe when Christmas rolls around it's one of the most depressing times of the year. Been in jail and prison ministries since 1982, and there's more suicides that take place at Christmas than any other time of the year.

There's just much depression going on. People get theirself into hock up to [their] eyeballs giving presents to people they don't even like.

Which, that's not that bad, because we need to love our enemies, and we need to humble ourselves. But I believe that Christmas is just a stench in God's nostrils. It has nothing to do with the birth of Christ anymore. I think it's just completely out of whack.

I don't see anything wrong with celebrating the birth of Christ. It's just the commercialism. That's the part that's gotten completely out of hand. I don't know if there's some significance why there never was pinned down to a date, why we don't have anything in the history books. There's nothing. There's nothing to pinpoint the birth of Jesus Christ.

I don't know if that has some significance, but I know that we're supposed to celebrate the death, burial, and resurrection more so than the birth. Because that is the significance of our freedom.

Explain to me the different levels of commitment. First you're born again, then baptism. Pull that all together for me.

Well, I would have to go back, of course, through the fall, the disobedience. The deception of Eve and the disobedience of Adam in the Garden of Eden. God said, you know, "Every tree you can eat of here in the garden." He only had one no-no, and that was not to eat of that tree that belonged to God. That was his. He said man could have everything else. He could eat of every tree, he could do anything else in the garden, but don't touch that tree, and they shouldn't've even gone near it, let alone taken the fruit from it.

But what happened, he said, "The day you do, you shall surely die." Well, God wasn't talking about physically, which it did mean physically, but he was talking about you're gonna die spiritually first. And the problems that we suffer, they always begin as spiritual problems. And I believe that, and that also explains why people years ago lived to be nine hundred years old and eight hundred years old, and it kept decreasing: seven hundred, six hundred. We're just reproducing mutant cells, so to speak, because of spiritual problems in our life, which reproduce physical problems.

So anyway, mankind died spiritually, which brought on a physical death as well, so through the years our longevity just keeps declining. So anyway, here we got the human race walking around in a spiritual death. The Bible even calls us the congregation of the dead.

So, in the Book of John, the third chapter, Jesus is telling Nicodemus, you know, Nicodemus is saying, "What must I do?" Jesus is saying, "You must be born again." "What do you mean born again? I can't enter my mother's womb the second time." And Jesus said, "You must be born of the water and the Spirit." You must be born of the water, he's talking about a fleshly birth. Because the next verse says that which is born of flesh is flesh, but that which is born of Spirit is Spirit.

Being born again is just becoming alive spiritually again. All of a sudden we're awakened. We are, we're just awakened to really what we're all about. We're all spiritual creatures, just clothed in an earth suit here, in this body that's gonna pass away. But our soul, our spirit's gonna live forever. Somewhere.

John the Baptist, the first message that he preached was repentance. That of repentance, to turn away from.

Actually, by the deception, by the disobedience of Adam and Eve, the Book of Genesis said that we were given dominion over the earth. Well, we lost it. We lost it through disobedience. We lost it through letting the devil deceive us. So the devil won legal rights to the earth. He's the prince, the power of air, the Bible says.

That's why we have to have faith. God wants to help us. God wants to be our knight in shining armor. He said he wants to be our shield, our sword, our buckler. But the Book of Hebrews says without faith, it's impossible to please God. Actually, what that means, without faith it's impossible to allow God to work in our life. We must believe in him. We must believe in order to receive. It takes a tremendous amount of faith many times.

When we believe, when we feel the tugging in our heart, when we feel that—and we do—sometimes we try to explain it away. I ran for years and years, and I just kept getting more miserable, more miserable in my search for what? To fill that void that I believe we're all filled with, a void in our heart that only God can fill. And we're trying to fill it with drugs and sex and alcohol and race cars and motorcycles and all kinds of stuff, in the pursuit of happiness, in the pursuit of freedom and joy and peace. We're trying to fill that void.

So anyway, in order to do that we've got to have faith. We allow God to work in our life. We give him legal right, all of a sudden, to work in our life.

So, comes baptism.

What is the point of being born again? Is that when you say "I accept Jesus Christ as my lord and savior" and turn your life over to him? And that's the moment?

Yeah, right. And that's a heart connection.

I believe that the true born-again experience is truly when a person, I mean they make the mouth confession with the heart connections. I mean, it strikes both. Both places. And the mouth confession is real important because we're making, we're confessing out loud. We're not ashamed.

To the rest of the congregation?

Yeah, to the world. To the world. And that's basically what baptism is. We're going on.

What's after baptism?

Well, somewhere along the line, I believe in the baptism of the Holy Spirit. Which is different from being just, being born again. The Bible says that we can't even come to God unless his spirit draws us. We can't even do that on our own. We can't even have faith. It's a gift from God, the Bible says. Everything that we do is from God. We really can't do anything that he doesn't give us the ability and the strength.

Here he is, drawing us, always drawing us and wooing us, romancing us, dating us. You know, singing under our window, trying to get us to come out, trying to get us, draw us into this relationship with him.

I had this, I hadn't been in a church in, gosh, so many years, and after I got saved, I had this desire. I found an old Bible that I won in a Sunday school contest when I was a kid. I dragged that thing around with me all my life. And I found it and I began to read it. I just had such a desire. I never read anything. I can read, but I just read the *Easyrider* magazine and the funny papers, that was about it.

But I wanted to read, and I did. The first year I was born again, I read the Bible all the way

though and about fifteen other books besides that. Just everything I could get my hands on. And God was teaching me that, you know, the other books that I would read. 'Course he teaches you how to, you line that up with the word of God, you learn to spit out the seeds.

Being baptized in the Spirit is just being immersed. It's like what happened in the Upper Room on the day of Pentecost.

Immersed, not in water?

No, just in the Spirit.

So, in an earthly, tangible way, what are you talking about? Speaking in tongues?

I personally, even though I was raised in a Pentecostal church, and that they said, you know, that you were not baptized in the Spirit unless you speak in tongues, I don't believe that.

I speak in tongues. I'm like the Apostle Paul. I praise God, I speak in tongues more than all of ya. I sing in tongues. I love—it's a pressure-release valve for me. When the word, "hallelujah," that's our highest form of praise, and it just ain't enough. I can say it fifty times, and it's just not enough. But whenever I just, I don't know, whenever I just feel the Spirit of God moving me, and I start speaking in tongues, it's a pressure-release valve for me that I can just praise God.

'Course you've been at enough of our services, you probably heard me sing in tongues and pray in tongues in the microphone. When our praise group, our music ministry, sings—I believe that the Apostle Paul, he devotes a whole chapter to tongues, talking about tongues.

We talk about the breath. Being born again was the breath. Spirit means breath. Well, we see in the Book of Acts that it came as a strong mighty rushing wind. [Laughs.] So it's the difference of a breath and a wind, and all of a sudden you're baptized in that.

The nearest comparison I can think of is, okay, the devil's counterfeit to that would be when we would get high or drunk how our bodies do stupid things, we do crazy things. Well, we do. We might do some crazy things. They came out of that Upper Room, and they was even asked. Well, they're all drunk. And, of course, Peter stood up and says, "These men are not drunk as you suppose. It's only the third hour of the day."

So they appeared to be drunk. They were just, whoo, whoa, man! So, then they ended up, they were speaking in tongues, but I think that the ultimate—'cause I've heard people speak in tongues, and I wouldn't even know, or you wouldn't even know, they were Christian; that's what changed my mind about that a long time ago. People depend, they all of a sudden, they think because they can speak in tongues that they're okay, that everything's fine. That's an outward manifestation, but I believe the more important outward manifestations of being born again, of being baptized in the Holy Spirit, is the fruits, the fruits of the Spirit.

And not only gentleness, peace, love, joy, faith, love, long suffering, gentleness, meekness, kindness, temperance, all these things, but I believe that if a person is baptized that they're gonna have fruit of sharing. He said that I've given you power to become witnesses. I've given you power to be bold. And all of a sudden, you've got the Dirty Dozen over here, the twelve apostles or disciples. I mean, they go from one day of fighting one another, I mean they're fighting, they're always arguing over who's gonna be the closest to Jesus. I mean, it's a motley crew. They're really a mess.

But then after the day of Pentecost, I mean these people, twelve of them went out. Or eleven. I believe that Paul was the one that took Judas's place. 'Course the twelve cast lots and Matthias was chosen as the twelfth to take his place, but God already had a man picked, and that was the Apostle Paul.

I believe that he was the one that God picked. But these men went out and literally just changed the earth. Just changed. I mean power. That's power. And people believed the words that they spoke. Because it says in the Book of Mark, sixteenth chapter, "These signs shall follow them that believe. They shall speak with new tongues, they will cast out devils, they shall lay hands on the sick and they shall recover, on and on and on. These signs will follow them that believe. And I believe it's talking about those that are baptized in the Holy Spirit. Because there's such a boldness there.

The Book of John, first chapter, I think it's the twelfth verse. It says that but as many as believed on his name, they received, he gave them power to become the sons of God.

Yeah, yeah, he gave his power. And that power was the Holy Spirit.

Both the church and the Unchained Gang are non-denominational.

Right.

There's a lot of terms that, not coming from a church background, I just always, at least vaguely, associated in my own head as being synonymous that I now know are not. I'd like you to explain. That's Pentecostal, fundamentalist, born again, charismatic, full-gospel, Spirit-filled, evangelical . . .

[Larry laughs.]

But they're not all the same thing, right?

Naw. They are and they're not. I mean, I think that they're all different terms. Basically, I guess basically, in terminology, they're supposed to be, but I guess people keep coming up with these new, the new phrases because people maybe will attach a stigma. Something will get attached to a group over here. Just like maybe, okay, the Nazarene church used to be called the Pentecostal Church of the Nazarene. But somewhere along the line, I don't know what happened, but they dropped the name *Pentecostal.* They don't have nothing to do with tongues.

So all of a sudden people come up, okay, now we're not Pentecostal, we're charismatic. Okay, we're very charismatic. Okay. And there is a difference, 'cause I came out of a Pentecostal church which had, oh, the Pentecostal churches have the best music, everybody knows that. Their praise is the best as far as denominations are concerned. The Pentecostal church has definitely had the best praise and worship and was definitely a lot more lively. But all of a sudden the charismatic movement started in, and then we started really seeing the body.

What's the difference between Pentecostal and charismatic?

Well, I think here's the difference was, they started using the name *charismatic* because of you saw more of the gifts being in operation. There's a lot of prophecy going on, lot of word of knowledge, lot of the different gifts, a lot more, even though in the Pentecostal church you saw a lot of speaking in tongues and a lot of interpretation. And a few times I remember some word of knowledge, but not really too many of the other gifts.

They were but they wasn't. I don't know how to say this. There was more, I guess the charismatic—the Pentecostal churches was, there was a tight rein. A little bit tighter rein on who was going to be used in the gifts. In the charismatic churches, it seemed like it was just the whole body. And because of stigmas, I don't want to be labeled as either one of 'em. [Laughs.]

Because of the granola Christians. I call 'em the fruits, flakes, and the nuts. [Laughs.] And they want to attach theirselves. Not that all these things aren't real—because they are. They are real, but you see a lot of flesh. A lot of flesh. People getting in the flesh. All of a sudden they want to show you how spiritual they are, and so, you know, you see, if you're in some circles, you'll see people laying hands on people, and people will fall on the floor. Well, I've seen people pray for people till the back of their head almost touched their backbone, because they're trying to push them on the floor. Seems like the more people that they can knock down on the floor, the more spiritual they are.

Not that these things aren't real, but people need to let God move. God is perfectly able to do what he wants to do without us helping him. I mean pushing things, making things happen quicker.

Okay, the term *full-gospel* or Spirit-filled is because I believe in the baptism of the Holy Spirit. Well, some churches, the Baptist church, the mainline Baptist churches, they believe that once you are born again, you've got all you're getting. They believe that as far as being baptized in the Holy Spirit, you got that when you became born again. So they don't do the tongues thing, either. So they stay away from that.

But what's going on here is pretty close to Pentecostal, right?

Yeah, it's real close.

I've heard people in the congregation say they don't see the difference between this and Pentecostal.

Yeah, well, basically, that's probably the best term. I just don't want to—I just want to say that we're a church out of the Book of Acts. So people won't label us with loosey-goosey Pentecostal churches or the legalistic Pentecostal churches. Because you got both.

The word *Pentecostal,* I mean there's so many different types of churches out there that are called Pentecostal, and right away, as soon as you say the word *Pentecostal,* my mind flashes back to the legalistic Pentecostal churches which I came out of. Which, whew, holiness is the way you dress, how high the women have the Ph.D.—the Pentecostal hairdo—piled up on their heads. The men can't grow any facial hair. You can't have any hair on the tops of your ears. I mean if Jesus walked in their church they wouldn't even know him. They'd throw him out for being a hippie.

But pentecostal with a small p, in the sense of restoring the Pentecost after the Tower of Babel.

Yeah. Yeah. Yeah.

And you have the hallmarks of music and the gifts of the Spirit and anointing with oil.

Yeah, yeah. Right. We do all of that.

I want to allow people to move in the gifts here, and I know that there's gonna be some flesh involved. Flesh is gonna be involved in all of it, because we're still in the flesh. So there's gonna be some fallacy in it, but I don't want people to think that we're a bunch of idiots, you know,

swinging off the ceiling fans and that there's no order.

I think Paul was very careful in speaking to the Church of Corinth, and he was trying to tell 'em, you know, Hey! I mean your communion services, they're just beginning to be drunken orgies here. I mean straighten up. You people are coming and speaking in tongues all the time. Why don't you just shut up and listen to the word being preached once in a while? Nobody's leaving here edified. Nobody's getting anything.

And there are churches still today that do that. You go in there, and, oh, they're down there amen-ing so loud that they're not hearing a word you're saying. They're just so hyped up, and, you know, they should have built their churches round, because they take off running. And I like to run, I like to march, I like to see people dancing and get happy, but still yet there's gonna be an order because I want people, I want everybody to be encouraged and blessed. Like I say, a lot of times churches like this will attract all the granola Christians, and I've been in those churches. It's sad. Then you get to the place where you're handling snakes. [Laughs.]

When I first came here, the first few times I was here, people made a real point of letting me know that there was no snake handling going on.

[Larry laughs.] So we don't do that.

Because you consider that an excess?

Yeah. It's nuts. It's totally nuts. I don't even believe that's what he's even talking about. Taking up serpents is being able to, I believe it's talking about the enemy. The devil's a snake, his demons are snakes.

Tell me about the role of music in worship.

Music is powerful. Even Aristotle said that music is the most powerful force on the face of the earth to put a message across. 'Course God knew that. God's the author of music.

Lucifer, which is, you know, Satan before he fell, he was the band leader. He was in charge of all the music. Music worship, we're finding out so much, so much about it. You can go back through the Old Testament and see how God would put the singers and the musicians in the forefront of the battle. He's saying, Worship me! Worship me and praise me with the right attitude, with a heart of thanksgiving, and I will defend you. I will be your shield, I will be your buckler. I will fight your battles. Worship me. And this is an act of faith. Just a release.

We see, man, we see people coming in here got demons hanging all over them, we just worship God. And the demons are running for the windows and the doors.

How do you see the demons?

Well, you can see a difference in a person's life when all of a sudden that demon has to detach. I've been in a deliverance ministry for a long time where we have actually prayed the demons of Hell out of people.

Then, through praise and worship, you don't have to go through all the slime and the flopping around on the floor. 'Course we still have to do that once in a while. If our church is setting the tone, if we're—it says that God inhabits the praises of his people. No devil in Hell could stand in the presence of God. It's such a powerful atmosphere of praise and worship. Just like the Walls of Jericho come tumbling down around a person's life and they're exposed.

So then once they're free of this satanic bondage, then they can make a clear decision: Okay, do I want to continue to walk with God, or am I gonna walk right back out there and jump on the devil's bus and keep on going down the pike with him?

It was like Saul being delivered of a demon spirit. Every time they'd have David to come and set before Saul, and he would play on his harp and he would worship God, setting there. And it said that Saul would be delivered of an evil spirit. Because through that atmosphere the devil can't hang around. He's got to leave.

Is it ever hard for you, because you're in charge of maintaining that atmosphere? When everybody else is slain in the Spirit, is it hard for you to keep playing guitar and keeping things together and conducting over the service?

No, I love it. I could go on for hours. I have to stop. I have to make myself stop. Sometimes I just want to just go on. I see what I have to do. A lot of times there's decisions I have to make because I know we come in here, and I try. I know we have visitors. I know we got a couple hours to do whatever we're gonna do. And if people are with me, if I can get our body and get the people who know where I'm coming from, if they can join with me right off the bat. I've had top-notch evangelists come in there, and they said, "Man, you guys, just go one-two-three-go and you're off!"

The quicker that we can get people into this arena of praise and worship and creating this atmosphere, the quicker, I mean we can get something done.

But I have to make a decision. When I see people not entering in, so then I say, Well, we'll

change the order of the service. We'll do something else. But if people can enter in, boy, it's
powerful.

It's like the waters of Siloam. You know, it said
the waters was troubled, just step into the waters. Just wade in there, take it by faith.

I guess that's what I was called to be first, was to
be a music minister. It's a part of it that I just
love, just love that part of it.

*What about the role of women in the church or in
the gang? It seems women have a different place in
different churches.*

Right. I believe that we're all one in the body of
Christ. The Bible says that it's neither male nor
female. I believe in women teachers. I believe in
women prophets. I believe that women have just
as much right in the church as the men do. I
know that sometimes I read the King James Bible, it just seems like there was male macho-ism
going on back in there. And a lot of stupidness.
Because, you know, they said they don't allow
women teachers, which that's not what the word
of God says. He does allow women teachers.

I did a whole study on it, did a teaching on it.
It's kind of funny, these same people, they won't
let women teach behind the pulpit, but they'll
send them to deepest darkest of Africa to be missionaries and fight lions and headhunters. And
they'll stick 'em into the dungeons of their Sunday school classrooms and the nursery and things
that the men don't want to have nothing to do
with, changing diapers and all that stuff, but
don't let 'em behind the sanctimonious pulpit
that sets there in the midst of the sanctuary.
That's a bunch of garbage.

*Do you see that sort of sexism trying to creep in to
the church?*

Oh, it's been in the church for years. There's so
many denominations—without even mentioning
the denominations—but there's so many denominations that they really oppress their women.
They're just a little bit higher than a dog.
[Laughs.]

*What about here? This is an essentially sexist cul-
ture that we . . .*

I've had people in this congregation that's come
against me whenever I took my stance, whenever
I taught on women teachers and how God has
called women just as much as he has men, that
we're all one in the body of Christ. Right here in
Galatians 3:28, "There is neither male or female,
for you are all one in Christ Jesus." Praise God.

I had a couple men came to me and wanted me
to stop this teaching. I said, "I'm not gonna do
it. I'm gonna teach the word of God. I'm gonna
teach all of it, as I see it, as God gives it to me,
and we're gonna go with it."

Some of 'em came up when I got done. There
was one, an older man came up, and he apologized. He said, "I'm sorry Larry. I was raised in
a church that taught against that. But," he said,
"I see it." He said, "I really see it. I just apologize for how I acted and what I felt." And then
all the rest of them that felt that way, they're not
here no more. They're all gone.

Because they left for other churches?

Yeah, but really they're not even in other churches. They're just out there—they just wanted to
run things. So God's moved 'em out.

I really feel good about it. It's easy to see that
the churches here in the United States, if it
hadn't been for the women, half of 'em
would've, most of the churches would have

closed down years ago because it was the women that kept them open. The men wasn't taking their place. So who in the world are we?

When all of a sudden, we're rising up now, saying, You women are just a bunch of dogs. You know, keep your mouth shut and set in the corner. If it wasn't for them, the churches would have been out of business.

Was that a hard adjustment for you to make?

No.

Was it an adjustment?

No, not really. Actually, the Pentecostal church that I came out of, we had women evangelists that came in.

I'm talking about from being a biker.

No, not really. I know how the bikers—and I used that, because I'd been—it was okay then but God just changed my heart. He really did. I'm thankful for the women that we got around here. They really make things work. All the men and the women. We just got a great bunch of people. They just make things work around here. Men and women working together. So it's really awesome.

CHICO

Monday nights I'm usually at the Monroe County Jail. Tuesday nights at the juvenile treatment center talking to the kids there. Every other Wednesday night I'll be at the Indiana State Farm. We have church services there. Larry Dyer and myself and Wes Powell will be there.

What are some of the instances that have really moved you?

When you see a big old boy get down on his knees and give his heart to the Lord. Come in there, looking like me: tattoos from one end to the other, look like they just come straight out of Hell theirself. And they drop on their knees and see them tears roll down their cheeks and give their heart to the Lord. I mean that's one of the rewards. Aw, man, it just gives you a feeling to see somebody do that. Just like when I gave my heart to the Lord, the feeling I had. At first it was a numbness, then it was like you was on fire. It was great.

And to see these guys come to church after that and keep coming. A guy that was there today and yesterday, a fella named Dave Matthews. I talked to him every time over there. He's out now, still going to church. He got him a job. And to see him keep carrying on what they were doing when they were in prison.

See, lots of times they'll get what's called "jailhouse religion." While they're locked up and everything, they'll walk with the Lord and go through all the whole motions like they're really on fire for the Lord. And some of them that get out will go right back to their old ways. They'll do this while they're there so things go easier on 'em, maybe get out early.

And you have that, but then you have the ones that are strong in the Lord, that stick with him when they get out, keep walking with him. Those are the ones that count.

Still yet, though, any time you plant those seeds, just tell people about the Lord, the word's like hot tar. Like rolling down the road on a freshly tarred highway. Or a side road. Some of the tar's going to stick, just like the word of the Lord, some of it sticks. You don't shake it all off.

People, when they get in trouble, you find out lots of times, that's when they call on the Lord, when they're in trouble. Outside of that, they don't. Sometimes you got to just get down to the lowest point, flat on your face to call on him. And he'll be there. He'll stick with you. He don't turn away from us. We turn away from him.

And nobody said being a Christian was going to be easy, 'cause it's not. You get ridicule from people. Just like when we go to the biker parties and stuff, there's a lot of people that don't want to hear the word of the Lord, but that's alright.

We talk about the things we go through. Look what Christ went through for us. He died on the cross. He was beat, his side was pierced with a spear. He was nailed to a tree. And we're not going to go through anything as degrading as that was. We owe a lot to the Lord.

He made the ultimate sacrifice for us. People talk about, Well, such and so got saved last night. Man, we was saved two thousand years ago when Christ died on that cross. They may have just acknowledged their salvation last night, but they was saved two thousand years ago.

And faith, you got to have faith. This guy asked me, "What do you think faith is?" We were talking, and it kind of stumped me at first. I said, "Well," and then it was like it wasn't me saying it. It was like I was hearing myself say it, but it wasn't me doing the talking. It's like the Holy Spirit was saying, "It's being able to reach out and grab ahold of something that you can't see and believing in it till you can see it." To me, that's what faith is. And we got to have that faith. You got to believe in the Lord, because he

give us the book, and all we got to do is read it, believe it, and stand on it. And that's what it's all about.

Going to the jails and the prisons and the other places, we're the only Jesus Christ a lot of them people ever see. So when we go, we need to represent him as well as possible, the way he should be represented. Show 'em the love that Jesus Christ showed for all of us. We just got to keep on doing that to everybody we meet. A lot of people think, you know they talk about going to church. They think of that building as being the church. Well, that building's just a building. The people inside that building, we're the church.

What God gives us in his word, we're supposed to take it out and share it with everybody else so they can feel what we feel. Give them what the Lord's give to us. It's not something you just keep yourself, because he gives it to us so we can give it to somebody else.

The Lord keeps a watchful eye over each and every one of us. Just like in Isaiah 49:16, he says that each and every one of us are engraved on the palms of his hands. Well, that means that then wherever before him in all his works and everything he goes to do, we're always there. He's sees us all the time. He never takes his eyes off of us.

RANDY

How did you meet the Unchained Gang?

I met them through going to church over there. I met Larry when I was in jail, at Monroe County. He come up and was doing some Sunday morning services, and I liked where he was coming from. I knew he had been down some roads. It's like when alcoholics are in treatment, they'll listen to another alcoholic before they will some-body that's come out of school that hasn't went down them same roads. And that was like with Larry. I could feel, see, and hear what he was say-ing, 'cause I knew he'd been down them roads.

I remember, Shalom started going to their church. They had it in the little house in Elletts-ville there. She says, "It's Larry's brother. You know, Larry Mitchell's brother?"* I said, "Oh really?" She said, "Yeah man." She said, "We go dressed as we are, we praise God as we want to." I said I'd check this out. So I went and then I went, then I went, then I went and I went and I went.

Then we moved in behind Big Red, Big Red Harley there, into the warehouse back there. So things fell in there. Things really came in. I was watching this and I was watching the Unchained Gang. I was looking for partnership, I was look-ing for brothers, I was looking for a closeness.

CHICO

People where I work, man, they couldn't believe the transition that I made. For years I used to run lottery cards. I'd go to Illinois and bring lot-tery cards in there and sell. I ran the biggest part of the gambling that was in there. I used to loan shark. Guys borrow a hundred dollars on Mon-day morning, pay pack a hundred and fifty on Friday.

What if they didn't?

I always got my money. I always got my money.

By scaring them? By hurting them?

Whatever it took. But everybody knew me and I never had any problems, 'cause everybody knew

what I was like. A guy borrowed twenty, he paid back thirty. That's just the way it was.

I didn't have any trouble with the foremen, 'cause they'd play the lottery ticket and stuff, and I didn't charge them, so they let me come to their departments and do my business.

Now people, they say, "I can't believe you've changed this much." Well, I have. And it's not me, it's the Lord. I talked to a lot of the guys there about the Lord, try to get them to come to church.

I had a guy tell me one day, "You know, church is nothing but a bunch of hypocrites anyway." I said, "Well, don't you think there's hypocrites out here? And a lot more of 'em?" He said, "Well, I don't know." I said, "Let's put it like this: I'd a whole lot rather go to church with a bunch of hypocrites as go to Hell with 'em." And he didn't have too much to say about that.

Used to, I never cried. I been to some of my best friends' funerals and never shed a tear. Now I get to talking about the Lord or get to talking about something, and the tears just start flowing. It's like you broke that shell that was around my heart. He softened a hardened heart is what he'd done. And now then, it's like the Lord, he squeezes on that heart, and when he does, then the tears come. Like a big sponge or something, I don't know. But it's great. I have never felt this good about anything or myself as I do now. I wouldn't trade this for anything.

We get to people that nobody else can get to. These people wouldn't accept a preacher coming in with a three-piece suit, tie and everything. Why, they'd eat him up and spit him out. They would. They'd just chew him up and spit him out. Whereas they'd take guys like us that've been there, and they can relate to us same as we

---

* Pastor Larry's brother, Steve, was the pastor at the time.

can relate to them. They'll listen to what you got to say.

What they got to say is not always positive. I've had people call me a phony. But I just tell 'em, "You just keep watching me and see what I do and find out if I'm real or if I'm a phony." They're watching. They want to see us stumble. They want to see us fall. It's not gonna happen. As long as we keep walking with the Lord.

SHALOM

The extremeness lies at everything I do. Everything I do. I cannot be happy or satisfied with mediocrity in anything that I do. And that's not patting me on the back. I wouldn't change my life today for anything at all.

Even the Big Book of Alcoholics Anonymous says you will not regret the past nor wish to shut the door on it. God has given me a way of that. Most assuredly I regret hurting people and all that. But God has a way of taking your bad experiences and turning them around so that I can use them today. I can go to the Bean Blossom Boogie, and I can go to where the most extreme hardcore bikers are, and I can understand, and I can talk to them, trust 'em, for the most part because of this [points to a facial tattoo].

I assume that you got that in jail?

Yeah, it's a time mark. Again, today, they say, "Oh, that's a mark for somebody that's killed somebody." Well, it didn't start out being that; it started out being a felony mark. It's a teardrop. It represents oppression. And it is a witness.

I used to feel like I was no good because of all the things I did, and I couldn't understand so much excitement toward that way of life. And

[Larry] calls it boot camp. And that's what I'm talking about when I say God just has a way of taking all that bad stuff and turning it around to be used for him and for those people who so desperately need good to get ahold of.

What are some of the things that you understand when you're talking to bikers that some other witness who didn't have your background would miss or mishandle?

I understand the woman chained to the motorcycle while the guy's off drinking and doing whatever else with whoever else, and she's chained there for one day or two days or however long it takes him to get drunk. I understand that she needs to be treated with dignity. I understand that she probably will not want to communicate with another woman.

How do you get around that?

This helps [points to facial tattoo]. It always helps to say I understand you probably don't want to communicate with another woman. It always helps. That's me and that's the way I do therapy, too. I don't hide anything. If I'm having some doubts about where you're coming from, I figure the very best way that I can find out where you're coming from is to ask you where you're coming from. Many therapists have to go through all this convoluted rigmarole to come to the light bulb kind of realization. I don't do that.

Lots of light bulbs go off [laughs], but it's out of direct communication. That's helpful.

I'm slightly past the age—well, this works both the good and the bad—I'm slightly past the age to be where they would feel a true camaraderie, and yet being a little bit past that age also takes me out of competition. So it can work either way.

One thing that I've noticed, especially on the trip to Texas, is a lot of people in the gang—and I think you will take this in good spirit when I say that you are among them—are not very good at organizing.

Oh God! [Laughs.] Well, you're wrong! [Laughs.]

It seems like the structure of Christianity is a welcome, appealing element.

I hadn't even thought of that! It could well be. The guidance. The trusted guidance. To me, guidance and structure, in this case, are almost synonymous. It's like all my life—whoo boy, there's not been very many people I would follow. 'Cause there was no trust. And so I only followed me, and I had no structure. I'd never been taught structure. Structure seemed rather Establishment, and I didn't want it. At one point in my life. Now it's too late. [Laughs.] So I can see that.

I think you were the one who spoke in a meeting a few months back about the specificity of prayer. Someone was talking about quitting smoking. You said you don't just have to pray to be delivered from smoking but also to not gain weight.

Yes.

It dawned on me that even if you remove the supernatural part of prayer, it's a mechanism by which people who are not naturally good at organizing things, really can organize and focus on what it is they're trying to do in a specific way.

You get yourself in a stance to go forward in that direction. Is that what you mean?

Yeah, even clarify just what it is you're trying to do.

It's a treatment plan. I deal with treatment plans all the time.

Watching you work with the woman the other day, that's very much what you were doing, just keeping her focused. Her mind was just going all over the place with different guilt and responsibility and excuses. Seems like prayer is a very internal way of doing that.

Yeah, I just have to agree with you. I can't say I ever thought of it before, but when you said it, it's like, Wow! I certainly know that most of us are pretty nonorganized.

MARY

She and her husband, Ron, are among the more middle class of the group. "I got on a motorcycle behind my husband when I was fourteen. He was a neighbor across the field from me. We were high school sweethearts. We were born in the same town, Oak Ridge, Tennessee. My dad was working on the Manhattan Project. His grandmother worked in Oak Ridge in the nursery department of the hospital, so his grandmother probably took care of me while I was in the nursery. We didn't meet until our parents both lived in Louisville, Kentucky, opposite one another. We met and went to high school together, married, and moved to Indianapolis. I was twenty, he was twenty-one."

Their background is not in the biker world but rather that of "motorcycle enthusiasts." "I get so much pleasure from riding. And it is, I think, the movement of the wind. But also, I guess for a woman, I have an unreasonable love of engines and not speed necessarily but power. And I enjoy feeling that gearing, that motor to take a hill. I enjoy figuring out where the apex of a turn is, leaning into that turn. I really enjoy that freedom. It's kind of a crazy thing. I tease some of the other church members because they say they don't pray when they're riding a motorcycle, and I say, 'You just haven't lived till you've ridden a motorcycle in tongues.'"

Sometimes it's hard to tell just what your role in the church is, when the church may or may not be operating where you think you're operating, at the same involvement in spiritual gifts. There's a thirst and a need for active participation in spiritual gifts in the church.

There are many who are hurt. There are many who are sick, and there are many who need to be listening to the heart of God for their lives. Those who are truly walking in the Spirit, who are tuned and desiring to know what God actually wants for them, every moment of every day; they want the people in the church to listen to what God wants for them every moment of every day. This is a tall order for John Q. Public.

So I guess almost from the first moment that I stepped into the church, knowing that I was operating at a gift of healing at that time, or gifts of healing, I should say—that's biblical: "gifts"—I knew that I was going to walk around laying hands on people. Because that's how you transfer that gift, and I know that's one of my purposes.

But I've been an intercessor. Biblically, Christ was the intercessor. He came to earth, and he died to intercede on behalf of all man who sinned before his father, that they might be redeemed and saved and forgiven. An intercessor on earth—Christ goes back to the Father, okay? And he intercedes forever on our behalf, saying, "Father, forgive them." And an intercessor on earth basically goes before the throne of God and says, "Father, forgive them. See that they are not where they need to be. Please reach your hand out and touch their lives in whatever way is necessary."

They intercede, saying, "Lord, please turn your forgiving, your forgiveness and your love upon this person and their life. Draw them into a right way. Draw them to yourself. Draw them to

where they can be led by the Holy Spirit and not by the world.

Do you intercede in this way for Christians and non-Christians alike?

Yes I do. Yes. And for the church. And I guess you might say intercessors end up praying all the time, 'cause there's so much stuff going on all the time. But it is a mark of intercessors that they wind up spending a whole lot of time in prayer. And it's not 'cause they say, I'm going to pray all day. It's because the heart inside of them desires constantly that the will of God be done. They know that if they pray about problems that come up, it gives the Lord permission—God has to have our permission—to move in our lives.

He gives us free will, so he has to have permission. So the intercessor prays, "Lord, please, we give you permission. Step in here and change this. Make this right, line this up with your word. Line this up with your will, that your will be done on earth."

Lots of times that's how an intercessor is defined, as one who prays that the Lord's will be done on earth.

So I pray a lot. That's a God-appointed position. I didn't volunteer. I guess I'm a pray-er, Rich. I'm a pray-er.

My father's family was Church of Christ. My mother's family was Presbyterian. So I actually attended a Presbyterian church when I grew up. And I learned to go to church dressed very nicely in my little white socks and my navy-blue dress and wear my white gloves and my little hat and sit quietly on a pew. Anyone who knows me now probably has trouble with that. 'Cause I come to church now in a leather vest and usually jeans, and there's no vestige of white gloves or high heels or anything like that, usually.

When my son died, we visited a church where a friend of ours was pastor, and he was the man who preached the funeral when my son died. We had met this couple. Actually, I should say my daughter met this young man at a biker rally, and his parents invited us to go to church and said, "Come on, you can ride your motorcycle." So, Sunday morning we hopped on the motorcycles and followed this man from Indianapolis to Ellettsville.

As we began to come, we went through Gosport, which has a windy country road, and I began to think, I don't know anything about this guy in front of me. He's dressed in leather, he has long hair, he's riding a motorcycle. 'Course, I'm on a motorcycle, too, but it didn't occur to me. He was on a Harley; I was on a Honda, so I felt like somehow I was neater and cleaner than he was. It was unreality.

But for a moment, I know now, the devil came up and tried to frighten me from going into this church situation. Because he'd probably been listening around the throne and knew what was going to happen to me once I got there.

We pulled into the parking lot, which is a steep hill, gravel lot, and immediately I dropped my motorcycle. My daughter is on the back of the motorcycle, so we both scrambled. But it was just like that. We were both standing up, and I thought, Well, I'm a short person, I ride a big motorcycle. I drop it. So I picked it up, I rode it up to the top of the hill. We parked and went in.

When we went in they were singing "I've got a feeling everything is going to be alright." Not a quiet, peaceful song the way it's done at the House of Prayer. Very energetic. I just felt this tremendous power there. And the people that we came with were sitting in the front row, so there

I was on the front row on the first time I'd been in a church like this in many, many moons.

And I felt that I had somehow come home. I felt like I had turned a corner and the real part of my life was about to begin. I don't know how to explain that to you, 'cause I thought I was living a pretty full life. But I just knew that whatever was going to happen to me, from that point on, was going to be the real purpose, the real reason that I was born. And it has been so.

From the first time, that first altar call that first morning, I was standing with my eyes closed, and I've always had, since I was about sixteen, I've had feeling in my hands. When people walk past, if someone's ill or really just if the Holy Spirit wants me to pray for that person I will feel that person physically go by.

An analogy might be to have a pair of matched magnets on opposite sides of the table, and one moves, the other one draws the other. That's how that person draws my hands. And I was standing with my eyes closed during the altar call, and all of a sudden I could feel people. I could feel there was something in front of me. And I thought, Oh, this is wild. 'Cause normally I'd only felt that in more private situations, where it might be a one on one. And I opened my eyes, and there were four people knelt down there by the altar.

I said, "Lord, whatever it is in your heart that you want for them, I'm just going to touch them, I'm just going to pray for them, that that will be fulfilled." And it has not let up since. Every time I'm in that church, there are people that I'm drawn to that way, people that I'm drawn to to pray their God's will for or in.

There's so much hurt that people don't think God can heal, but he will prick the senses of an intercessor and draw that person to them. And that's what he does to me. I may not even realize there's something going on in somebody's life, or they're sick or whatever, but if I follow my hands, now he raises it up in my heart almost. If someone's really hurting, he'll raise it up almost like a feeling of mourning, like a deep cry inside.

If I go to that person and hug them or just take their hands and pray for them, he gets his chance to do what he wants to do in their lives. I'm just a tool. And what happens to me is just a matter of flipping on the electricity so the tool works. It's an honor.

Is it a burden?

Is it a burden? Well, I don't really think it is. Some people would look at it and might think it is, 'cause I get calls at all times of the day or night. But Christ, who is in me, who is in every Christian who is born again, and the Holy Spirit answer the phone. I don't really have to supply the energy. As long as I'm doing what he's asking me to do, he just pours the energy in. I mean, I get to the point where I'm going, Ah! Somebody come touch me and take some of it. 'Cause I am just power-packed. And it's his energy, it's God's energy.

People who talk about having gone to Heaven, they talk about instant communication. They don't really say things. That tremendous energy that can do that, we're only getting as much, just a little teeny bit of what our earthly bodies can handle. When I pray and I feel that energy come into me, I know that he'll keep working on me till I get to the point where I can handle more of it, 'cause I can handle a lot more now than I could before.

It's not really a burden; he doesn't make anything you do for him really be a burden. That's not his way, not that I could discern.

What was your life like before you were a Christian?

Well, I joined the church when I was twelve, the Presbyterian church. One doesn't get born again in the Presbyterian church, no. No, one does get sprinkled, and one makes a commitment. I don't know how exactly I came to be—yeah, I do.

I think a lot of times a person who is going to operate at an intensely spiritual level will be attracted to the occult. And there was a time in my life when I told fortunes, when I read tarot cards. When I searched for why I knew things that other people didn't know, how that fit in—and truly I know now that it was distorted. It was Satan trying to prevent me from moving into intercession and into the prophetic, which God would bless. I've just known things.

I thought that was the answer. I thought it was the gift that I had in my life, to be able to do that for people. I never, never ever had any interest in drugs. And I believe that's because my mind was always hyperactive. I was always into some bizarre thing in a thought process.

As a teenager, as a college student, I was a civil rights activist. As a young married mother I took part in a women's group that went into prisons and went into the various places. It was made up of a black, a white, a Christian, a Jew, a Roman Catholic. It was called Panel of American Women. We would go into places where there was either religious or racial strife, and we'd mediate a discussion.

And I really thought I had works going for me that were sanctioned from on high. I knew things that other people didn't know. And I felt like I was a little psychic because of that.

But I had an experience that awed me and frightened me a little bit. I think there's a little bit of fear involved in awe. I played euchre in a neighborhood group of eight women. We never had eight women. We always had seven women, so the person who hosted the group always had to bring in a substitute.

So we went one night to play euchre, and I sat down next to the substitute. The woman who sat across from me knew that I read cards sometimes, and she says, "Mary, see what's in the cards for me." And I'm kind of plumbing my psychicness and thinking, I don't have anything, Lois. But at the same time, the woman sitting next to me was raising this feeling inside of me.

So I said to her, "What about you? Would it be alright if I tell you what I'm feeling coming up about you?" I started. I laid out eight cards, but I realized that what was coming up inside of me didn't have anything to do with what I thought the cards ought to mean.

I'll just try to tell you real fast what I said to her, 'cause it's indelibly imprinted in my memory. I said, "You have two sons, blonde-haired, blue-eyed. One's seven, one's nine. You're living with a man who you're not married to. He's dark-complected, dark eyes, but you're very much in love with him, and he is in fact the person you were meant to spend your life with. Your father has a brother nicknamed 'Red,' 'cause when he was young he used to be a redhead. He lives in Colorado, and Red is in the hospital, and they've discovered he has cancer, and he's facing surgery, and he's facing death. But if your father will make contact with Red, whom he hasn't talked to in eight years. Your father being a Christian, if he'll make contact with Red and go to him and

share Christ with him. Red will believe, and Red will move to Michigan where your father lives, and the two of them will live on the same street and walk to church together for the rest of their lives."

I didn't know this woman from Adam. I had never seen her before. When I quit, there's tears running down her face, and she said, "I have two little boys, blonde hair, blue eyes, seven and nine. I'm living with a guy. I'm divorced, but I'm living with a guy that I'm dearly in love with and he's dark-complected, dark hair, dark eyes. My father has a brother named Red, and I don't know for sure where he lives, but I know that my father hasn't talked"—and she just started, you know—"for at least eight years, but I'm going home and tell my daddy to call Red."

Six months later she called me and she said, "I have to tell you this. I had to hunt up your phone number, 'cause I didn't even know your name. My father and Red are living in Michigan. Red has been converted. Red has been healed of cancer or at least all the cancer has been removed. And they're going to church together. They live on the same street, three houses away from one another."

And you could have wiped me up off the floor. At that time, I said to my husband, "Where would that information—how does one have, how does one touch into information like that?" When one doesn't even have any kind of relationship with that person. It's not like I picked up anything that belonged to her. I was flabbergasted. And I was frightened.

I really didn't want that kind of power. I didn't want that kind of information. I was afraid that I'd walk up to any perfect stranger and have that kind of information about them. And I rejected it. I burned the tarot cards, never picked up a deck of cards again to do that kind of thing. I just couldn't. I couldn't. And I wouldn't.

I went to my brother-in-law, and I said, "What do you know about this kind of thing?" And he says, "Mary, you have a gift of prophecy. You have a gift of word of knowledge. God intended what happened to happen. He knew, even though you didn't that the time was right in those people's lives. And he just set a seed. It was always their choice to do the things that you told the woman about. It was always their choice to decide to go or to go to Michigan or whatever," he said. "But he just used you for a tool to trigger that, to give them the opportunity to change their lives."

And I began to look at that, began to pray about that, and I began to ask, go back to God, and say, "Take these things that don't even feel right to me away." The tarot cards, the interest in the psychic, the idea that I was psychic. I didn't have any other explanation for those kinds of things, because in the Presbyterian church one doesn't operate in gifts of the Spirit. I knew nothing about gifts of the Spirit.

And I didn't even really understand what my brother-in-law told me, except that I trusted him because I felt he was a very godly man. And I just shut down, from the standpoint of I just wouldn't touch anything that wasn't real, right here like this table. I wouldn't even respond to ideas and thoughts and process. I had always known when my children were in trouble. I knew one time when my husband stopped and had a flat tire and changed the tire. I knew what time it was when he stopped and what he was doing. And I just shut that down. I wouldn't even receive it.

And then my middle son got into drugs. He wasn't coming home, and I began to say, "Lord,

please just show me whether or not he's alright. Is he okay?" And if he was okay, I would just get this sense of peace come over me. Sometimes it would be two o'clock in the morning and I would say, "Lord, just please, if he's okay, have him call me." The phone would ring. In just a few minutes the phone would ring.

And I began to find a different way to use what Satan had corrupted in the fortune-telling. I began to pray for my son. I knew that he used to go back into the woods behind our subdivision, and he'd get high, take pot with him, or whatever it happened to be.

One night I knew that's where he was. And I went out into the front yard, praying, "Lord, please, please protect him. Don't let him do something really stupid. Just bring him back home and let him sit up. I'll sit up and talk to him all night. His heart's hurting." I said, "I'll talk to him. Now show me what I can do." This was the kicker: Show me what I can do to change this situation.

God loves a request like that. He loves it. And I felt, it was just as if I drew up—I'm only five foot two, okay?—I drew up, my arms came out to my sides, and I drew up my fists out beside myself, and I felt like I had suddenly gotten to be tremendously powerful and about ten feet tall.

And I said—now I never thought about angels, okay?—I said, "Angels, go forth and make war on that which comes against my child! Go defend my child!" And it was like this militant person came up inside of me, ready to fight, ready to make war.

And I could feel inside myself that in those woods there was a battle going on between good and evil for that child. He wasn't a little kid, he was sixteen.

And I didn't know anything about spiritual warfare. I never knew there was such a thing. But that's what the Holy Spirit inside of me, that's what God showed me to do, that's how he answered that prayer, "Show me what I can do." That's what he showed me. And after I stood up there like that, with that vengeful-mama pose, after a little bit, I just got this feeling of peace come over me. It was like, Okay, that's done. And I knew that he'd be home soon. And I went back in the house, set down at the kitchen table, and in about fifteen minutes he walked into the house.

And he said, "Oh, you're still up." He says, "You know, the woods was really different tonight." I said, "Yeah, I bet it was."

That's how I kinda got from being off on one track, and I think really being deceived by Satan into using things God gifted me with in a worldly way. It was like the Lord taught me as I tried to defend my son in the drug situation. It was like he taught me spiritual warfare when I knew nothing about it. I do a lot of it now, but I didn't know anything about it then.

When you're instrumental in healing somebody and it doesn't go the way you expect it to, or it isn't as simple as someone's sick, you lay on hands, and they're well, how do you feel?

Well, it's not me when it happens and it's not me when it doesn't happen. There are lots of different things that can prevent somebody from receiving the healing. The Bible says that he wants all of us to have health. When we accept Christ, with our salvation comes our healing. Christ died. He was flayed for us. The stripes that he took were for our healing. But it takes faith, it takes a lot of faith to believe against what a person has been taught all their lives, which is that only a doctor can make them well. Or that they have to live in the pain that they have. Or even, many people have been taught that their suffering is somehow sent by God, that they might become more Christ-like.

You asked me a few minutes ago if I pray for people who are not Christians. Yes I do. My own father is a good example.

Although he grew up in a church with a great deal of church activity, he professes not to be a believer. I guess it's been about ten months ago now. He's a very big man, weighs—shoot, I don't know what he weighs, but I know he weighs well over three hundred pounds. He was upstairs in his bedroom, and he had blood vessels rupture in his stomach, and he began to hemorrhage.

I came home from work to find my husband—I mean I was working like after six o'clock—I came home to find my husband, my son, my neighbor, all sitting around the kitchen table. They had just received word that the ambulance had come and they were taking him to the hospital. He was hemorrhaging prolifically, and they did not know whether or not he would live or if they could stop it. And because of his size, surgery would be risky.

And about fifteen minutes later my sister called back and she was in the hospital. She had been following the surgeon down the hall, who was supposed to operate on him if they decided it was a go. He didn't know she was there, and he said, he was saying to his companion, "This really big guy that they just brought in, who is bleeding so bad, I do not see how we can save him. I just don't see how we can save him. We can't get enough blood into him fast enough, we can't get him into surgery fast enough, and even now, he's just, it's come up again. He's lost all of his blood."

Well, she had just kind of backed away and gone off to the phone and called and was hysterical, really. And I looked at my son and my husband and my neighbor and my daughter who had wandered in, and I said, "We are going after this in prayer right now." Everybody got up, we went into the family room and made a circle. And my prayer was from my own point of view. I asked for his life for me. I said, "Lord, I believe you can heal him, and I know he's an unbeliever, but this is a man that I love. This is the man who taught me to love. That's my father. He's one of the most loving, giving, self-sacrificing people that I know, extremely intelligent, very talented. He doesn't understand you. Please, for me, make yourself known in his life at this time. Heal him, save him, that he might know who it was, whose hand was in his life. I will go and tell him."

And the prayer was fervent. Everyone's voices were raised. And as that prayer ended, I burst into laughter. Laughter! Giddy, hysterical, crazy, nutty laughter. And my husband looked at me, and I said, "It's just joy. I know that God has done this. This is already done. He is healed. Right this moment he is healed. 'Cause the God of love has heard my plea, and he has answered that. He's done that for me, and I'm gonna go tell him."

So my son and I hopped in the truck and drove to Louisville from Indianapolis, and it was eleven-thirty at night. I walked into my dad's hospital room—they had got him kind of semi-stabilized—in my vest. He was extremely weak, and he kind of opened one eye and looked at me, and he said, "Oh, hi." He says, "You came a long way." I said, "Yeah, I was praying for you, and I had to come and tell you that you are gonna be well, and you are gonna be healthier than you have been for years." And he said, "What is

that you have on?" looking at this [her Unchained Gang vest]. He could see this.

I said, "It's my vest, Dad, from the motorcycle ministry." I said, "I walk around with Jesus' name on me so nobody'll mistake who I serve." I was just being bold and almost to the point of ridiculous, but at the same time I knew that if I was bold enough it would retain in his memory.

I've been really sick and weak before, and I know that it's almost like there's a fog between you and people who talk to you, and when you go to play it back you get a vague memory, but if that person was loud enough and adamant enough about what they said to you, you can get that memory back. So I was being like that with him, and I said, "You are healed! You are gonna be well! It's already in motion, Dad. You just lay there and let God do his thing." And he said, "Okay, that's all I feel like doing is just laying here."

So I went into the waiting room, and my mom and sisters were sitting there, all mopus droopus, and I said, "Dad is gonna be alright. He's gonna be alright. I know he is." Well, they think I'm crazy. They had done a scope picture. They went down his throat and took a scope picture of his stomach, and it had a big hole in it, and they were giving him medication to kind of soothe that, hopefully to promote healing. And they were doing the transfusion, and three days later he was so much better that they decided that they would take another look in his stomach and see if they could project how far along he was. And they couldn't find the hole.

What was your family's reaction after that?

They haven't given me a whole lot of flack about believing that he was going to be healed. At first they just thought I was nuts. They really did think I was nuts. I said, "God intends not only for that stomach to be well but for the quality of his life to be improved, that he will be able to get around better, his health will improve, the arthritis he's got in his knees will improve. You're gonna see a man whose quality of life is improved, because God has answered a prayer I made."

And sure enough, even right now, he is losing weight. He's lost another fifty pounds, gets around better. The arthritis has come under control. He's different, and today we were in the church for that funeral, and I watched his face, and I watched him listen to the minister who talked about the Christlike qualities of his aunt. Tears come down his cheeks. God is changing that life. He's touching that life. And he's being glorified there.

I know that Dad will figure out who the head and the beginning and the end of all things is. He'll get in touch, 'cause he's already been touched. We love him because he [God] loved us first. And I think Dad is seeing that he has been loved, he has been touched.

Do you think that will happen with the rest of your family?

Sure. I'm claiming 'em all.

Does it create friction?

It doesn't actually create friction. I guess 'cause I'm the oldest child and I've always been, well, they tell me I've been bossy, but I think I've— well, maybe I have.

I don't tell them what to do, but I do try to make sure that they know who I serve. My next sister, who is five years younger than I, she has Christian leanings, but she has never stepped into lining her life up with what God wants.

She's just lived in what we refer to as a permissive will: Yes, I believe in Jesus Christ type of thing.

My brother, who's a year younger than her, same kind of thing. Searching as much as anything else. And so I share with them. I'm not gentle with them in that I share my experiences. I share what Christ has come to mean to me and the things that he does, the things I see happen.

She's thirsty to know more and more, and it allows her to step out in faith and begin to step into the gifts God has for her. Likewise her fiance. He was raised Jewish, but he has become a Christian. And yet the richness of his Jewish heritage, the teaching, the training that he had in shul, he's able to share that biblical knowledge with her, and I love to sit and talk with him about Old Testament, because he has it in a way that I don't think Christians get it when you're raised Christian. That Jewish heritage, that Old Testament is just, he can just make it come alive.

One of the things that surprised me when I first came to the House of Prayer was how many people were wearing Stars of David on necklaces, the banners on the walls. There seems to be a real current of Judaica there.

It's hard to separate, in my mind, Christianity from Judaism because we came out of it. In essence, the Gentiles were God's second choice. His chosen people were the Jews. And when he couldn't get them to listen, then he settled for the Gentiles, hoping, I believe, that eventually the Gentiles would get back and convince his chosen people, and I see that that happens.

When I first came to the House of Prayer I was surprised to see that. But it spoke to my heart, because back in my old days when I was reading tarot cards I used to believe in reincarnation, and

I used to think, oh, you know, in some former life I must have been a Jew, because I love things Jewish. I relate to the Jewish people so much. When I came into the House of Prayer I thought, Well, this is kind of neat, because basically all the Old Testament was written to and about and for the Jewish people, and if we're going to study that and understand that we need to understand the Jew and how he was and what he came from, what his heritage is. I really think that's what we're doing at the House of Prayer. That's why you see that.

Plus some of what you see is, there's a banner that says "El Shaddai." That's just one of God's names, and the symbol—forgive me, I can't think of what the name of the . . .

Menorah?

Menorah, that is there is a testimony unto God's power to save.

When I began to understand what it was, what the symbols were, it just was even more appropriate, actually, that the Christian of this day understand that God's power has gone all the way back to forever, to the beginning, to all the people that he tried to reach out to, the Jews being his chosen and cherished people. I think it would be wrong for Christians to not respect that. If God wanted them, we best be wanting what God wants.

Do you have much contact with Jewish people?

Yes I do. I used to work with a lady who is Jewish, Russian-Jewish. And she called me about five years ago and said, "I'm starting a small company. Will you come and work with me?" We'd always been really close. And she has two daughters and a son. The son has completely rejected Judaism and Christianity. One daughter is what

she refers to as a "completed" Jew. She has become a Christian. They think of it differently. Jews who convert think of themselves differently. It depends on how they define that process.

But Sandy, my friend, has no desire to become a Christian, and yet she said to me at one point—her daughter, her oldest daughter, has cancer—and she said, "Mary, if God would heal my daughter, I would believe."

I said, "I don't know that you can strike a deal like that with God. I really don't. I think he would ask you to believe first and then see what he will do." And she was saying, "I can't, I can't do that. I believe, I was always taught that we are waiting for the Messiah, that Christ might have been a powerful and awesome prophet but he's not the Messiah."

And so for a while, for three years, as my own faith and my own experiences built I shared them with her. She was interested in them. She wanted to hear. I continued to pray, "Lord, if I'm here, if I'm working here so that she can know something of Christ in a personal way, I'll stay." I was unhappy in the job, but I was feeling that I was supposed to be there. And she and I, in everything but religion, were very close. We liked to do the same things.

We mothered one another. When you get older and your mom is in some other state, or in her case her mom's dead, older women mother one another. We'd do nice little things for one another here and one another there. Her nice thing to do for me was to cook Jewish for me.

But there came a point where I felt I couldn't push her anymore, that she needed to make a decision. And she drained me. The manifestations of ministry and the Holy Spirit that you see come from anointing from the Holy Spirit. Every

Christian is anointed, but a person who flows in anointing and ministers in the Holy Spirit can be shut down by being around somebody who is negative and just demeaning of Christ. You can't stand to hear your savior put down indefinitely.

You can witness through him with a lot of power. Perhaps it's just me. I was not strong enough at that time. There came a point where I had to walk away from it. I had to say, "Sandy, we'll be friends, but I can't work here anymore. I can't be everyday coming into a situation in which all that I believe is demeaned. I would not do that to you." You know, I'm not pressing my Christianity on her, I'm just . . .

She would joke about spiritual gifts, and she would joke about whether or not Christ was actually Christ or not Christ, and she would make religious jokes. She hadn't been that way in the beginning, so I almost began to feel like the Lord was working on her. It was a self-defense mechanism. I felt I had to pull out of that job, so our contact is more on the telephone or we go maybe and have lunch or something together. Under those circumstances she doesn't do that. But at work it got bad.

I have a Jewish neighbor. We take joy in God, and I trust that who I am and what I do and when I share my own spiritual experiences are sufficient witness to him. But we share joy in God first together. There are several people down at church, as you know, who come out of a Jewish background.

There's nothing more beautiful than to hear Deborah sing worship chants, sing prayer chants in the church. It's like God can't resist coming and sitting on the stage and listening. You just feel the presence of that ear of God wanting to hear those songs of praise—in the Hebrew! To me, some of it is lost when we begin to try to sing it in English. The Hebrew is what makes it awesome. Wish I could read Hebrew.

I used to think the most beautiful thing was to hear a cantor sing. But I haven't heard that in many years. I've heard Deborah; Al* doesn't that much that I'm aware of.

Tell me about your son.

Which one? I've got three.

My oldest one is active in the church. The middle one is the one who took his life. And the younger one lives in New Albany, and he and his wife are—they're not Spirit-filled, but they're very active in the church. They teach a Bible-study class.

In our house there was always prayer over meals. We never sat down and ate without prayer. And my youngest son said to me, and this is through all the card reading and everything, my youngest son said to me not long ago, "Mother, I'm having trouble in my Bible class because I have a very personal relationship with God. That's the way we were taught. We weren't taught religion, say, we weren't taught the Bible, but we were taught a very personal relationship with God. The people that I teach mostly have some kind of a nebulous relationship with God who is some stern father who is up there, and they don't understand how to bring him right down with them. And I'm having trouble."

And I realized when he said that that my middle son, too, had that knowledge of a personal God. He had done drugs. When he was twenty-one, he was married and had a little boy, three months old, and graduated from high school in the year when he was twenty-one.

---

* A member of the church who, like Deborah, was born and raised Jewish.

There was a great deal of pressure, but he pushed himself in order to be able to graduate. In '91 his marriage was just not doing well. And his wife and he were separated. The little boy was with him. In an effort to try to heal the marriage, he had invited her to go out to dinner, to take her out to dinner so they could talk.

When they did that, she was supposedly living with a girlfriend. She told him where she was and everything. Later on that evening, he went to the house to talk to her, and she did not expect him, and there was a guy there. They were sitting on the couch. And the knowledge that there had been a man in the house when her girlfriend was not there and that she technically was still married, he was just devastated. He didn't find her doing anything untoward, he was just devastated.

And he felt, I believe, that there was no hope for the marriage, that it would be destroyed.

Kids now and kids for the last twenty years have lived with so much. Well, let me just back up and say very few people, maybe a third, who have lived in a secure family situation, and usually that has not been an ongoing experience for them. It may have been a five-, ten-, eight-year experience not a thirty-year experience. And he grew up in a solid marriage. My husband and I have been married thirty-one years.

He did not want, he just did not want that to be torn up. He wanted it to be put back together, not torn up. She had come out of a whole different attitude about marriage, where it was a temporary thing that you did until you got tired of it, then you switched partners.

It was like two o'clock in the morning on a Saturday morning, and he said, "Mom! Mom!" And it woke me up. I always told my kids, "I don't care what time it is, day or night, if you got something on your mind you want to talk about, you're welcome to wake me up." And the urgency in his voice awakened me instantly. When I went in to sit down at the kitchen table with him, he was shaking and crying, just sobbing. He told me what had happened, told me what he had seen. And he wanted to know if I had any Excedrin or something. He had a splitting headache.

I got him some Excedrin. I went in and sat down at the end of the bed. He laid down in the bed for a moment. Then he said, "Mother, pray for me. Pray with me." And so I did. I prayed for him. I prayed for her. I held him in my arms, and he cried and cried. His heart was just broken. His expectations were devastated. Human beings don't do well when our expectations are devastated. We just don't do well with that.

He fell asleep, the day progressed, his brother and his wife were there. The oldest son was at the hospital, visiting somebody in a coma. We had ordered pizza, which was delivered. And when that pizza came, Lee walked into the kitchen, walked past the table. People were kind of serving themselves from the box. He got a drink out of the refrigerator and walked back out of the kitchen into the bedroom and shot himself in the head.

My husband was back in the bedroom, and the two of us met outside of that bedroom door. We had heard that shot, and we both knew, just knew, what had happened. He would not let me go in. He says, "I don't know what you're going to see, and I don't want you to see it. You go call 911."

So I went and did that, and he went in. As I was talking to the people at 911, they said, "Is he breathing? Have you got a pulse?" or what have you. I went to ask Ron. He's trained in CPR, and he had done a preliminary checking for pulse, looking for heartbeat, whatever.

So he went to talk to them on the phone, and I knew. I had set with my father-in-law when he died, and I was not afraid. I have a strong stomach. I was not afraid of what I was going to see, because my child's body was precious to me and I just wasn't afraid of what I was going to see. As a result, there was nothing to see.

The bullet had ricocheted in his head and torn up his brain, but it had not burst the skull. There was no mess. There was nothing to see. I knelt down beside the bed. He was laying sideways across the bed, and I lifted his chin, thinking I would start CPR. My fingers went down his chest to find the place over his heart, and I saw blood just trickle out of his ear, and I knew that his brain was torn up.

My only thought, my only thought was that having taken his own life, he had sinned against God, and it just came up out of me like an ache: "God forgive him. God forgive him." His heart was beating under my hand. I said, "God forgive him. Come to him. Jesus, come to him, in your unconditional love. You love us, no matter what we do. In your unconditional love, Lord, show him, show who you are, how deep your love is. Forgive him, please forgive him. Please, please forgive him."

In my mind I just saw Christ. It was like he was coming from a distance, like this—his shoulders, his hands, open and reaching down. I just saw him come. And I knew that I knew that I knew that in those dying moments that Christ had once again offered himself and offered his forgiveness.

When the family gathered with the minister that was going to do the funeral, each of us had dif-

ferent tidbits of information that we didn't know the other ones had. And my husband was just heartbroken because he felt that because he had taken his life that he was damned. So he said to the minister, you know, "Tell me, he was never baptized." And my son says, "Yes he was, Dad." I can still see the shock on my husband's face. He said, "He was?" He said, "Yes. When he and Cindy decided to get married in the Baptist church, he went to the preacher and he said, 'It would be hypocritical of me to be married in the church if I'm not under the church's authority.' And he confessed Jesus Christ as his savior, and he was baptized. That's why they went that one night when they didn't have to go, was so he could be baptized."

I though my husband was going to be a big puddle. The minister said, "Are you concerned that because Lee took his life that he still would not be taken to Heaven?" And Ron said, "Yes, I am."

He had been depressed. The doctor had been trying to treat him for depression for probably six months. He said, "He was under doctor's care. The illness that was wrong with him was affecting his ability to make decisions." He kept saying, "I don't think God would hold that against him. I don't think he would."

And I said, "I got another key." And I told them about what had happened in the bedroom the night he died. That moment was God's gift, not just to Lee but to the whole family. We all had peace with knowing that God had made a way. He always makes a way of escape. He made a way.

I wouldn't want to put down anybody's grief. Grief is grief. But from the reading that I did, trying to heal myself and gain understanding of grief and the grieving process, I've always been one to try and check and see: Are you coming along? Are you growing? Are you stagnating? What's happening with you? I read a lot about grief, and I tried to decide in my own mind what I thought Heaven might be like.

I read a bunch of stuff about near-death experiences, everything I could get my hands on. Because the other side of death is an unknown quantity to us. And that's where my child was. He'd gone someplace I couldn't go and about which I really had little factual information. I wanted to know. I was an inquiring mind. And I just, it was everything, anything. I would get discouraged, 'cause I knew that I couldn't ultimately know where he was, what was going on.

Grief, I think, can be the most painful human emotion. We traveled on a motorcycle a lot during the year after he died. I've always loved to ride. I ride my own bike. This was in January that he died, the twenty-fifth of January. I ride in the winter, too, as long as there's not snow and ice on the ground.

I became numb. The cold didn't bother me, the heat didn't bother me. I didn't smell anything. My sense of smell went completely numb. And every so often I would come up out of that frozen state of mind and emotional senses. It seemed like when I did what happened to me is that I would just be hit with that tremendous sense of loss.

We're a real huggy family. We always scrunch in together and hug one another. The thing that happened to me that was the worst was that I couldn't touch him. There was nobody to hold onto. When I missed him, I couldn't hug him. And the loneliness, the longing was just excruciating. I would double up in tears, just in a knot of pain, holding my sides 'cause I thought my body was just gonna burst.

And I say that and I describe that 'cause probably one of the most intense experiences that I've had is my own personal healing, that grieving. I loved that child, as moms love children. I would have rather died than him. I would have rather borne the hurt that he had when he found his wife and was crushed by what was going on. But that is not something you can do for your child. That's really not something you can do for any other person. And I was just torn. I was just breaking inside.

I would cry for a while. I would allow myself to grieve for a while, and then I would say, "Lord, this is going to kill me. And I know that is not what you want. I'm going to stand up. When I stand up, you meet me there and you get me on with whatever I'm going to do. If we don't get anything done but putting the dishes away out of the dishwasher today, Lord, you help me do it. Help me do something. Help me stand on my feet. Please, I can't collapse on the children. I have a daughter who's ten years old. She's got to have a mom. I've got to function."

Every time I did that, I stood up. Right there I would find strength. I don't have any idea how it came except that it was God's answering my prayer and giving me enough strength to operate. Gradually, as I began to do that, I began to get better and better. And a year after he died, in January, one morning I came around the corner Sunday morning, my husband was making coffee. And for the first time in a year, I smelled it. I came around the corner of the kitchen, and I went, "Man, I can smell! I can smell! I can smell coffee!" And I knew that I had come to a point where I would be able to get back to life. I'd be able to put death behind me, and I'd be able to come forward into life. And that's only by the grace of God.

I never, I thought—my husband and I said to one another—we'll never be the same. There'll never be any real heartfelt joy in our lives again. How can you—you can laugh, but you can't . . .

Kahlil Gibran wrote a beautiful book, and one place he says, "You may laugh but not all your laughter, and cry but not all your tears." It's like living a half-life. You're so hurt that what's inside of you can't ever get completely out. You just get a little bit of it. You don't get a gut laugh, you don't get heartfelt tears. You just get, you skim the surface. I thought I will never laugh again. It'll never just come up from the gut. Real joy. I'll never be able to walk around with a smile on my face again. Wrong! That's not the way God operates.

What was the change?

When I came into the House of Prayer. Lee had been dead about a year and a half when we first came.

The minister that did the funeral, we started going to his church, and we drove almost an hour to his church like we drive an hour to Ellettsville, and it just got to be complicated to do it. So we quit doing it. We had not been for maybe six months when we went to Ellettsville.

And there was no hand-lifting in the Methodist church, and there was no—we sang traditional hymns which worked for me because at that point I was drawing back on my Presbyterian background, and the Methodists were just a hair or two looser than the Presbyterians, so I thought.

When I actually lifted my hands up to the Lord, as I craved to do, because I knew he had rescued me from just literally dying in that grief, just withdrawing into myself. When I lifted my hands, once again, he met me. God is faithful to just meet you. You set out, he meets you.

Every little bit of praise that I offered, every time I did what I felt inside myself what I wanted to do, raise my hands, not one hand a little bit here but way up in the air, each thing I did, he met me and he filled me. The little thing that I did, he filled me with his own healing to the point where I got where I was so full of joy that I would just burst out laughing in praise. I was so excited. I was so happy. And I realized that I had begun to do what I didn't think I ever would be able to do again. And so had Ron. We had joy back, we really had joy back. You know it's gone way beyond that. We're not just talking joy. We're talking about dancing. And the Bible says, "He'll turn your mourning into dancing." Boy, he has done it to me. He has literally, literally done it to me.

I get so full of the joy of knowing he is my God. He has saved me, my family, my child. He has imbued me with enough of his presence that I can go share that with other people. He allows me to serve him by ministering to other people and improving the quality of their lives, because that's what he wants for them. I just get all excited and I get weird. "Peculiar," I think Larry likes for us to refer to ourselves.

When your son died and you prayed over him, you believed he was in Heaven when he died. What in your grief were you responding to then?

Missing him myself. Missing him myself.

Even though you knew you'd see him again?

You could liken it to a wife, a daughter, a mother, a father going overseas for six or eight months. When you're used to seeing 'em every day and being able to hug 'em or whatever.

Someone that you're really close to, if they're overseas where you can't talk to them, you can't call 'em, you can't touch 'em, letters don't get through very well, they get eaten by the alligators or whatever. That's how you feel during that, or that's how I felt during that, six months.

It must be stronger than that if you're talking about not being able to get on your feet without God's help.

I could ride a motorcycle. Now this is crazy: My motorcycle's anointed. It ministers to me a certain amount I guess. I could go and ride a motorcycle and enjoy the fellowship of the people that we rode with, come back into the house and be okay, and then all of a sudden be hit with the fact that I wasn't going to see him again. At least not for a long time. At that point, having always seen him, most all of his life, seldom more than a week or two going without seeing him, the sense of loss was just, it was just hard.

And I would basically say, "Lord, I know I'm going to see him eventually, but it's so long. It is so long to wait. Years and years and years without seeing him. It is so long to wait." And that would just wipe me out, and I would have to battle that. I'm not going to get hung up in that. I'm not going to succumb to that thought process. I'm going to go another way.

I'm gonna say, "But I am gonna see him, and I'm going on with what I have to do now for that ten, fifteen, twenty years, whatever, however many it is. And then I know that when I get to Heaven he's gonna come and meet me."

I had two dreams about him and that was all. In one, it was kind of nutty because—I dreamed I had taken his son out to the country, set him down—at that time he's about three years old—he's running in through the farmyard, and I was at the truck trying to get stuff unloaded, and this horse had cut loose and he was running through the farm yard, just about to plow over Rusty, my grandson.

All of a sudden Lee appeared. I couldn't get to him around the truck or anything. All of a sudden Lee appeared, grabbed that child, and there he was standing at the end of the truck holding his son. And I'm just looking at him, saying, "How did you do that?" And he said, "God allowed me." And he put the child down and he ran off to play, and it was like you look at somebody and it's heart to heart, heart and eyes to heart and eyes. I said, "Can I hold you? Can I hug you?" He said, "No." I said, "Okay. Okay."

Two years after that, I had another dream that I recalled. I was walking up this sidewalk. He got out of a white limo at the end of the sidewalk and was dressed in white except for a navy-blue tie, and he had—Do you know those old-fashioned white leather suitcases that had straps on 'em and stuff? He had this white leather suitcase.

He just looked really nice. He was a handsome kid, and he looked really good. And I walked up to him, and I was careful not to touch him. And I said, "Can I hug you?" And he put down the suitcase and he said "Yes!" And I just took him in my arms, and we just hugged on one another until we'd had our fill.

I stepped back from him, and I looked up at him, and over his eyes was like an iridescent, pinky-purple, eyeshadow-type-looking stuff. And I looked at him, and I said, "Son, is there something about you that I didn't ever know that I need to know?"

And he said, "My eyes?" And I said, "Yeah." "No," he said. "I see things differently. I see across time, and I see things much differently." That's all he said.

He was so full of joy. It was like what was around him was bigger than him, because he was just so full of joy, which he never, or seldom, seemed to know on earth.

He said, "I've got something for you." We were walking down the sidewalk into the house. And when we got into the house, he handed me a video tape. I started to put it into the VCR, and he said, "I can't watch it right now," and he left.

Well, the background of the thing about the video is that we had three different videos that he was pictured on, and that was it as far as having any video of him. They had been lost. None of them could be found, nor had they been found since his death.

The day when I woke up from having that dream, I was moving some furniture in the family room, and I found one of the videos. It had him and his son and his wife on it and some stuff from their wedding, some pictures from their wedding. I set down and I cried. I thought, I'm not gonna sit here and cry. I'm gonna watch the stupid video. God's good.

Let's talk about motorcycles.

There'd be people who have more mileage than this, but I don't think there are a lot of women who have much more mileage than this. I've probably ridden between forty- and forty-five thousand miles since I had my own motorcycle, which was five years ago.

I discovered that after I received my prayer language, one of my favorite places to pray was on the motorcycle, buzzing down the road. And I would pray in tongues riding a motorcycle. It's wonderful, it's just awesome.

Lately, it's like the Holy Spirit has given me these little songs. I can be riding the motorcycle, and I'm singing some little song that sounds

kind of like a Spanish nursery song or something. I don't know what it is.

Everybody needs to have something that feeds themselves, some form of recreation that feeds the spirit inside of them. And for me, riding a motorcycle really does that. It doesn't seem to make any difference that I'm short on one end and could stand to have a couple or three inches of leg to ride, maybe handle it more efficiently. I don't worry about that. I really don't. I get teased about the things that I do and the choices that I make, but I know how to pick a parking space that'll keep me and the motorcycle upright, and it may not be where everybody else is parked. I get ribbed about it. It doesn't detract from my joy. I love, I just love, to ride. Feeds my spirit.

I have an anointed bike. Anointing is a very special thing, when the Holy Spirit touches your life and allows you to minister, but he allows me to minister through that bike. And I didn't know that it was going to turn out to be that way when I got that old brown Gold Wing. From the time I put the fish and the dove on the back of that trunk it has just started to attract people. I can take it anywhere and it finds me somebody to minister to.

Most people say, "Is that a hog?" which is a slang term for a great big Harley, and I have to fill 'em in on that. And that's a good place to start. "No, it's not a Harley, and it's not. It's a special bike."

We brought this big, gorgeous, green bike home. I was a little bit intimidated by it, 'cause it is a big bike. I took it out to try to get used to it, riding circle eights and all the things you're supposed to do to get used to a new motorcycle.

There's a Christian rally scheduled first week in May in Terre Haute. And in addition to that, I had committed before the church to take people to Atlanta to an Intercessors 500 meeting, and I know the power of the anointing that would be in that meeting.

It was to be toward the end of May. I knew I was taking people that would come back, and what they had learned was gonna change and minister the church. And I knew that my husband and I needed to be at that Christian bikers rally in Terre Haute.

I was riding the green bike, and we pulled out of the filling station, just having filled it up. Two people had made a pathway for us to come through, and there was a double yellow line beside the van, which was the outer vehicle. My husband went on around the van, and somebody came up beside the van, passing, heading into a turn. He wasn't supposed to be there, that suffices.

When I came out from behind the van, it was front end of motorcycle to front end of car, and I went over the windshield, hit the hood of his car, and slid off into the ground and just kind of laid there, trying to decide if I was all there or not. When I realized I was, I just said, "Glory to God, I'm alright! Yes! Thank you, Lord!"

Just to praise him, I just started to speak in tongues, just started to praise God. Which is how the EMTs found me, speaking in another language. Well, their first question, and I suppose they ask this to everybody, "Do you know who you are?"

Yes! Redeemed in the Lord! No, I didn't do that. I wish I had of. I told 'em who I was and what had happened, and I said, "Everything seems to be just fine, just fine." And they said, "How come you have blood on your face then?"

I reached up and realized I had a little nick in my nose here and a little nick here and a bruise on my right cheek bone. And I said, "Well, something hit my face." And the EMT looked real deep and said, "You ever had a broken nose?"

The first thing that happened to me was in my spirit I said, "Don't you speak a broken nose over me. I'm not going to receive any broken nose. God has looked after me. I haven't got anything that's broken."

My hand went up to my face, and I felt and I said, "No I haven't, and I still don't" He said, "Well, why are you bleeding?" And I said, "Well, I got a little nick here, I got a couple little cuts and they're just bleeding a lot I guess. I don't know. I can't see myself."

They checked me out, and when I stood up I looked across the hood of the car that had hit me, and there was a young man standing there, just holding onto the car, just shaking. I mean he was just, just shaking. I walked over to him, and I said, "Look at me." And he looked up at me. I said, "I am alright. I am perfectly alright." He said, "I thought you were dead. I thought you were dead."

"I am alright, I am perfectly alright. The God who looks after me has protected me this day." He said, "I ride a motorcycle, too. I have never had an accident, not in my car, not on my bike, nothing." And I just talked to him for a while.

My husband had checked on me and he had gone home. We only live two or three minutes from that filling station. He had gone home to get the car, come back, and get me, and when he came back he approached the car and I heard this guffaw. I heard him laugh from the gut, and he walked up and he said to me and to the young man, "I should have known that she would be here. Has she prayed for you yet?"

And he looked at me and he looked at him. We both had on our vests, sprouting 100 Percent Jesus all over the place, and he said, "No, but I think maybe somebody should."

I got to talk to him for just a minute. I just told him. I said, "Don't beat yourself up about this, don't get involved in guilt 'cause you hit another biker. Just don't go there 'cause I am fine. I have no grudge. I know that the insurance companies will figure out what to do about the motorcycle or whatever."

He said, "Yeah, they will." I said he could just consider that somehow that was what was meant to happen this day. Please just don't be concerned about it. Don't be beatin' yourself about it, that you made wrong decisions or whatever. Don't be doing that, don't get into that. Just let the insurance companies sort out the damage to the vehicles. Forgive yourself, forgive me for getting maybe too impatient to get where I was going.

I hate to see somebody walk into guilt. It's the devil's tool. It beats people up, it saps their energy, depresses them. And if you're a Christian it's a sin against God. You're to trust God and not be guilty about stuff. That's another story.

But I have to say that we went on to the rally, and that evening our pastor and the praise team were playing music. And at one point I felt that I needed to turn to the lady next to me and pray with her about something. That's what the Holy Spirit was telling me. So I turned to her and I said, "Is there something I can agree in prayer with you about?" My hands were all tuned in to this woman, and I'm trying to be obedient.

Well, she said, "Yes, I feel like my ministry is changing. If you would pray for me that I stay in God's will where that's concerned." And suddenly, inside myself, I just thought the Spirit of the Lord just come up and said, "You are receiving an awesome gift of healing."

I had just found out that my other grandson had—the doctors said that he had a hole in his heart. I said, "I have a prayer need, prayer request. Will you stand in faith with me and pray for the healing of my grandson? I need a woman who will meet my faith that this healing will be done."

You just felt two spirits come out and collide. Faith met faith. The power of that prayer was—I get tired of using "awesome." We got to come up with a word that really sums up God, and that's as close as I can get. The power of that prayer grew in intensity while we prayed. I just felt so much of God's love, God's energy, God's purpose being fulfilled in that prayer. And as we got to the end of it, I realized that not only was he going to heal Luke but he was going to move in my son and daughter's life, that they would get to be Spirit-filled, that they would get to move into the full love and the full function that God had for them, and that the whole family would be able to relate that tight-knit understanding, where everybody walked in the Spirit.

And the power of it just filled me up. Nobody touched me, nobody said anything. I thought I felt this cool little puff of air come from kind of from my right against my face, and the next thing I knew I was over backwards and there was nobody to catch me. And I tell you what, the Holy Spirit decked me a whole lot harder than that automobile ever thought about, and it broke the triple-tree on my bike.

And I was on the ground, and I felt the impact when I hit. But as soon as I hit I also felt peace and joy just wash through me, whereas in the physical I hit and I felt that impact. It was instantly gone.

I just started to laugh. It happens to me. I get giggling, and people think I've gone off the deep end. But I just started to laugh. I was so relieved. I was so excited all in one fell swoop. Laughter like that, do you remember my saying that I laughed when we prayed for my father and I knew he was healed? Laughter sometimes is an indication when it comes spontaneously like that after an intense prayer. It's an indication from God that a prayer is completed. That's not always the way that you know that a prayer is completed. Sometimes you have peace or you have a release from a need to pray anymore. Sometimes, when something is really broken loose, you just—it ends up in laughter.

So there I am, laying on the ground, laughing. My husband is being beaten up in the Spirit, 'cause twice in one day he's not been there to protect me. I bless that man. He was actually hurting because he didn't prevent the motorcycle accident. He couldn't prevent the motorcycle accident. And he didn't catch me, 'cause he didn't think I was gonna fall. He thought I was praying for the other woman. He says, "You're always praying for somebody, and I figured you were praying for somebody else. I didn't realize that she might be praying for you" or with you or whatever.

And he said, "I was just sitting there going, 'I'm just not any good at this. I'm not being a good husband, I'm not being this I'm not being that. I didn't catch her.'"

Audibly, inside of myself, all of a sudden he said, "The Holy Spirit said, 'I caught her.'" He said, "I never get that kind of thing. That doesn't happen to me. But I knew, just instantly, that guilt that was working on me," my husband was saying. That guilt that was working on him released. He said, "I knew that it didn't matter that I hadn't prevented the motorcycle accident. It didn't matter that I hadn't caught you, 'cause the whole thing was about God and God's purpose and what he is doing. And it had nothing to do—I didn't do it wrong. God did it. Then I could really get with joy into the rest of the situation."

I was walking around in that rally, the afternoon of the accident. I knew that I knew that I knew—you hear Christians say that kind of garbage—I knew that I knew that I knew that somehow in the spiritual realm there was a shield around me that literally prevented Satan from taking my life in that accident.

The experienced riders kept saying to me, "I don't know how you lived through that." And the pastor said, "There are thousands of angels up there in Heaven, Mary, going [huffs and puffs]. And I knew that it was true. You know how you know inside yourself that you have no right to be walking and breathing, but that wasn't the way the story was written so you're walking around and breathing?

When I went to Atlanta, the first service, there was a woman sitting diagonally in front of me, a young African American woman. When the service ended we were all hugging on one another, and she moved toward me, and I knew inside of myself, I said, "You have a word for me," meaning you have a word of prophecy or a word of knowledge or something to give me. And she just kind of checked her spirit for a moment, and all of a sudden this stuff started to roll.

I can't repeat it all, but the thing that hit me so powerfully was she said to me, "You have a shield around you. You have an impenetrable shield in the spirit around you, and the fiery darts, the attacks of Satan bounce off of it. It is a blood shield, a blood covering, from Jesus. And it is because of your obedience, the Lord knows where that obedience is taking you." She didn't know I'd been in an accident. But her last words to me were, "The shield is unto life against death."

I had a real hard time standing up after she said that.

Every two weeks, the gang holds services at the Putnamville, Indiana, Correctional Facility.

NANCY

She is a prospect with the Unchained Gang.

I had a life that a lot of people would have considered a good life, but it wasn't going to make
it for me. So I woke up one morning, uncontrollably crying. Wheezer and me, laying in bed.

I just sat up and I told him. I had been telling
him I wasn't happy, that I didn't want to drink,
didn't like his drinking. As long as he drank, I
couldn't not drink. He wasn't going to pull up
off the drinking, so it was becoming real appar-
ent that I was going to have to leave that relationship for good, for the last time.

I just woke up bawling and crying and sat up in
bed and shaking my head. I just told him, "This
isn't gonna work." And he just patted my leg,
and he said, "It'll be alright." He did not understand. I couldn't quit crying. He left for work,
and I had to call my dad to tell him I couldn't
come in to work. I just can't quit crying.

I cried for probably an hour and a half, and I fell
to my knees and just did what I knew was asking
God to give me another DUI. 'Cause I had been
praying. I had been praying and saying, "Lord,
please help me quit drinking, but don't let any
harm come to me." I was kind of praying to God
to do something but limiting him. So I wasn't
getting an answer to my prayer at all.

When I fell to the end of my bed, I just fell on it
and just prayed and told God, "I don't care what
it takes." And I knew, I knew that that meant it

was a DUI, another one, that was gonna make me have to go through the system, have to go through the IOP* classes and all that stuff that I skirted around the first time.

So when I prayed that, it was a week to the day later that I got my second DUI. Then I stood in the jail cell and paced back and forth and said, "Lord, I didn't mean it. I didn't mean it."

I had always had the Lord in my life. I always believed in God and loved Jesus. But I was brought up Catholic, so I didn't know how to pray. I didn't know how to have a correct relationship with God. All I knew was God was my father, so he had to love me. And Jesus was my brother, so he had to do big-brother things was what I thought. It was strange.

You said before that you were sexually active since you were thirteen?

Yeah. Very much. Seems to be my hardest thing to overcome. I thought the drinking would be. All my other vices, like my drinking, my drug addictions, the stuff that I wanted to control or get out of my life, they were harmful to me in very visible ways. And harmful to other people and this and that. But the fornication, to me, I never sat down and held my head in my hands and said, "Oh! I wish I could quit doing this for the rest of my life!" I have, however, sat down and held my head in my hands in despair and said, "I wish I could never do this again. I don't ever want to do this again." The drinking, the drugs, anything to do with that. But I never did do that over sex.

When I first joined the church after I got that second DUI—of course I did a couple days in jail and then I got out—they made me go to the treatment and all that stuff. Or they were going

_____
* Intensive outpatient.

to make me, but in the meantime the courts take so long that I went to the mental health clinic and told them, "I need to start counseling now. I'm going to have to do this anyway, might as well do it now, because I need help."

I'd been in AA for four years, trying to quit and couldn't get the job done. Just could not. Actually, three years, because it was three years in between DUIs. I'd been going three years hot and heavy to AA and doing all that kind of stuff. To me, when I stayed three weeks sober the first time I thought that was a miracle. When I finally made it to three months, I went out and celebrated and got drunk.

I was so tickled with the three months, I just felt it was a miracle. But then I wanted more. It was like, Man, if I could just get a year, I know I could get some of my brain cells talking to each other again.

I used to be a very, very highly intelligent kid. My mom, when I came home from school, the teacher had a spelling list, my mom had one just as big, and I had to write every one of those words ten times, put 'em in sentences. She made sure I was able to communicate well. And I lost a lot of that. I lost a lot of that with extensive drug use. When I finally hit my bottom, which I did several times, but the last time I couldn't talk. I had a total nervous breakdown. My parents put me in the back room in their house, and Mom came in and fed me once in a while.

I could walk to the bathroom, but I couldn't say anything. I could hear people talking, but I couldn't even think a full sentence. So it scared me, 'cause it lasted for about four weeks. When I finally came out of that room and ventured down the hallway, and Mom was in the kitchen, she just, you know, she turned around and it was like, Oh, my gosh, Nancy's come out of that room.

I walked in the family room and just watched the birds in the birdbath outside the sliding-glass doors. I remember Dad putting his guitar down and asking me if I was okay. I just stared, and he said, "Nancy, do you want us to get you help?" And all I could do was shake my head no, because I was scared.

He said, "What do you want?" and I could not get two words to come out of my mouth. It took me about fifteen minutes of sitting there, and finally I said, "I'm scared."

That's when he said, "Do you want us to get you help?" All I could picture was them putting me in one of those straitjackets in the mental ward, and I didn't want that. I shook my head no frantically.

Mom came in, and she was like, What are you scared of? What scared me the most was that I couldn't pray, because I couldn't even think a full sentence. And always before, anything I had ever done to myself, as bad a shape as I had ever been in, I could always still communicate with God. And I couldn't do that, and my mind knew I wasn't able to do that, but it wasn't able to go any further.

I sat there probably another fifteen minutes before I got the fact out that I was scared. I told my dad and mom, "I'm scared I'm not going to come out of this." But I said it in like five words.

When I finally came out of that, that's when I started trying. It's hard to explain what's up with alcoholism and addiction. It is not a physical thing. I mean the physical thing occurs and the physical addiction occurs. But if that were all there is to it, then you could just go to detox, get dried out, and be okay. It's a thinking disease.

I had struggled with it for a long time, and when I got that DUI, that second one, I knew that would make me get on the ball with it, and I started going to the mental health clinic. She was like, You need to get to an AA meeting. I told her, I said, "No, that's not what I need. I need something more, and I don't know what it is. AA gets me this far. What AA did was help me get back in touch with God, which I had kind of fallen away from, but it didn't take it far enough."

Like the marriage to Wheezer, it didn't go far enough for me. A lot of people would have thought it was a good thing.

Through that whole ordeal, the DUI, I started going to the mental health clinic and started talking to Connie Henderson. When I went in there, I told her, "You know, the first DUI I got I came in here and told you all a story, that I had never drank in my life, that I had just gotten divorced from my husband, and that all of a sudden I was drinking. And you all didn't deem me an alcoholic and blah blah blah." I said, "I want to lay down the truth, and I want you to help me."

I told her everything. I said, "I been drinking all my life. My grandfather owned a still. From the time I was able to drink out of his cup I was drinking moonshine and whiskey."

He gave it to me. I was his favorite. I was his first grandchild. We were inseparable, and he was a huge man. Huge man. Like six-foot-four, 275 pounds, and just loved me.

What I'd do, I'd take a drink and I'd make a face. And he would laugh. He was pickled all the time. And he'd laugh and I'd do things like dance for him, little ballerina. "Look Papaw, I'm a ballerina!" And I'd dance for him. Get him laughing, and I'd take another drink and make a face.

My mom said I was three years old before she realized I was making the face to make him laugh, that it wasn't the taste of the whiskey. I told this woman, Connie Henderson, so the drinking's been all my life. I been a junkie since I was fifteen. Had been doing hard drugs and everything from thirteen on. My parents threw me out at fourteen years old, which was not the smartest thing to do 'cause that just put me on the streets to get even worse off than what I was.

Like I said, I met the girls' dad when I was fifteen. I was a smart cookie and very, very honest. And I knew I was a little-bitty thing that needed somebody pretty big to—I could take care of them financially, but I just needed someone big to protect me from being raped and all that other stuff. Russell fit the description, and then he kind of grew on me and I fell in love with him.

He got in trouble with the law when I was seventeen. We went to New Mexico then. The rest is history. A friend of ours said he knew a town we could hide out in and they'd never find us. There was no law in that town. Farmington, New Mexico. And there wasn't. There was a lot of bikers.

When I was going to this therapist I stayed sober for I don't remember how long. Maybe, oh, a month, and went out and drank. And I was so totally and utterly upset.

I got the DUI in May, and I went out June eleventh. It was June eleventh. And I got drunk, and I just, I lost it. I was seeing the counselor. I was begging for help. I was begging for answers. Somebody tell me why this keeps happening. And don't tell me it's because I'm not strong enough.

I've been hit by a lot of things in life and really lived through a lot of things, and I just could not figure out why anyone who could live through what I've lived through could not do a simple thing like quit drinking.

So, here it is, June eleventh. I go out and drink at the bar. I go to a bar, I'm drinking. All I can talk about at the bar to the woman sitting next to me is the fact that I'm real unhappy about being there. Probably ruined her night.

The next night I looked up a friend of mine, Hubie. He was going to the House of Prayer. I knew he was sober. Him and I had been tight. We always will be. I may not see him for ten years, but I will always have that bond with him. I knew he was staying at the Ramada Inn, renting one of those efficiencies, and I showed up at his door. He hadn't seen me in forever, a year maybe.

Knocked on the door. Another thing he had never seen was me cry. Because your emotions, you get pretty hardened after that many years of using. And I had spent more time with Hubie than I think anybody, including my husband. He'd never seen me cry.

I walked in, and he gave me a hug, and we sat down, and he asked me how I was doing, and I had a smile on my face one second and just boom—just started bawling. Uncontrollably. Told him, "I need help." Through my crying, I got that out.

When he finally got me to quit crying enough to talk, I told him the whole thing. I don't want to live like this anymore. I don't want to live like this anymore. I want to be able to feel again. When there's a beautiful sunset, I want to know that emotion that normal people feel. I was so dead inside.

He got me to quit crying. He said, "You can go to church with me." I said, "I don't know." "Go to church with me. You know everybody there. It'll be okay." And that's back when there was only thirty people, tops, going to the House of Prayer.

And I did. He said, "Nance, most of 'em you see, you don't hesitate to go to AA meetings and see their faces. You'll go with me this Sunday. We'll sit here and I'll pray with you now."

I said, "You know, it's not working. I've been praying." He said, "It will." So he prayed with me, and that was June twelfth. And that became my sobriety date. I went to church that Sunday and I have been there ever since, of course.

The funny thing is, Hube and I sat there and talked for a long time before we prayed. We prayed and everything, and on my way home from Hubie's, I started praying by myself in the car, and I told the Lord, I said, "I promise you, if you'll just give me one year, Lord, if you'll just give me one year to get my brain—cause as bad off as I had gotten, brainwise, I knew it. I had enough brain cells to know that I had lost a lot of my intelligence. Not only my feelings but my brain working, period.

I told the Lord, I begged him, "I'm begging you, if you'll give me a year and take away the desire, so that I'm not sitting twenty-four/seven thinking about whiskey, I will read your word, I will read the whole Bible. I will read everything. I will study it, I will learn it, I promise you. I will do this, and then at the end of the year I'll have enough ammunition and tools that when I get hit again with the obsession, I'll be able to fight it, Lord."

And everybody laughed when I went to church and told 'em. I told 'em about a week later at church. Because that was my problem. I couldn't even read the Bible. I couldn't read a paragraph without my brain going off in la-la land about whiskey. Nothing would stick with me. I was too obsessed with wanting a drink.

I had gotten about a month's worth of sobriety and then gone out and drank. I got my second

DUI and could not believe a month later when I drank again. It just, the despair was undescribable. You just can't know the feeling.

It's like if you, literally, started wetting your pants and couldn't quit it. Couldn't, even if you watched your clock and every fifteen minutes went to the bathroom to try to do something about it. Still, you just had no control over— people think, Just don't drink. Well, it does not work that way.

In fact, I couldn't even, I couldn't even read. I couldn't do anything without that gnawing, obsessive thinking and feeling of wanting a drink.

Here, I'd gone a month after that second DUI. I wound up at the bar, then I went to Hubie's and begged him for help. At this point, I was just going from person to person to place to place. Anything I could think of and begging for help. Because I knew it was available. I knew it was out there.

Larry Mitchell, if he could do it, so could I. Don't ask me why I didn't go to him, except that I think pride. I love Larry. I respected him so highly, and I wanted him to respect me, and I didn't feel respectable.

And there again, that's where your brain's not working enough to say, What are you talking about, girl? Here is the man that's done it. Go to him! And has everything you know you want. I wanted Larry's spirituality, 'cause I had known God. At fifteen years old, I don't think Oral Roberts had a thing on me. Even if I was Catholic, I had a spiritual, spiritual heart and was the sweetest, kindest, most loving person that you'd ever meet in the world, other than my grandma. And of course she's dead now.

I had it going on, and I wanted it back. I knew Larry Mitchell knew how to get it, but I didn't. I don't know, there's a pride thing there. I didn't want him to know that I was in such bad shape.

So Hubie was my last stop before I—he took me to church and I realized I was home, at this church. Not only did I know half the people there, but it was like they were so happy to have somebody to pray for. Instead of looking at me with pity, the way counselors will look at you and you know the world looks at you.

I think that's what caught my eye. Nobody looked at me with that pathetic look, pity in their eyes. Instead it was, Praise God! You've come to the right place and you're gonna make it!

In their eyes I saw their knowing that I was on my way to victory. I was home. And I did accomplish the victory, through this ministry and the people in it. I know, and I give God all the glory. I know if it weren't for God they wouldn't even have the victory to have passed it on to me.

The sermon last night, that Kenneth Copeland gave, did you listen to that? Adam is the one that made Satan the lord of this world that God created through his actions. He made Satan lord of it. And God, through Jesus and tricking the devil into taking Jesus to Hell, where he could kick the devil's butt for us and take back the world so that we'd have a choice, I just, I don't know. I mean if it weren't for God, I wouldn't want to live. I wouldn't want to be. I know that it's God and all his glory, but God has anointed Larry Mitchell, and he has anointed Carl Beadle. And Randy, Randy Wagner. We've all got our faults, but there's anointing on us.

When it's needed, 'course God can use a jackass—that's in the Bible—to minister and spread his word, but this ministry has given me my way back to God in my life. 'Cause I was dead. I was everything but physically dead. I was dead mentally, intelligently, physically—dying, killing myself.

Have you had moments of difficulty since then?

Yes. In fact, when I said that prayer on the way back from Hubie's house, it didn't immediately—it's not like a lightning bolt. I hit Hubert's house, he talked to me, he prayed with me, and something inside me knew I was on my way, where I wasn't getting that feeling talking to the counselor. With her it was more like, Come on, woman, hurry up! Give me something! I've been here four times, you've sat and shook your head and listened, Yes, yes, yes, listening to everything I've told you. Now I've told you my life story, give me feedback. Tell me something how to quit. I didn't get any feeling like I had when I left Hubert's. I felt like I was on my way.

On my way home from his house in the car, I was talking to God. I said, "Lord, I swear I swear, if you'll just give me the peace of mind from my addictions so that I can drink up your word." I had never read the Bible, but I wanted back what I had with him when I was fifteen, plus more.

I wanted that spiritual relationship with him plus knowledge about him. I'd always been just kind of okay and comfortable with the fact that, Well, God knows me and I know enough to know he loves me and he's there for me and that's all I need to know. Well, at this point it was like, No, I want to know. I want to know God. I want to know his word. I want to know him personally. Instead of just what he can do for me. I want to know what I can do for him.

I said that prayer and it didn't happen overnight, but it happened pretty quick. The next day wasn't so bad. I went to work. And normally I could make it through the day at work, but around four o'clock—it's like I knew when it was four o'clock, 'cause I had an hour before I could get a drink.

That was actually pretty good, for me, to have a job and be working. The next couple days, I didn't obsess so much on the drinking. It was a lot less, it was about half as bad, which was wonderful.

I went to church, and I told a bunch of people what I had prayed, and they laughed at me. And I was standing there thinking, "What's so funny?" Al Lavine patted me on the shoulder, and he said, "Well, hon, the thing is God doesn't deliver you from anything to give it back to you. You're sitting there telling us you asked God for a year, and then when he hits you back with it that you'd be able to fight it with all the new knowledge you have." He said, "That's what's funny. Sweetheart, if God delivers you, you're delivered. You're free. He'll set you free. You're free. Don't be talking a year thing. God doesn't work like that."

So I walked away and kind of thought about it and looked up to the sky and told God, "Well, I'm still asking for that year. If you don't see fit to set me free for my whole life, consider that year thing, God."

It didn't take long. I can't remember now, but it seems like it was just a few weeks, and it dawned on me, sitting at work, that I hadn't thought about whiskey once an hour. I hadn't even realized it was four o'clock. I didn't even desire a drink. And I was in shock.

And I had been reading the Bible and been able to read like at least a chapter before, which was good for me. I couldn't hardly even read a paragraph without having to read it five times, 'cause I couldn't get my concentration to stay.

That was another thing, my attention span and my concentration were so pickled and gone. That's hard for someone who used to be intelligent, too. I think it's probably easier on people who never were originally, because I knew that I used to be able to do this, and now I was having to struggle with it. It's humbling.

I had been reading the Bible for a couple weeks and getting better and better at it to where I could read a whole chapter, stuff like that, and contain what it had said.

Seven months went by of bliss, absolutely not a desire in the world for the first time in my entire life was I not bound to that. And it hit me: I was sitting at work, seven months of freedom, I was sitting at work, and I smelled it. I smelled whiskey. I looked around. I thought maybe my dad was, you know, having a bad day. I don't know, put whiskey in his coffee. I don't know.

I could smell it as plain as day. I sat there, and I thought, No. Finally, I asked him, "Are you drinking whiskey?" and him and his partner both looked at me. I said, "I smell whiskey." Boy that night, I went home, I changed clothes, I couldn't get it to quit, so I decided to go to a meeting, an eight o'clock meeting at Trinity* on Kirkwood.

When I left there, I wanted a drink even worse. I thought, "Well, I'll take a walk," you know, on Kirkwood. Oh, I walked alright, for forty-five minutes, back and forth in front of Nick's,** telling myself, Fight him. Fight him. Struggling with Satan, because he was like, Wonder who's in there, Nancy? You probably got some friends in there. Just go in and talk to them.

Yeah, I could do that. I started crossing the road. Man, it hit me: No, no, no! I know what's in there. I know what's in there. I don't want it. For forty-five minutes I walked back and forth in front of that bar, struggling, crying. Finally I got

---

* Trinity Episcopal Church, where a number of AA meetings are held.

** A bar across the street from Trinity.

in my car, went home, called the AA clubhouse, the twelve/twenty-four club, and Kenny answered, a friend of mine.

I talked to him, and he was like, "You want me to come over?" "No, no, no. I don't want that." He's a single, good-looking young guy. I'm like, "No, I don't think so, man. I might have another problem on my hands."

I hung up the phone, I paced back and forth. And it was like my brain had a cloud around it and it was visible to me. I could almost see it. Because I knew there was something I needed to do. I couldn't think of it, and I knew it was a simple thing. And then I looked down and there was my Bible. And I thought, Yes! God, yes! That's it! Open that sucker up. I opened it up, and the words—and I'm telling you, I was under attack by Satan. I didn't think about it at the time, but afterwards. 'Cause I looked at it and I could not—the words were scrambling, like I was having a flashback from some drug. I could not read the words. They were blurred and moving. And I started crying, and I just said, "God, *please* help me! I know if I can read something, if I can just read something this would go away." And I don't know why I knew that either. And I don't know why it's like that.

It's like the words stopped moving, the cloud went away, and I sat and read that Bible. And it went away. I didn't tell anybody about it for like a month because I was ashamed. Everybody at church was so happy for me. I was doing so good for seven months. I didn't want to admit that I possibly had slipped in my spiritual walk enough that that happened to me.

I finally was sitting in a Chicago Pizza with Larry Mitchell and just couldn't not tell anybody any longer. I told Larry, "Something happened to me and I got to tell you about it." Because I was

also at that point, then scared to death that it was going to happen again and I wouldn't be able to fight it. I had never, never had such a wonderful seven months in my life, and the thought of losing it had me in panic.

So I did eventually talk to him there at Chicago Pizza, and I told him, I said, "What, what am I gonna do if it happens again?" And Teena* said, "I don't care if it's three o'clock in the morning, call, and we will pray over the phone. We'll come over there."

Larry kind of made me feel better about it. He said, "Nancy, that was Satan's biggest gun with you." There were a lot of things Satan couldn't get me to do, because it was just imbedded in me. I wouldn't steal. I would starve before I'd steal. I went through withdrawal several times off of heroin and different things 'cause I would not steal to get anything, to get drugs or to do anything.

But that alcohol, that was Satan's biggest gun. Larry told me, "You've got to be prepared because Satan's gonna start. He's probably real good and mad now. You been serving him all this time. You've turned your back on him. He's gonna hit you with everything he can." And that made sense to me, and I could see it from that perspective. And I felt a lot better.

Then I started telling everybody and letting them know if this happens to me again I'm gonna call. We can all pray and come against Satan together. At all costs, don't let him have me again.

Like I said, When I first got sober, I wasn't able to read very well. A lot of things I had once been able to do, I couldn't do. I knew I just had to work on it.

_____
* Pastor Larry's wife.

Hubie said, "Don't start out with Genesis." He said, "Start out reading the Book of John, and then go back to Matthew, Mark, Luke, read those, and on through the New Testament. But start with John and then go to the beginning of the New Testament and read all through that and then go to the beginning, to Genesis."

That was good. I'm sure he got that advice to give me from God. Especially to an addict, or someone with the same types of problems addicts have, when we first get sober it takes a while for our brain cells to build up. You don't want to give us something too hard, like reading the Old Testament. That could get very discouraging, cause us to want to give up.

I read it all that way, starting with John, then the rest of the New Testament, then the Old Testament. But I've got this little voice in me saying, "You need to continue."

Used to, in fact, a year ago, I could quote you Scriptures. Not like Larry can, but I could quote the Scriptures that I speak. Now I've forgotten that, and it's like, Man, I need to get back to reading every day.

Philippians is a favorite of mine, and Ephesians, and I like Romans. I just need to get back to reading them. I need to make time for that, and I need to start—the girls have been in school long enough now that they're starting to get used to this routine I've set up for them. They need to start being responsible for getting things done without me having to supervise.

One thing I like about Philippians, it's a small book. It's got four chapters to it, so if I came home and was tired but wanted to read my Bible I could read Philippians and have read the whole book. Whereas, like if you read Romans, it's kind of hard to sit and read Romans all in one reading.

So what was going on when you were thirteen, fourteen, and fifteen that made you such a wild child?

My personality, period, was always very aggressive, very achieving. My mom said she could not get me to sit on her lap when I was a baby. I was too busy. Where my sister, in contrast, was very hang-on-her. It was just a personality thing there.

I was very independent. I love knowledge. I'm curious, a very curious person. I like to know about everything. I was very intelligent, I was very athletic. Always, always, always on the go. And my mom had always just let me run loose.

I'd leave in the morning after breakfast, and she may not see me till that night. I'd get on my bicycle and I'd be gone. I played sports, basketball and all this stuff. Well, my mom had a brother, my uncle. Him and I were very, very close. He didn't spend a lot of time with me 'cause he was a junkie. And a drug addict.

He'd show up and he'd have a tie-dyed shirt he had bought for me. What I didn't know is that his wife was sitting at home with no electricity and no formula for his baby. But he had, in his drunkenness, stopped and bought me a tie-dyed shirt. So to me he was the greatest, and nobody bothered to tell me.

The things Mom tried to protect me from really hurt me in the long run. Bottom line is she was cutting things off with him. He was a lot younger than her, and she had raised him 'cause he was the last of my grandma's kids. She was cutting him off. She was afraid, because I was turning twelve. I was starting to develop, and all of a sudden my mom's going nuts.

To be honest with you, at twelve years old I didn't even really notice boys. It didn't phase me, but she started freaking and thought that— and she could have been right—that my uncle was getting a little too close to me. I was developing into a young woman and . . .

So she threw him out of our lives. I didn't like that. And she started accusing me just out of the blue. She started accusing me of smoking, of doing drugs. And I wasn't—yet. I'd always drank, but that was nothing.

Her and I started butting heads, and it got bad. She also, her nerves were bad, so when she was mad at my dad she would take it out on me. 'Cause she's really a frail woman. If you yell at her, she'll cry. She's that type. And she's very scared of my dad 'cause he's pretty blunt and nasty verbally. He can be that way. So instead of taking out what she wanted to say to him, he'd go to work, and boy she'd lay in on me. My name became Moron.

Looking back, I know that over the years, when my mom was short-tempered and nasty to me and called me names, even when I was a kid, I look back, and it was her nerves. She couldn't say what she wanted to say to my dad. She didn't feel like she could, so she'd take her frustration out on me. And at twelve years old, it really, really alienated me from her.

Then we moved back in town, and she really wanted to know what I was doing all the time. We clashed so bad. And I did start. I went and bought a pack of cigarettes. She had yelled at me for something Dad had done, and I left the house and made her mad there. She was like, "You don't walk away from me!" I just kept walking. I thought, Screw you.

I went and bought a pack of cigarettes. And from there, I don't know, I got a high off of 'em. And I wasn't seeing my grandfather anymore, so I started hanging with kids that were drinking. It just escalated. My personality had

something to do with it. The fact that my mom was not in her right mind at the time. She was dealing with things that, she needed to do a lot of growing, which she has done now thanks to me.

Her problems with my dad, my problems—my dad, since he was using, he wouldn't help her when I did start using. In fact, he kind of gave me the impression, "Nancy," he told me. He said, "I'm getting real tired of your mom being down my throat. Now I do everything I do, and I just don't get caught." In other words, he was telling me, Do what you're doing but don't flaunt it in front of her face.

And I was like, Well, but I'm the type, any time I'm doing anything I believe in what I'm doing. You know what I'm saying? This was the '70s, too. I was wearing marijuana-leaf earrings and stuff. Hey, when I do something, I do it full-force. I'm a hundred-percenter.

When I was in school, my mom didn't really have to egg me on too much. If I'm gonna learn this, I'm gonna learn all of it. I don't do anything half-way. Except, of course, I did my relationship with God half-way all those years. But I didn't know any better. Being raised Catholic, I thought that's all there was to it. You go out, you drink, then you go to confession once a week, and that's what the Lord expects you to do: Go be human, 'cause that's the way you were made. So go be human and then just make sure you get into the confessional, and that's your duty to God, to confess. Then that's it.

You can imagine at a fifteen-year-old—shoot, I'm thirty-four and I still have a lot of teenage tendencies. I like to play hard, and I like to work hard, and I'm adventurous.

Did you meet up with Russell right away when you left home?

No. No, I left home at fourteen.

Is that when you got into heroin?

LSD. I don't think I did heroin till I was fifteen. LSD, pot, LSD. Fourteen years old, I was just kind of the new kid on Kirkwood, and I was just such a little, little girl. I weighed eighty-five pounds. Very curvy. Very curvy but tiny.

People's Park was hippies and stuff. And, basically, when I first left I stayed with a girlfriend of mine and her parents, who were extreme alcoholics but very wealthy. There again, that escalated my drinking. Up until I was thirteen I just drank around the family. They all drank, so I drank.

But when I left home and moved in with Sarah and her parents, oh my gosh! We'd get home at four-thirty in the morning, and they'd get home at five-thirty in the morning. They had two stocked bars in their house, so it just escalated. Plus, there was absolutely no structure to my life at all, where at least Mom had a very structured house.

I wound up drinking a lot. Then, of course, it doesn't take long to meet characters in low places. They have nothing to lose, usually, so they're usually pretty open people. I wound up on Kirkwood, and this man named Gary McDonald took me under his wing. I was very trusting. If somebody did rip me off, it didn't bother me too bad. It was like I felt sorry for them instead of feeling mad about it.

Man, I was a sweetheart. Very, very sweet, giving, little girl, very trusting. And Gary picked up on it right away and said, "Oh my gosh!" 'Cause he was walking down the alley, and I was sitting outside of Rocky's, smoking a joint in the alley. He's walking by, and I was just, "Hey, you want a toke?" And he couldn't believe it. "It's three-thirty in the morning. What are you doing in this alley, let alone talking to me? I could rape you, girl."

He got at my trust and my openness. I had it in my mind that I was gonna go when I was gonna go and God was my buddy. God wasn't gonna let anything happen to me. I really did. I wasn't scared of anything. He decided right off, 'cause Gary knew there was stuff to be scared out there of, because he was it. He was a very mean—well, he's dead now, but he committed murder several times, he ripped off anybody he could, his mom included. He'd rip his own family off. But he liked me.

So he took me under his wing, and he kind of took care of me. He was twenty-one or twenty, and I was fourteen. He was a year older than Russell. I mean he didn't follow me around everywhere, but when he saw me he let everybody in town know that I was his sister. 'Cause all of a sudden I'm on the scene, and everybody's, you know, Who's that? He told 'em all I was his sister. I still have people today that don't believe me when I tell them we weren't really blood, 'cause he made 'em think it.

So I went along with it. But he introduced me to Russ about a year later. I was shooting pool in Rocky's, and I was pretty and I knew it. I was pretty, I was capable, I was very good at shooting pool. Anything I did, I was good at. Anything that I tackled, I could do it very quickly and very good.

He brought Russell up, and I just wasn't too interested. I was, you know, "Man I'm shooting pool. It's nice to meet you. I'll party with you sometime," but he looked like a big old dumb hippie. And I had enough people I was seeing at the time.

But man, he just kept hanging around. He told me that Gary had told him that he knew the woman for him and that we belonged together. And as I got to talking to Russell, he was very intelligent. He had gotten out of boy's school at fifteen years old, sixteen. They sent him to a half-way house here in Bloomington, and the people that were running the half-way house immediately realized he was very intelligent. He was one of those book-smart-but-not-a-lick-of-common-sense, couldn't-blow-his-own-nose type but very, very intelligent. They took him and got his GED and took him to IU, and he got accepted into IU at sixteen years old. And then blew that because of his drug use.

When I went to school was when everybody went to bed, at the sleeping rooms. And Gary and his girlfriend had one sleeping room. It was four rooms upstairs. Me and Russ had one. Dude named Cowboy had one, and then Greg Anderson had another one. So we were all like family up there. When I came home, the party was on again. I eventually quit, 'cause all I could do was sleep through that, the school.

Russell just didn't quit coming around. He just kept showing up, and it didn't take him long to realize that if he showed up with a bottle of whiskey I'd spend a lot of time with him. I wouldn't go to bed with him for a long time. He just kept coming around.

But I liked his intelligence. One of our pastimes when we moved to New Mexico, when he wasn't at work and we were sitting around the house and doing our thing, I could be doing the dishes, he'd read to me. He liked *Omni* magazine. He subscribed to that.

He'd read. And if he'd read something that he knew I didn't know anything about, he'd read the paragraph and then he'd explain what he was saying. 'Cause I'm real good with math, but science was never my thing.

With Russell, he played a lot. He didn't the first two years, when I was fifteen to seventeen years old, in Bloomington. He wouldn't have gone out on me for the world, because Bloomington was my town. I didn't have to have him. Once he got me two thousand miles from home and convinced me that if I went back, that I would be an accomplice to his crimes and even the ones he committed on the way to New Mexico, he more or less had me scared to go back.

In my heart I just felt like God loved him so much and that if I just could somehow explain to Russell that. I would pray for him when he did that stuff, thieving and stealing. I never could. That was wrong.

Dealing drugs was not wrong because—unless I would have dealt it to little kids—but you know, to me, I did business with forty-year-old men. They were gonna get it somewhere. Why not me make the money?

Yeah, Russell got me two thousand miles from home. Then I started getting into some hairy stuff. It was bikers. Like I said, Russell was a thief. Well, in Bloomington, Indiana—and Gary and all these guys—I could pray for them and pay off their debts if need be. 'Cause it was usually chump change, small stuff, never more than fifteen hundred dollars.

We hit New Mexico, and they started dealing with these bikers, and I would get people coming to my door. Big, mean people that killed people daily, wanting five grand. You know, "Your old man owes me big bucks." And I'd have to pay it.

Finally it got to the point where it was the principle of the thing with Gary. And the Dead Men, president of the Dead Men came to my house out in the middle of the desert, him and his body guard. He told me, "I've worked it out with my people. You've got two days to get out of here." And he said, "Gary's done. And if I were you, I'd leave that old man of yours with Gary and let us take care of 'em both."

I was crying. I didn't cry, but I was whining about it. I said, "Gosh, no, Terry, don't do that." He just told me, he said, "It's the principle of the thing now." 'Cause it was only ten grand. I told him, "I've paid you that before. I can do it. Give me two weeks, I can do it."

Gary didn't rip him off a second time. He ripped off his buddy. I had paid a ten thousand dollar debt of Gary's once. I pulled up to a liquor store window, drive-up liquor store window in New Mexico. Farmington. I was making a liquor run. I was nine months pregnant. Russell was with me and one of the Dead Men.

Well, we got surrounded by Barons on motorcycles, and they decided to pull us out of the van. They shot the guy that was with us. I don't think he was dead, I think they just shot him. I saw him go down. I could see the pool of blood forming in my peripheral vision, but I wouldn't take my eyes off the guy that did the shooting.

He went to pick his gun up and point it at Russell, and I just stepped in front of Russell, big belly and all, and said, "You take him out and you're gonna have to take me too, 'cause I." Well, I didn't even go into why 'cause. I said, "You take him out, you're gonna have to take me, too, but I don't see that as solving your problem any."

And that guy, I got his attention. I looked him straight in the eyes, just dead-set, and said, "I

tell you what. I don't know the figures on this little escapade here, but I get the gist of the thing. You've let this guy rip you off." I said, "This"—and I pointed over to the guy laying on the ground—"ain't gonna do you no good. You done made one mistake by letting someone that looks like this even in the position to rip you off. Now you gonna make another mistake and just kill him? Whatever the amount is, man, you let me know, you give me a time, I'll pay you. But I'm gonna tell you right now: You let this m-f into you for a nickel, and you come to my house for a nickel, you might as well shoot my ass because the first time's my mistake for marrying the man. Second time's yours. I'll go down over a nickel."

You know, I was just right up there. I caught his goat, and I kind of thought I kind of tickled him. I was still a little-bitty thing with a humongous belly. And out there, women didn't talk intelligently. There weren't any women anyway, and the ones that were out there were sad. Very sad. Illiterate, no self-esteem.

And he was got. He looked over, and they spoke in a different language—Mexican or whatever—for a while. And I could tell what they were saying. He was like, What do you think, compadre?

I think the dude that he was talking to told him that Terry Duncan, who was the president of the Dead Men, had had the same problem and that I had paid him off. The guy just put his gun down and looked at me and said, "Ten thousand dollars. Two weeks. You got two weeks." And he was laughing the whole time. He couldn't quit laughing and shaking his head at me.

I guess it also looked funny, humongous Russell back there, letting me do this. But Russell was just like that. He was like a big old St. Bernard. You know, Duh do, duh do, which way do we go? He wasn't a bad person. Russell was a fantastic person, and in fact every one of these men, every one of these men, had beauty inside them that I felt God privileged me to see.

Doug, Russell's buddy, Doug, despised and hated and for good reason. He was a thief, he would screw your daughter. He's just bad news. But there were good things inside of him that not everybody had a chance to see. He would do anything for you. Of course, at fifteen and sixteen and seventeen that's what I saw. I went to him when Russell got in trouble with the law and he ran. I knew where he ran to, but I didn't know how to go get him and where to go. So I went and got Doug, and I said, "Doug, man, this is what's happened, and we need to get Russell and get him somewhere and hide."

He had broken into a home and ripped off a bunch of silver and stuff, and he got caught. They found out it was him, and the cops came to our sleeping room. I guess some of the pieces of the different things were in the room. And I had gone on an excursion, which I did every once in a while. I'd just start hitchhiking and be gone for a couple days, and Russ'd run hisself rampant looking for me. And I'd just come home after two or three days.

I was a whore, to be honest with you. Not a slut, because I had class. Not a prostitute. Nope, like my drugs, I mean, this stuff was so good, how could you put a price on it? To me, drugs were just, oh my gosh, how could you put a price on this stuff? In fact, when I started dealing drugs I didn't make any money off of it. I wasn't making no money. So everybody loved me. 'Cause I wasn't even charging.

I was into that free love. I just loved everybody, and I just didn't see why not. Very sexual. Very, very. Drugs doesn't help that situation, you

know what I mean? When you're fifteen, you're bored with the world, you got all these new drugs to try and all these new heights to reach, and just how many orgasms can I have a day? I was just carefree. If it feels good, do it. And this really feels good!

I did understand some things. And one of them was that I had the world by its toes. I had it in my clutches. I was fifteen. And I used to say this freely: I love fifteen. I love this age. I'm old enough to know how and young enough to not be accounted for it. And to me, it was my time. That's all it was.

Even at first, I did not understand that I needed a big person to protect me. I figured, and even after Gary and Russell kind of pointed it out to me that I did, I still thought, How sad for them that they don't realize that God's bigger than anything. And my whole outlook was, this is my time. I probably won't even live to be twenty-one or twenty-five, to where I have to start thinking about being responsible. I didn't have the desire to. I didn't have the desire to die; I didn't have the desire to live past a certain age. It wasn't important for me to live long. It was important to me to live fully.

Anything that was out there, I wanted it. And I didn't want a piece of it. I wanted to know it all. I was fascinated with poor people. Fascinated. I wanted to live with them. I wanted to experience it.

This one old man that let me and his daughter stay in this storage room outside his apartment, he was from Kentucky, and he worked for the city. He kept Karst Park mowed and taken care of. He'd get up at four-thirty in the morning, and he'd drink a pint of whiskey, and he'd go to work. He'd come home, drink his Red, White, and Blue, and his daughter was a real large, huge, cut-throat. She'd rip you off for anything. And she was a prostitute, and I had met her on the streets and didn't have any place to stay, and she was, you know, "Well, you can stay here." So that's where I kind of made that my home.

I could have gone home and lived in a fairly, you know, the money and stuff. That's not what I was interested in. Kind of like you with your wandering around, you've got to know what I'm talking about. You want to capture these things. You go one step further: You want to capture these things you want to know on film. And you want to communicate them in words on paper. I didn't even want that. I just wanted it. I just wanted to travel. I wanted to meet people. I wanted to experience different religions. I wanted to know cultures, different cultures.

It's really pretty sad. Ha! pretty sad? It's the saddest thing I know, that I was an addict, that addictions were involved. Because had I not been an addict, I could have led such an even more interesting life than what I have.

And I wouldn't have lost so much along the way. I lived with Navajos. I know their lifestyles, and I could tell you some stuff about their predicament. But it would have been nice, had I not been an addict, I may have been able to get it together enough to take pictures of this and maybe publish some of what I lived through. I went to their medicine man, their church or whatever they called it. I can't remember now. I wish I'd have wrote all that stuff down.

I wanted to be an architect. At fifteen years old I called Odle and Shook* and made myself an appointment. When I walked in he said, "You are my appointment?" I said, "Yes, and I want to speak to you. Do you have a minute?"

_____
* An architects' firm in Bloomington.

I think I floored a lot of people back then. And I knew I did. Not just sex. I don't think I needed that. My stature and posture and my confidence for being that age. You look at fifteen-year-olds now, they don't have that. I had the confidence of a forty-year-old woman at fifteen.

I just had all the confidence in the world that I—why worry? Why be self-conscious about anything? The most a person can do is tell you no. Or if you get raped, so what? You're raped. They raped your body. It's not like they sucked your memory out. They can't take that away from you, your spirit, your soul. Why give it to 'em, just since they took your body?

I was raped once and it hurt, and it did take me a couple months to get over. It hurt more because it was someone I knew. I was passed out and would have never known had my girlfriend not told me. I was out. I had been up for four or five days doing some of that real good coke, came in humongous rocks.

I was, I was, shoo, couldn't get any higher. And I took a handful of downs, but before I did I asked her to be with the girls when they woke up in the morning. "You know what I need to do is go to sleep. And I don't want to call Mom. You want to stay here and watch the girls for me?" And she said sure.

So I took a handful of downs and knew I'd probably be out for twenty-four hours at least. And I was. When I came to, she told me that Bob had been partying with—we'd known him for years. He'd spent the night, he'd lived with us off and on.

I wouldn't have done something like that and left someone in my home that I didn't trust. Had I done that and I didn't know the guy, I would have told him, "Hey dude, the party's over." In fact I did that. I had cleared everybody out but him. He was one of Russell's best friends.

It was three years after I left Russell, or two. I just never dreamed in a million years. The rape itself, I'm sure the guy had seen me naked, that didn't bother me. But that he would do that to me, it hurt.

I tell you where I come from, I didn't handle hurt and anger very well, so I had the capability of turning it into feeling sorry for the person. I think that's more what I was about. If there was an emotion that I didn't care for—it sucks to be hurting. It sucks to have someone rip you off, and you get your feelings hurt over it; instead, it's easier to feel sorry for them.

Did the rape change that?

It was part of what hardened me. Growing up, period. And maturing gives a person a little bit of knowledge to harden a little bit on a lot of things. But New Mexico really did it.

I witnessed four murders down there. The first one was within the first two months. We hadn't been there long. I think it was about six weeks into being there.

We reached there, and we had gotten split up from Doug. So it was just me and Russell. We got there by a trucker from a truck stop, took us on in. He got us a motel room and then fed us dinner and he took off. And he told us, "When you get a place, here's my number. When I go through this route, you can let me stay with you." That was a nice thing. Along the road you meet some really good, giving people.

We stayed, and the street people got to know us real quick. They started out telling us, "Man . . ." They'd sit and smoke one joint with us, and it

would be like, You guys are gonna have to be careful.

This one dude, he took us under his wing. He had been in Vietnam. I can't remember his name. Warren. He took a real liking to us, and he said, "Here, I'll show where you can sleep." And he looked at me and says, "I'll let you use my sleeping bag." He takes us across town in this nasty alley, and he pulls out this sleeping bag. He said, "Can you believe somebody threw this away?" Come nightfall it was cold out. You know how it gets cold at night? I was welcoming that sleeping bag, and he took us up on top of the Moose, and there were several street people up there.

Russell got a job within three days. A trucker. Then his boss started lending him money towards his first check so that we could get a room at Motel 6.

Within about six weeks we had met a lot of people. We met these boys within like two or three weeks that had a house. They had an extra room, and they said, "You can live here and split the rent with us and stuff." So we moved in with them, and they took us up on the cliffs one night.

We said, "Where are all the parties?" And they said, "Well, there's always a party going on up at the cliff that overlooks the town." I said, "Let's go there." They said it's real pretty and all that stuff.

So we go up there, and I've got my fifth of Jack. And, by the way, at ninety pounds I drank two fifths of Jack Daniels a day. And you figure I slept six to eight hours of the twenty-four. One fifth of Jack Daniels I saw kill a man. He drank the whole thing and keeled over. It was too much. And he was much larger than me. But that's the tolerance I had built up.

Anyway, I was standing up against the car, just looking out over the city, the town, all the lights and how beautiful it was. And there was a bunch of people up there, a bunch of rowdy Mexicans and stuff. I'm standing there with a bottle of whiskey in one hand and a can of Coke in the other, which was my thing. The bottle of whiskey would be gone before the can of Coke.

I'm standing there, and I looked over at Russell just in time to see a couple of Mexicans throw an Indian off the cliff right behind Russell. I knew they were getting rowdy, that's why I looked in that direction after I was looking at the town and the lights, and I heard 'em getting rowdy. I looked over just in time to see them, just politely, I mean it was just like nothing. They just threw him off that cliff, and all you could hear was that scream.

I dropped my Coke. I never ever dropped whiskey, ever. Couldn't shock me bad enough for that. I dropped the Coke and I stood there, and I was waiting for the scream to stop. 'Cause I had been on that cliff during the day. I knew how big it was. The scream did not stop for a long time. Later on, like two months later, I was up on that cliff and realized why the scream never stopped. The echo. You could yell off that cliff and it would echo for three minutes, four minutes. It really laid heavy on my mind.

That was the first murder I saw. It's like I saw it, I watched them do it, but I never went to see the body. For years, up until about two years ago, that was one thing I told that therapist I wanted help with. I could go along for a year or two just fine and then it would hit me. I would have a problem with that one.

And I watched two guys drown a guy one time. Right there in front of me. And I watched a guy get shot.

Bikers took a Navajo. Out there, it is a pastime to kill Indians. There is no law except the Dead Men at one end of town, the Barons at the other. And their pastime in bars is to stab, shoot, beat up the Indians. They just do. Or Mexicans. Or the Mexicans kill the Indians. It wasn't just one group, they all killed each other. The Navajos, they'd get so drunk that they vegetated. Instead of getting violent, they vegetated.

The first violence I did see was in Bloomington, though. That was Gary and Russ. Gary had been hired to make an example of this guy that had ripped off this drug dealer. I didn't know that. I'm in the back seat of the car, smoking a joint. I got two speakers in my ears. I can't hear a thing the guys are saying. All I know is that we pull over to pick up this guy.

I saw Gary see this guy, and he looked at Russell. They went, "Yeah." So he pulls over to pick this guy up. He turns down the radio, he says, "Hey man, want to smoke a joint? Come on, get in."

They put him in the back seat with me. I'm thinking, "Yeah, we're going out to Griffy Lake to smoke this joint." No, we get out to Griffy Lake, they pulled over, and Gary got out of the car. And he said, "Hey man, come here I want to show you something." Russ looked at me and said, "You just stay here."

I didn't think nothing about it. I had whiskey between my legs, I was fine. I was toking, drinking. And I heard, I heard them start pistol-whipping this guy. At first I heard him just going, "No, man," in a scuffle. When I turned around, Russ had the guy. Gary was doing things I had never seen. I don't even think at that point you saw that kind of stuff on TV. The blood.

They broke every bone in his body. They mutilated his face. Frankly, it was so loud, the screaming and the hitting him. When Gary hit somebody with his fists it was a loud thing. I don't know why that is. You wouldn't think it would be.

I remember that was my first time, and I threw up. After so many minutes of it I held my hands over my ears, and I couldn't get the guy's screaming out of my—I could still hear it. He was screaming. I could hear the bones breaking. It was grossing me out. I got nauseated and wound up on the other side of the car, throwing up.

Gary, when they stopped, he left him for dead. He thought he was dead or close to it. And he was. He come around the car, and it was like he went from that and what I was hearing to coming around the car and, "Oh, man," and he put his hand on my back. He said, "Nancy, you alright? You got to quit drinking, girl."

He had no idea. None. And I started crying. "How could you? How could you do that to somebody? I've never seen anything like that."

And Russ realized that I wasn't throwing up and getting sick from being drunk. Russ told Gary, "She's not throwing up because of the liquor, man."

That's kind of how I was raised by them. It started out them telling me, "Man, you are so trusting. We have got to do something about you." And it was like lesson after lesson.

They both apologized. Russ said, "I'm sorry, Nance. The guy ripped him off. The guy's a thief. He ripped so and so off." I don't care if he committed murder. Nobody deserves that. I'd rather be shot. That guy went through pain. I imagine people that were tortured under Hitler sounded like that. I don't see how anybody could stand that.

I got in the car, and I was sick for a long time—half an hour. And I told him, "Don't ever do that in front of me again."

That's where that kind of came into effect, that, Don't do this kind of thing in front of me or with me there. And then it grew. They would do things on and off. I would have to tell them what was acceptable to do in my presence and what was not. If you burglarize this house, don't do it while I'm with you. But you can bring the stuff home and sort it out, and I'll stand and pray over you. We kind of just got a feel for the way it was done in our family.

I was the mom. They were like my guys. Somebody had to take care of them. They just didn't have it together enough. They were going in a bad direction, and somebody had to love them. And somebody had to be the stable part of their lives. They in turn, I received the thrill of life, I think is part of what that was about. A lot of learning experience, life experience, even though it was negative.

The second, that guy they drowned, man. Sandi Marie was a baby. Everybody had the day off. We were all going to go to the lake and have a picnic. I had packed a picnic for the whole oil field crew. We all lived in one house out in New Mexico.

What I noticed happened to me out in New Mexico was that I became, is the word *ambiguous?*

Ambivalent?

That's it. Ambivalent to the whole thing. By the time I watched them drown that guy, it really didn't phase me like the time I saw them throw that guy off the cliff.

When we got to New Mexico, after Russ had worked as a trucker for a while, we turned around and went back and got Gary. Got Gary, picked up Pat, so we took a bunch of people we knew out there. They all got into the oil fields, so it was kind of like the whole oil field crew lived in one house and I took care of them.

My job was to collect their money when they got their paycheck, buy the groceries, fix the food, clean the house, for these five men.

It was me that wanted the picnic, I want out of the house, I want to spend time with you guys. I packed a humongous picnic lunch. We had our coolers, and all of us were there. Had Sandy Marie in a punkin' seat. She was just months old.

I looked out and I saw them, I saw them leading this Navajo. Two bikers, looking at their buddies back on shore, waving. Each one of them had one of his arms, and he was just walking. I looked away for a while. It was real shallow water till you got way out.

I looked back, though, 'cause I realized that was kind of funny. What are they going to do with him? As they got further and further out and they're looking back at their buddies and laughing, ha ha ha, I looked at Russ, and I said, "Russ," who was playing frisbee. "Hey Russ!" And he stopped. He knew that look on my face. "What are they doing with him?"

Russ turned around and looked for a minute, turned around and looked at me, and said, "Start packing the stuff." So I started packing, and while I was packing I watched them hold him under.

I think what bothered me more than anything was knowing that I had gotten ambivelous to it. It did bother me, but it was almost a why? Why? I've been wanting this forever, this picnic thing. And why do they have to do that? What is the fun? And then I also realized I could remember when that meant a lot more than that. That bothered me a little bit, but not enough to do anything about it. I do remember realizing, You're worried about your picnic? That guy's

dying out there, but it does kind of suck that I have to put all this stuff back!

After my second DUI and I was talking to that girl, I said, "I feel like there's a lot of things that I needed to come to terms with in my life." I had done a lot of things. I wound up being pretty violent. You had to be. You had to be.

I've hurt people, I've beat people up. I choked a girl badly one night and yanked her off a bar stool with the belt off my coat. I yanked it off. And I'd do these things in blackouts. I didn't remember doing it. I don't to this day. I know that I did. Everybody said I did. It was my belt off my coat. She was in shock. I could have broke her neck. I tried.

I was drinking very, very heavily. She was flirting with my old man. I watched her for hours and I didn't care. But I was the type who could be drinking and just be happy-go-lucky and not care and then, Boom! But if I got mad, whew, it was not controllable. I didn't like it at all.

I know that I was standing at the jukebox one minute and the next minute I'm standing in the middle of the room, and she's trying to get this belt off her neck and crying and choking and saying, "Why did you do that to me? Why'd you want to kill me? You could have broke my neck." And I'm standing there laughing. I got no idea what I just did. I looked down, and it was like, Oh, my God! What did I just do? But I was drunk, and I just played it off.

That's one thing that kept me alive all those years, my acting ability. I was pretty good at it. I think the key to acting is to not act but to be able to really have a good enough imagination. Like a child, when they're playing house they're not acting. They're not purposely acting. They are playing "mommy." I would play "hardcore."

Like when that girl was—I remember thinking, I was at the jukebox a second ago. What is—from jukebox to girl standing in front of me, crying, screaming hysterically, everybody's standing off away from me, What is this? But hold your composure, you know you're cool. I meant to do that.

I did, though, tell her, "What are you talking about?" Getting my belt off from her, and she got it off, and I grabbed it from her, and, "Aw, shut up." But it bothered me. I just didn't let anybody know it, but it bothered me later.

And I told the therapist, I got a lot of stuff in my life like that. Not having raised my kids perfectly or even close. I told my therapist, I think I've got a lot of guilt. I think I've got a lot of guilt at the amount of time that I wasted of life, in bar rooms. When I was fifteen years old I was so much more mature than when I was twenty.

At fifteen, I could look at you and say, "Why would you want to fight? Even drunk." But after New Mexico it was like I regressed. And I did things that were beneath me. I was not raised like that. I was raised up here, and I was living down here. And I had gotten caught up in it, and I didn't know how to get out for a long time. So I just stayed there and decided I'd be the best "here" person. Alright, if I've got to be here, I've made my bed and I got to lie in it, I'll be real good at it.

The violence thing, to me it was such a waste of time. And it is now. There's nothing constructive comes from it. Nothing constructive. And I've got this real hang-up about life being constructive. I can't stand it when it's not.

I can't remember what the fourth time—I always do that, too. I saw four. There was the guy from the van shot, the guy drowned, the guy, oh! The

guy that keeled over dead. Nobody really killed him.

When we were hitchhiking to New Mexico, Russ made a lot of money, and—when we got there—Russ made a lot of money off me and my drinking. Out in Texas and New Mexico, there's a lot of men in these areas with a lot of money. Oil field hands. They make a lot of money, and they got nowhere to spend it on. Or nobody. Because women don't live out in those areas. It's too rough.

You could go from bar to bar and encounter drunk roughnecks with lots of money, nothing better to do than to bet it on whether that little eighty-five-pound girl can drink more'n me. We would do that. We would go from bar to bar, and we'd sit for a couple of drinks and watch and just, Who's our victim?

We were hustlers. There's an amount of honor between hustlers. At least you're hustling somebody. You're not thieving them. We would sit and we would watch and we would pick out the guy that was probably the drunkest, most boisterous, egomaniac. We'd go stand next to him and have a few drinks with him. You know, sociable.

Russell would get the guy going: "This little girl could drink more than you, man." And the guy'd mouth off to me or something. Next thing you knew, Russell was, "Hey man, a hundred dollars. Hundred dollars shot for shot, this girl could do it." Everybody in the bar's in on it by this time.

I was tiny. I weigh twenty pounds more than I ever weighed in my life right now. And I'd do it, shot for shot, every time. Every time. I never lost, ever.

Except one night, I had a stomach flu. It was at a party we went to. I told Russell, "I can't do it, man. I can't." But he was drunk, and it wasn't even a money issue this time. It was an ego thing coming out of him. He didn't like this guy, and he wanted me so bad to prove this guy worthless. I told him, "Russ, I can't, I can't. I'm sick to my stomach." And sure enough I vomited. He wasn't too happy.

I could live just fine without a lot of where I went. I could do without having seen the guy thrown off the cliff. I could have done without seeing that guy drowned, just blatantly drowned. I could have done without seeing the knifings.

That's just the deaths. Every time I turned around I was nursing wounds. Gunshots, keeping pressure on the wound until the ambulance or whoever could get there. After a while I don't know how nurses take it. It's depressing to me. I'm such an upbeat person. That was my main thing about my personality. My daughter's got it. I insist on being happy. I insist. I don't think it's constructive time to be sad or depressed.

Boy, after a while in New Mexico I could not get that accomplished. I couldn't get my mind to go there. And I was so good at getting my mind to go places. That's always been my best defense. I could take any situation and make my mind not act but literally go there and be there, and then live through it.

Like when I would be attacked in bars in New Mexico by women bigger than me, I could literally picture that person kicking my two-year-old daughter twenty feet in the air. And it was real to me. And I could make it real to me. And I'd kick the living daylights out of someone three times my size, out of sheer rage at that thought.

It's something I did several times when I was attacked or—yeah, attacked. There's no other word for it. You got someone coming at you with a pool stick, you pick up a pool ball and bang 'em in the head. That was another thing I had going for me. I had pitched for a softball team. I could hit anything I aimed at. Anything. A whiskey bottle? You could be thirty feet from me, and I could hit you in your nose with a whiskey bottle. That was back then.

I went through that with the therapist. And there again, she gave me some good feedback. She was able to answer some things for me, because at the time I was like, Can you tell me why someone with so much going for her wound up there? I was pretty! I was little but shapely. I had the body going. I had the personality. I was sweet, I was nice. Everybody liked me.

When I was in third grade, my mom heard of this Girl Scout thing going on and decided to take me. It was at Cascades Park. We pulled up, and it was like a hundred little black girls. My mom didn't want to let me out. She said, "Oh no, you don't want to go here." "Yes! Yes! This is exactly where I want to be. Now this is looking interesting." First it was just a Girl Scout thing.

That was something that fascinated me. Hey! People I don't know! I always had that really wonderful adventurous—I thought it was kind of neat, you know?

What did your therapist say?

She said, basically, when my grandma died and my family fell apart and I was just left with my mom and dad who are emotionally deprived, she said that I was searching for a family, that I had a deep sense of needing to belong. That's how, when I wound up fascinated with the poor and they took me in, I had told her, they literally made me their family. I was one of the family.

I was got by that. Then, as the years went on, my business being what it was, and Russ and Gary, one of the things they also taught me was to make money off my dealing. It blew Russ's mind, it really blew Gary's mind, when they found out I didn't make any money when I dealt drugs. They shook their heads, and it was like, Oh, we got something else to teach her. And they did. They did a good job at it. So I learned to start making money from this. And that came natural to me, and I was real good at it.

When we hit New Mexico, I realized the law in that town was those bikers. It was good to be in their family. This was organized crime, bottom line. And if you don't belong to the family, then you don't survive. So the bottom line was because then you'll be out there selling to anybody and it could be an undercover cop.

Gary prospected. I would not. Terry Duncan, who was the president at the time, took a grave liking to me. These bikers that you meet in Indiana ain't nothing. Even the ones in the world, they ain't nothing. These guys out there killed daily. They killed each other, sometimes in drunken fun. I mean this was an eighty-member group out in the middle of the desert. What the biker world calls one-percenters. They live, eat, breathe, work, everything's "club."

They do not work outside of the club. They run guns over the border. Terry started hanging with us, and it was one of these, you know, he'd come in the house, and I'd start gathering up all the glass and lamps and getting them out of the way because those guys got wild. It was, yank off their chain belts and hit each other. They were wild. They were very much more than you can even imagine. And I had a great imagination, and these guys went far beyond it.

Gary, who was a very large man, huge compared to Indiana—bigger'n you, much bigger, three times your size—out there he was small, next to those guys. They grew 'em big. Gary left our house and started living with them and was prospecting for Terry. Terry would come over, and he liked me, to begin with, just because of my business head and my confidence, my overconfidence. Women weren't like that out there.

Then, his old lady got pregnant at the same time I did. I was completely junked out on heroin and crank. I was doing highballs and synthetic heroin. And I was drinking two-fifths a night of Jack Daniels. I don't know if you know anything about withdrawal, but it is not pretty.

When I found out I was pregnant, I quit everything cold turkey. Period. That can kill a person. In fact, I couldn't believe that Sandi Marie lived through it, that it didn't kill her. For about three weeks Terry watched me. He watched me. He watched while his old lady continued.

He had several old ladies. Susan was his main old lady. She was the number one, top dog. And the others, one was given to him, Angel. She sat and told me how her dad was the president of such and such club—I can't remember now—but he gave Angel to Terry. And that was in the same conversation she proceeded to tell me that he made her have sex acts with a great dane. Like it was nothing, she said, "Do you have a dog?" "Uh, no! No!"

So you never participated in the legendary stuff?

No, I was an old lady.

Explain what that means.

In Indiana terms, see, that's a one-percenter club, in New Mexico. That was, everything is club property: your Harley, your woman, everything. That's the one-percenter club.

The men have to prospect, the women just have to do whatever they say. The women are property, bottom line. If you want to take a hammer to your bike, it's your property, you can do that. If you want to take a hammer to your old lady, she's your property, you can do that.

There's some clubs that come in between the one-percenter and the club like what I was in, where your old lady's your property. You're to take care of it. If she causes problems in the club, for the club. Say your old lady makes it a habit of when the club goes to a bar, she likes to flirt with other men and cause fights between these bar men and the club. Nobody is to go to the woman. They are to go to the club member and get him to take care of it.

It was in the bylaws. I used to tell Wheezer, 'cause I had a problem with one of the club members wanting to kick my butt all the time, and I told Wheezer, I said, "Man, don't let Dan hit me. I'm your property. It's right here. It is written, dude. Number one, I'm not doing anything. But if I was, and he had a legitimate—what's a word for bitch that I can use?—complaint about me, then he could go to you, he could complain, and you could make me sit my butt at home. But," I said, "this deal of him just wanting to hit me, you better get on it. It's your job."

Did you really see things that way?

Why, yes! And so did everybody else in the club. You were either an old lady—with the Cloven Hooves, you were either an old lady or a turn-out. Bottom line.

A turn-out is . . . ?

She's someone that is brought around—or allowed to hang around—because she's a slut. Well, let's put it this way: When I filed for divorce on Wheezer and I left, he took up with Pam. He put Pam on the back of his bike, took her up to the Terre Haute clubhouse and turned her out. Put her in the back room. Anybody want her? And they basically stand in line and just, you know, fuck her. To me it's gross, but whatever.

Your old lady, on the other hand, is your property and your responsibility to take care of. I didn't see it that way at first, but I grew to . . .

By the time I met Wheezer, we had come back from New Mexico. We got back here because things were just too nuts out there for us, and neither one of us—the money was good, but what good is money if you're dead? So we came back. Russ could not get a job worth a crap. Nothing. So he took a job with cable, working two months gone, home a week. Three months gone, home a week.

The last year and a half of our marriage was like that. Well, Russell being Russell, he's like a big kid when it comes to money or common sense. He can't handle his finances. So it wound up me and the girls living in Bloomington on welfare while Russ was making minimum five hundred dollars a week and jet skiing in Florida with blondes.

I put up with that for a year and a half. Basically because I loved him and he was the father of my children. A part of me wanted to just wait it out and hopefully he would grow out of it. And we would get a little older and mature and blah blah blah.

Well, I got so lonely, and I got to where I felt like where I was dying. I wasn't going anywhere. I had a three-month-old and a three-year-old. I had no money. I tried waiting tables for a while. I didn't get AFDC because I made minimum wage waiting tables and tips. I made two dollars an hour. I didn't get Medicaid 'cause I worked full time. My food stamps went down. I didn't make enough to cover the benefits I lost. So I had to take it back. I just felt like I was dying.

My mom kept trying to give me twenty bucks to take the girls. She hated Russell. She wanted me away from him. She wanted me to meet somebody. Well, after about six months I took her up on it. And I didn't plan on meeting anybody. I didn't think there was any way I'd be able to take my clothes off in front of another man.

I'd been with him so long that it was like I just couldn't even see that. But I went to the Union Jack, and I took Doug's wife, Brenda, with me 'cause Doug was working with Russ. Called her up. I said, "Let's go out. Mom said she'd give me twenty bucks. I'll buy."

And I just planned on drinking the twenty dollars worth and going home. When we got there, I sat down. I ordered a drink, and I told her, "Bring me a double. Just keep bringing 'em until I tell you."

She brought the double. She set our drinks down, and before I had it half-way drank—and I'm a fast drinker—had about a third of it drank, and she set another one down. And I said, "Hey, whoa, whoa! Let it get this low." And she said, "That's from the gentleman back there." And I turned around and I looked, and there's Wheezer sitting next to Honeybee and some other bikers. He's waving at me.

I turned around real quick and looked at Brenda. I said, "Oh, my God! Oh, my God!" I said,

"What should I do?" She said, "Drink it." Okay. So I drank it, and they didn't quit coming. I never spent another penny. They just kept coming.

He sent a couple girls over, friends of mine that I knew. Kim, she came over. And I didn't have a friend that Russell hadn't screwed. So she comes over, and she's talking to me, and she says, "Man, Wheezer's telling me he's got a liking for you. He likes you a lot." And I said, "Well, tell Wheezer I'm married." She said, "No you're not. Geez, Nancy, when are you gonna—? Russell's not married so why should you be?"

And I sat there looking at her, knowing she had been with him several times. So had Debbie, so had everybody else. And I was kind of the joke of the—you know?

But I looked at her and I said, "You know what? Just because Russell does something stupid, doesn't mean I need to. Two wrongs ain't gonna make a right, and I ain't doing it. So go tell your buddy, F-off."

It just made him like me even more. He kept sending the drinks. By the end of the night I was drunk. I hadn't drank in a while. I was drunk, and I heard 'em call last call. I looked around for my little buddy and didn't see him. I thought I better go get my drink.

So I walked up and told Cowboy, "Hey! Give me that triple to go." Cowboy started to make that triple, Wheezer pops his head over my shoulder and says, "The lady'll have a fifth and I'll take a case of Bud."

I just looked over at that guy, and I was so lonely. I walked over to Brenda, handed her my keys, and I said, "I'll see you in the morning."

I got on that bike with Wheezer, he took me to Deckard Plumbing. He had the key 'cause they're buddies, and they've got hot tubs there. And he thought it was cute that I wouldn't get undressed in front of him. I made him turn around.

I got in that hot tub, and we weren't in there two minutes, and I was like, This does not go well with being drunk on whiskey. I pulled back and I told him, "I can't do this." No, wait, I looked at him and I said, "Don't you have anywhere else we can go, like a bed?" "Yeah!"

So we got out. We went to his place, and I've got to say, I'll never forget that night. I let loose on him. I had the ability to make love to a stranger as if I knew them all my life and deeply did, deep down inside, love them, every inch of their being. And I gave it to that boy. I missed it so bad. And I was drunk enough that to me he was Russell.

He just fell in love. He fell in love.

I woke up the next morning in total shock. I sat up in bed like you would envision a dead person. Stiff, and sitting up, you know, really stiffly and start—"Oh my God! Oh my God!" I just couldn't withstand it.

I looked over at Wheezer and, Oh my God! Oh! I put my head in my hands. I couldn't believe what I had done. I was looking for my clothes. I was putting my clothes on. I said, "Don't look at me. Do not look at me." I was putting my clothes on. I told him, "I don't do this." And then I looked at his tattoos, and I said, "Oh my God! And I don't do it with bikers! I hate bikers! I don't do this!"

After they killed Gary, the bikers out in New Mexico, I swore I would never have anything to do with another biker. And here I was.

And Spanky was living with Wheezer at the time. I ran out to the living room and I says, "Spanky,

take me home. Now! Get me out of here!" And on the way home, Spanky told me, "I hate to tell you this, girl, but that boy is in love with you." I said, "That boy doesn't even know me, and he's a kid, and he's a boy, and he's a biker, and I don't like him! I'm not ever coming back. I don't know how I'm going to live with this."

Bottom line is, Brenda told Doug, Doug told Russell. I got beat. I got beat over that. Russell put me through a wall, beat the hell out of me.

Had he ever done that before?

Only once in the six years we were together, and that was my fault. He came in on PCP, and I lost it on him in his face before I realized he was on PCP. It was too late. And he couldn't stop. He didn't even know it was me. He just knew he needed that person out of his face. He beat my head into a toilet.

I, frankly, had started it. I had pulled him by his collar down into my face. I probably had hit him, too, I don't know. I was so mad.

No, he did not abuse me. He didn't even mentally or verbally ever, ever abuse me. He loved me with all his heart. But he had a sex drive he couldn't control. He couldn't imagine living without me, but when he was on the road and stuff it was like, She'll never know what I did.

We're talking about getting back together. The only thing he does now is smoke a little pot. He's held a job for six years. He says he's been faithful to this woman that he's with for four years. It could be. He's almost thirty-nine now.

We've both—I've changed tremendously, so we're going to get together and talk about it. He's got a job still where he's gone, but he's gone during the week. His boss now has a jet that flies him back home for the weekends. That's what he does.

So you got divorced after that?

Oh yeah, I had always told him, I had always told him, "I'll not leave you. I will not leave you. And I do not want another man unless you physically hit me. You're twice my size and ain't no man a man that hits a woman."

In my family that was a big issue. Our men may have drank and done whatever, but they did not hit their women. I had always promised him. I promise you: don't think I'll give in. And frankly, I don't think I would have ever gotten rid of Russ had I not run into somebody like Wheezer.

That was just a freak happening. Here was a kid. Wheezer had never had a real woman. He's six months younger than me, and we were twenty-one. Where I had been on my own since fourteen, he'd been from his mommy's house to—he was in the Cloven Hooves because his older brother was. He's a child. He still is. He's still a child.

Frankly, to be honest, I think I was the first real woman. I mean he had had a bunch of turnouts, but those women are just, they got no soul to 'em. They got no feelings, emotions, to their sex, to their anything. And I blew his mind.

He didn't care about Russell whatsoever. Plus he had thirty guys standing behind him. It was the first time I had encountered anybody that said they weren't scared.

After Russ beat the crap out of me, and I called the cops, and they got me out of there I went to find Wheezer. I talked to Cowboy, I talked to somebody else, found out where he lived. I went to tell him, "Hey, my old man's gonna kill you." You know, warn him? He laughed.

I said, "Hey, he's gonna sit down at the Union Jack and wait on you till you show up. This isn't funny. My old man's mean."

He laughed, and he said, "Well, I'll be there." He showed up, of course, with thirty guys. He called the Terre Haute chapter. There were thirty of them all together, between the clubs. And they all showed up at the Union Jack. Of course, Doug saw this and called Russell and told him. Russell just called me, and he said, "You can call your dogs off." But I was so mad. Then I was getting into it. It was like, Ha ha! Ha ha!

Russell had always told me, "Who's gonna want you now? You got my kids. Who's gonna want you?" And I believed him. So it was kind of like, Ha ha! Somebody did want me, and they're not scared of you.

I had had several men tell me over the six years that I was with Russell, the last four when he was running around on me, I had several men tell me, "Man, you're a good old lady. You deserve better than that. And if I weren't so scared of Russell, I'd go for you." He used to tell guys he'd eat 'em for breakfast if, you know.

He was a hippie but he looked mean. So he could pull off looking at somebody and saying, "I'd eat anybody for breakfast that even looked at my old lady." He could pull that look off because he was big and he looked mean. But if you really knew him, you'd know that he couldn't even hurt a bunny.

When Russ beat the crap out of me over Wheezer, I think he was scared. I had never gone out on him. He had always had me bluffed. I think it dawned on him, 'cause Doug really told him, "Man, let me tell you who Wheezer is. He's got the means to take your place, dude."

Russ, it blew his mind. So he came off with this, If I can't have you, nobody can. And I think he seriously contemplated killing me several times. 'Cause he had gotten some of New Mexico's attitude also. Me and him both came back from New Mexico totally different people.

The only difference, I didn't like the person I had become. I had to be that where I was living. When I came back here, I didn't want to be that person anymore. But it's not just an overnight thing to get rid of it.

It kind of gives me some understanding on—just a minute understanding—of how it is for Vietnam vets. People that go to war and see what they see, and they're trained to live a certain way, and then they got to come back and live in society. It's a lot of baggage to carry.

But that's another reason that I've done so well since I've joined the church instead of AA or anything else. As a Christian I've learned that I can forgive myself and God can forgive me. He not only forgives it, he forgets it. It's gone. It's like, What are you talking about, Nance?

If I go back to ask him for forgiveness again, he doesn't know what I'm talking about, and that's the way I need to be. Hey, it happened, it happened.

At one point in my life—the hardest point in my life—was when I honestly came to terms with feeling as if my life, other than giving birth to two of the most beautiful kids in the world, the rest of my life was nothing. Nothing. Not a constructive thing from it, not one good thing, could come from my past.

It came to a point where I was starting to feel that way. I had that in the back of my mind for a long time, but I was getting to where I couldn't keep it in the back of my head. Then my mom splurted it out, crying, told me I'd be better off dead and so would my kids. The whole world would be better off if I'd just die. There was nothing at all positive that could come from my past or my life and that I was beyond repair.

When she said that, it hit home because I had been suppressing that and trying not to allow it to come up. It was almost like the truth hurts.

I took my two girls in each hand and took them over to a girlfriend of mine's house, 'cause we were living with Mom and Dad after my divorce. I told Susie what she said and just cried. At first I told Susie, "She's right. She is absolutely right."

And I got my crying out for about fifteen minutes, and Susie handed me a cup of coffee, and she said, "She is not right" and started naming off—'cause Susie's known me all my life, we've been friends—she started naming off good things. I started coming around. I said, "You know, if it's the last thing I do, I'm gonna prove her wrong." I've been working hard at it since then.

How do you get along now?

I'm thirty-four now, and when I was thirty-one, no thirty-two—it's been about two years, because my DUI was two-and-a-half years ago, or, well, my sobriety date—my mom and I, about two years ago, sat down at MCL* and we talked. I basically told her what I felt was her part: I understand women in your generation didn't divorce. They didn't talk back to their men. Blah blah blah. But you taking out your frustrations with Dad, and what you couldn't do to Dad, you did to me. That I'm unhappy about.

She kind of wanted to make amends because she told me, "I feel bad because our family was the traditional family. The eldest male was the boss." And my grandfather, she said, "I just let him kind of . . ." like when I was drinking out of his drink, Papaw's drink. She said, "When I did start trying to make you stop doing that and saying, 'No no, Nanny, that's not good,'" she said, "I

---

* A cafeteria.

should have stood my ground with him when he said, 'Leave her alone.' I just never stood my ground. It wasn't thought of to disrespect the eldest male, my dad."

She said, "Frankly, I didn't think it was hurting you. I didn't know you would grow up to—in our family the men did what I did. She couldn't believe it when I started doing it. It was like men drink, not you.

She kind of said she was sorry for that. I told her, "That's not what I'm concerned with. Where I'm at is: Hey, what about all those years you took out on me? What about all those years my name was Moron? Someone said 'Moron,' I listened. And that's not right."

She never beat me or anything. They didn't whip, spank. I got grounded.

She said, back then, people just didn't put kids in mental health. It wasn't as popular. She went to apologizing for stuff when I was two and three years old, letting me drink out of Grandpa's drink. I said, "That ain't nothing. What I got honked off about over the years was you taking everything out on me that belonged to Dad. Also, y'all had the resources to do something with me, when I needed help."

I think I was twenty-five before I told her I had used a needle. She said she had just realized it a couple years before that.

I think it made her sick to realize that Dad knew all that time. Because when she said, "Well, he never told me that," I looked at her, and I said, "Well, not only that, but he got in my car for something and found what he quoted as my 'works bag' in my glove compartment and let me know I was lucky you hadn't found it."

That was when I was twenty, twenty-one, when he found that. No, twenty-two. So I said, "Give

me a break. The man's known for a long, long time." The conversation kind of petered out there. She couldn't even eat. She went home.

Then—this is two years ago—I was working for my dad. It was like the next time I came into work, two days later. I came into work, and Dad made it a point to explain to me that he thought that I was just going through a phase, when I dropped that needle out of my pocket when I was fifteen.

He said, "I didn't really think a whole lot about it. I thought, 'Well, she's just going through a phase she'll grow out of.' Of course, then the years went by and you didn't grow out of it and I thought, 'Well, hell, what can I do now?'" The thought of turning me in or getting me help from a mental health clinic, it wasn't popular back then, anyway. So I could tell Mom had talked to him, but he didn't apologize. He just let me know why.

What's it like working with him everyday now?

It's not good. I'm looking for a career change. Him and I are two totally different people. He's a very slow, methodic, simple person. Just not real excited about a lot. Not ambitious. Pretty dang simple.

I started out working there because I was a mess six years ago and couldn't get anything other than Burger King or Marsh Deli. I worked part-time for him, then it went to full time. Then I got licensed. I've been there almost six years now. Five and a half.

The thing that was happening, though, right about the time that I was getting good enough to go to work for someone else and make lots more money, was about the time that I decided I need to be home. Sandie Marie started experimenting with pot. I was working three jobs. I was working [at her father's insurance office] full time, Marsh Deli part time, Burger King sometimes and then after that got a job cleaning the surgical center. So I was doing that and working Saturdays for my brother-in-law at his [insurance] office.

The thing is, I intended on going into the insurance business like my brother-in-law did, but with my dad it's a female thing. He just can't see giving me that break. And frankly, if you don't have a break in insurance today, it's not the big money-maker that it was.

In my dad's day, he just stood at the booth in Sears and there was a line. There was no going out and selling. He just stood there and wrote it up all day. Well, it's not like that anymore. If you don't start out with a good deal of business, you lose money. You cannot make it before you go under.

Our claims adjuster just became an agent. He had an inheritance that he had just gotten and some money put back to boot, so it's like he said: I can afford to lose money for a couple years to build up the accounts and start making money.

Well, I can't. I got kids, I got me, I got to make that money. The looking for a job at another insurance agency, I kinda didn't want to do that, because at least I may have been making less money, but I could leave when I wanted. If the girls needed me to come to school and pick them up, I could do that without hassle. Also the flexibility. Bottom line is, I don't like working with him. He doesn't like working with me either.

Did he hire you out of guilt?

No, no, he hired me because Bob* had hired his daughter, who's my age. We grew up together,

_____
* His partner.

and when she moved on to somebody who could actually pay money was when I was needing that job, so it was kind of like why not.

He figured it'd be a temporary thing and I'd find a better job. Instead I decided to go to school. Because I cannot get the job I want and make the money I want to make without the schooling. So I just figured just do it. Do it now or I'm never going to do it.

What do you want to do?

I wouldn't mind being a professor, of business. And an addictions counselor like Shalom. In fact, exactly what Shalom is doing is where God blesses me. But he has also blessed me in the business end. When I first started thinking about going to IU, I thought, Man, I can do something romantic like a plant biologist, and I can be this really neat herbalist. These things I'm really interested in, I love it as hobbies, and God seems to make it stay there, as a hobby. I never get off the ground with that stuff.

In New Mexico I grew herbs. Oh man! I can grow some pot! I can. I grow some stuff. I'm real good with plants, and I'm interested in it. Anyway, it's not where I get blessed.

I see myself teaching, counseling, and traveling. Traveling is definitely something I see me doing. I think I will probably always have a home in Bloomington. In fact, I know I will. I've bought it, and I do not plan on ever selling it. It's going to be a retirement thing. I only owe thirty-eight grand on that. I could pay that off by the time I'm fifty and have it to rent out. Frankly, I could pay that off in no time if I ever got married and had someone else's income included.

I want a cabin in Montana. If I had my own place here, as far as the rest of it, a cabin in Montana would be nice. But as far as the rest of it, just like this ministry, Cecil told me—I talked to him last night. He pastors a church in Oklahoma, and he was telling me the troubles he's having: "They're all new Christians. They're going to the bars with their patches on, trying to tell me they aren't drinking." He says, "I know they are. They tell me they're ministering."

So he's telling me all this stuff, and I sat there and prayed for him. I can do that with someone outside my own—I don't know, I'm getting less self-conscious about it. For a long time I couldn't pray in front of anybody. I'd never done that. I was Catholic. You prayed quietly. I've gotten to where I'm pretty at ease with it.

I prayed for him. And, man, it's just blown his mind. He said he feels it. I did. I asked God to bless his congregation and bless his efforts. Boy, he just perked up. He told me, "You got to come visit in November, we're doing something." I can just see myself flying to Arizona and staying with a group of bikers there, Christian bikers, flying different places or getting a Winnebago set-up-type deal.

At first, when Russell called, I just couldn't even fathom what he was saying. But the more I think about it, and I prayed before we got to Eagle Mountain that God's will be done with this Lou thing.* When we got there, Shalom wanted to go to the laundromat, and she said, "I'll have Gracie go with me though, 'cause I know you want to wait here," and winked.

I looked at her, and I said, "Not really. I'm not going over there. If he wants to see me, he can come see me, and I'm going to kind of let God guide that as to whether he does or not. 'Cause if he does, I'll consider something. If he doesn't, I'll kind of figure maybe I need to give Russell some serious thought."

_____
* A prospective romantic interest.

The more I think about it, I love Russell's intelligence. He's real healthy, got a good—that was another problem between me and Wheezer: He was such a gulger, of food. He got fat and pretty inactive because of it. And I'm active. When Wheezer and I were together at first, he was skinny, and we were always on the run. Wheezer traded his bike in for a fishing boat. But Russ likes to travel. He's real good at communicating with people. He's a people person. If he could just keep his dick in his pants.

So what happened with Lou?

Nothing. They weren't there, and when they did get there, they camped up on the hill. Frankly, I told myself I think what Lou's going through is, he likes me but he's got this relationship going with her, and he's trying to figure out what to do. Frankly, I'm not willing to have him cut off that relationship for me. He mentioned to me, "I wish you lived closer." And it is. It's a three-hour-away thing.

And Cecil?

Cecil's way far away.

I know, but how does he fit into the picture?

I think Cecil could handle an old lady in Indiana. I like Cecil. A lot. Man, you should hear him preach. You should hear him preach. He's good. And I could see myself doing that, but he's a lot older than me. A lot. I've done a lot of time with men a lot older than me, and I've been thinking here recently, it would kind of be nice to have someone a little more my own age. If they could keep their dick in their pants.

Is that very Christian to say? Penis? How should I put that? If they could be faithful. There you go. Loyal and faithful.

This is something I'm deciding is time for me to work on in my walk. That's why you find me stuttering a lot here lately. When I was fifteen years old, you couldn't believe you were talking to a fifteen-year-old. I was so immaculate in the way I spoke. Somewhere along the way, well, you hang with illiterates all your life and you're going to become illiterate.

I spent a lot of years with some pretty ignorant people, so my language has gotten bad and my terminology. I need to get back to figuring out how to say, "If a man could be faithful" rather than saying "If he could keep his dick in his pants."

See, my dad uses that terminology, that lower mentality. And I don't want to work around that anymore. Shalom has done this in the last two years. I've watched her decide and make the decision: I'm going to grow past this certain thing.

Her and I, we're going to take golf lessons next summer. That's where all the business deals are made. Prominent people play golf, and I want prominence. And money. And I've always wanted to learn how to play golf. I've always wanted to do everything except skydiving. I have no desire to do that.

There's several things involved with me having a husband. Number one, I get treated a lot different with the Unchained Gang. Shalom, now, since I've put my head to it and I went to her about this. I said, "You know, nobody calls me when the club's doing anything. If I don't have a 'boyfriend' that's involved with the club, nobody contacts me when they do things or this and that." It's like I don't exist unless I have a husband. So I had to quit prospecting again, because I got rid of my boyfriend.

Why did you have to quit prospecting?

You have to have a motorcycle. You have to have a motorcycle to prospect for the Unchained Gang.

So it counts if you're going out with someone who has one?

Yeah, Hubie and I were supposed to get married. He asked me. I had said yes, and then he moved in, and I realized he was still a mess. Even without drinking, he was sour inside. I couldn't bring him to stop it.

Anyway, I got rid of him. Then Al came along, and he looked really good because he could preach so well. Everybody fell in love with him, and he picked me. I thought I was the lucky one. So I started prospecting under him, and it didn't take me long to figure out that he had some real bad problems in his life. I got rid of him and had to quit.

I took up with Jim. He wasn't from the church. He didn't have a bike, so during that seven months I kind of pulled away from the church a lot, period. Worst seven months of my life.

I don't know, I got rid of Jim and I just kind of isolated for a while. And then Al* called, after about six weeks of my isolating, six or seven weeks. I was ready to go out, number one. And then when Al just showed such enthusiasm about this lifestyle and told me, "I want to be a part of your life and a part of this."

I even told Al I wasn't in love with him. That was true. I loved him dearly. I still do. I'll always love Al, I just do. I told him I was not in love with him. Simply, merely for the fact that we hadn't been together long enough. But if he continued in the direction that he was going,

---

* A different Al.

which was my direction—same direction I was going, let's put it that way—that I would fall in love with him. And I was very honest, I believe that with all my heart.

If he had continued to love God and serve God and get into the Bible and into the word and been a Christian, I would have fallen in love with him. And I promised him I would always be faithful and always be loyal and that I would fall in love with him as time went on.

In my case, it was the sex issue was why we got married so quick. It was like, Well, let's go ahead and get married. If you're going to go in this Christian direction, I know I'll fall in love with you.

I just couldn't see how any man could spend that much money and not go through with the marriage. So I thought for sure that he was serious.

FELLOWSHIP

The Unchained Gang was started in 1988, when a group of ministers, including Larry Mitchell, himself a former biker, noticed how many of the people being saved in their prison and jail ministries were from outlaw biker clubs.

Since then it has grown to two established chapters in Indiana: one in Monroe County, the other in neighboring Greene County. There is a chapter forming in Indianapolis, and through the efforts of missionaries there is also a chapter starting up in Ireland. It is primarily the Monroe County chapter that is represented here.

Although it started on its own, it is now one organization in a growing movement of Christian bikers. No official numbers show the scope of that movement, but there are a few indicators. The Christian Motorcycle Association, which is the largest Christian biker organization although not an umbrella group, has more than sixty thousand members in five hundred plus chapters. In addition, there are small independent clubs like the Unchained Gang throughout the country and abroad.

The prerequisites for becoming a member of the Unchained Gang are to be a Christian; to be drug- , alcohol- , and nicotine-free for a year; and to own a motorcycle, 650cc or more. In a blend of traditions from the biker world and Alcoholics Anonymous, there is a three level process for gaining membership. One begins as a "hang-around." This is relatively informal and is allowed by a general consensus and sponsorship by a member.

After a minimum six-month period, a sponsor may ask members to accept a hang-around as a "prospect." That is done by majority vote. During this period, the prospect receives his or her rockers (the patch at the bottom of the vest, below the club insignia), which, unlike the patches

of world clubs that identify specific chapters, say "Servants of Jesus Christ" for the men and "Property of Jesus Christ" for the women. Here the gang has the opportunity to evaluate a newcomer's commitment, watch his or her Christian "walk," and see if the prospect has the right stuff.

After at least a six-month prospect period, when the sponsor feels the prospect is ready, he or she may bring that person up for "full patch." With a unanimous vote by all members present, a successful prospect receives his or her patch and full membership into the Unchained Gang motorcycle ministry.

This process serves a number of functions. It gives new Christians an environment in which to be as they learn a new way of life. It also works to weed out the uncommitted, the insincere, and those they consider to be a poor witness in taking God's word into prisons, to biker rallies, and onto the street.

There are those who do not make it through the full process. Some "go back to the world," and some remain Christians. There is no shame in not becoming full patch, whether by one's own choice or by the group's decision. One's salvation is still recognized; he or she is just deemed not appropriate for this ministry. A phrase often heard about people who do not stay with the gang is "God will still use him."

Highway 1 in Florida.

Shalom's birthday party.

Nancy and Shalom at the Boogie.

At a biker rally, members of the gang talk among themselves about the old days and their salvation.

Prayer, praise, worship, healing, and gifts of the Spirit are not confined to church services. "Oh, you should have been there," Chico mentioned before church one Sunday. "Me and Harley was at the IHOP (International House of Pancakes) up in Indianapolis when Harley got slain in the Spirit. Man, it was something!" Here, the gang prays for a member who was "laying down his patch" for personal reasons.

Paul at a gathering after church.

CHICO

And there's been some of us, some of the people that have started out with us that are not with us now because they've fell away. The ones that are strong in the Lord, they'll stick there, they'll be there. Like I said, a lot of my strength that I get is not just—well, like I said, my wife, she's got a strength in the Lord that just won't quit.

Becky, she can recite Scripture and verse. When I first started my walk with the Lord, I had so many questions, and I could ask her, and she'd tell me what this meant or that meant. The old me'll start to pop up from time to time, and I'll cop an attitude. She'll say, "You think the Lord'd do this or that?" She keeps me in line. She helps me everyday. I don't know what I'd ever do without her. There's no doubt about it, the Lord sent her to me. That's all there is to it. The Lord, before I ever started going to church, I quit smoking. I had quit the drugs, and I'd quit drinking. It's like the Lord was cleaning me up before I ever started going to church.

I can't say that there wasn't times when I thought I'd like to have a drink or just a line of toot, but I didn't. When I'd feel that urge, I'd just pray and it'd always work. Thing of it is though, that didn't last no time. I mean, no time at all. It was a temptation right straight from the devil is what it amounted to. And it didn't work. That part of it was the easiest part, the quitting all the junk.

What was the hardest part?

To keep on keeping on, staying with it. There's been times when I'd get discouraged, and I just want to throw both hands up. That's when the fellowship with the guys in the Unchained, that I ride with—'cause then I had them to talk to. I had Becky to talk to—kept my mind off all the junk.

RANDY

I ran into Shalom, the first time I ran into her, was in—she had been in detox over here, in Bloomington. This is so weird because she was pretty blown away, too. She was a drug addict and an alcoholic. She went into this detox. I can't remember, she had kind of purple or green hair or something like that when we first ran into each other. I remember we met at the club. We looked at each other, and she said I was the first person—she said she was not able to understand what people were saying, her head was so—she said I was one of the first people that she was able to comprehend what I was saying.

Anyway, we got pretty close. Ran pretty close together. She never was my woman. We was just always good friends. Always. And Gracie knew it, my wife, she knew that. So that's all right. Still today that's fine.

So that's just kind of how that went. But we drank together and fought together. Our relapses, you know. We was gonna rob a bank together once and never did make it because we got too drunk. [Laughs.] But that's kind of the way it was. We was I think still trying to carry on that old lifestyle that wasn't happening. It wasn't there no more. But also we didn't know how to live the other one. That's what I'm saying, God kept doing for us what we couldn't do for ourselves. He could get us sober.

She got sober probably like five, six years before me, on a constant basis. Maybe five, maybe four. I don't know. A few years before me, she got sober. We had started getting sober around the same time, and we slipped numerous times together. But then she got sober for good. She's got eleven or twelve years, something like that. I've got eight.

SHALOM

Something I've heard you say a number of times is that although the purpose of the Unchained ministry is to minister to bikers, not to forget to minister to one another.

Amen.

Most assuredly my trip to Daytona was the most powerful. I can't tell you how that happened or how it was, but it was almost like—there's like a half a million motorcycles down there.

It felt kind of like floating on a cloud kind of thing. It was just so wonderful. It was me and Larry Joe and Jim Burris and Crispy and Rusty and Mary and Terry Bayne. That may have been it. I don't know what happened. Sharing, getting to know each other's spirit. It was just wonderful.

In the beginning it was Hubie, for me. When I first got saved, because Hubie never let me out of his sight hardly. It was like he knew how completely ignorant I was of anything. I'd never read the Bible. I just had this real desire. Just a real desire. Steve Mitchell was my pastor, Larry's brother. I told Steve I felt like I had an iron plate in my chest or something. It's like I see all these other people all happy-smoochy, hugs.

I want that, but I feel there's just this iron plate that just, you know. Well, Steve kind of recognized that. So did Hubie. Hubie had definitely been a world biker. He just took me under his wing, and he did not let me go. And him and Larry Joe Mitchell even taught me about my jewelry. I was wearing jewelry that was not appropriate at all and didn't know it. The situation was not that they believed that jewelry was gonna hurt my salvation or anything like that, but it might be a real bad witness to people that worship crystals. That kind of thing.

I was just sort of groomed by Hubie. And Larry Joe. 'Cause Larry Joe was not the pastor then, and therefore he was traveling with us everywhere. So Hubie ministered to me, and Larry in the most literal way. Every day, every day, every day.

I just think sometimes we get out there, trying to do what we feel God wants us to do, taking the word out and trying to lead people in, and we can have some people sinking in our midst, and we don't see it. Sometimes, I believe. We need to be really careful about that.

I've been one that almost sank. I feel like I was probably down to two and a half on my way down the third time. And it's like Nancy and Larry Mitchell just sort of came by and swooped me up at the last minute. And Larry's not left me since then and neither's Nancy.

What did they do?

The whole thing with Gabby and Texas and all that.* A lot of people—if you don't know the truth to just make it up as you go along. And there was a lot of that going on. Not necessarily among the gang and not necessarily not among the gang.

The truth was bad enough. But to enhance that with things that weren't even close. And it just got bigger and bigger and bigger as gossip will. Gossip is an insidious disease. I can see where it kills people off.

It got bad. I got real—like, I didn't want to deal with anybody. I didn't want to go to that church

---

* On the way home from Kenneth Copeland's Eagle Mountain motorcycle rally, Shalom and Gabby began a romantic relationship, although they were both still married to other people. When they returned home, they began living together before they married each other. This created quite a controversy in the Unchained Gang and resulted in disciplinary measures for both of them.

anymore. I didn't want to be around the guys anymore, nyah, nyah, nyah.

What did Larry or Nancy do?

Love me.

Did they call you on the phone? Did they come by your house?

Well, Nancy's always here. I hadn't spoken with Larry, but I found out Larry was kind of feeling a little bit funny too. Nancy called Larry and said Shalom's about to go down here—see, Larry's my sponsor. He's my gang sponsor. And he's just a major part of my support 'cause Hubie moved away and all that. Larry never changes. He never changes. Other people change. Other people get angry or stick their lip out. Me, too. My relationship will change with other people because of my own feelings, but Larry never changes. And he'll just talk to me and just love me back to where I'm at now.

And I'm real comfortable with what's going on. I'm under a year's correction with the gang. I will not be able to wear my patch for a year, but I am still a full-patch member.

My pride had me say, Let me tell you what you can do with this patch. My God had me say, Thank you for caring enough about me to do that. I really believe that correction here is better than correction there. [Laughs.]

I feel like when we make things right here, we won't go into that judgment. He loves me enough to chastise me. My brothers love me enough.

Every September since 1992, television evangelist
Kenneth Copeland has hosted the Eagle Mountain Motorcycle Rally, an international gathering
of Christian bikers, held in Newark, Texas. Copeland claims attendance of twenty-three thousand,
with more than fifteen thousand at each of the
services. On the way to the rally, the gang holds a
prayer circle after breakfast in Rolla, Missouri.

Gabby at a flea market in Fort Worth.

Kenneth Copeland Ministries.

Christian bikers at Eagle Mountain.

Bike rodeo at Eagle Mountain.

A poster of Kenneth Copeland.

Kenneth Copeland on stage at the Friday night service.

Prayer circle at the end of the Eagle Mountain weekend.

SHALOM

I was moved by the whole experience. I was also moved by that experience in Texas two years ago and three years ago.* It always is a filling station. It's like so many times we go places, we're expected to be the filling people [laughs] instead of to receive that.

It's almost like a synergy thing. Most places we go, if there's any Christians at all, it's like maybe half Christians/half not Christians. And that's unusual. Usually it's one Christian to every twenty, twenty-five non-Christians. And when we go there, you know, for sure, that like 95 percent of those people are sold-out, born again, radical Christian people. Christian bikers, for the most part.

And it's just a feeling of going in there with folks with the same energy in the gut, the same love and the same goals and a lot of the same or similar experiences. Strength and hope. All that power together. To me, it just makes like a dome of power.

What about Kenneth Copeland? One of the things that really surprised me was that a group that had come from such a renegade outlaw background would connect with a TV preacher.

He connected with us. He is the one who put forth all that energy, all that money, orchestrated that whole thing, specifically for bikers, for Christian bikers. Because him and Jesse Duplantis and Jerry Seville have all ridden for years, which I never knew until three years ago. But they're all fairly expert motorcycle riders. And they wanted to step out of their three-piece suits and come into the biker thing. And I don't know why. I don't know if that was led by God

---

* Attending the Eagle Mountain motorcycle rally.

or led by recreation. Whatever it was, it's sure not a bad thing.

Even though I know how deeply God's in those messages and how deeply, deeply moved I have been by like Jesse Duplantis three years ago, life changing. Gracie got saved down there. Anyway, all of that. Even with that, it appears to me that the messages from the platform are the minor part of being there. It seems like more ministry goes on through the day and through the night with each other and moving from camp to camp and the fellowship and the praise. Seems like that's the major part.

I heard grumbling down there—maybe grumbling is not a fair word—that the fellowship was the only reason they came, that they didn't like Kenneth Copeland and thought—they called him a false prophet or at least suggested that. That the Bible warns against false prophets and thought that he was a businessman.

I'm sure he is an astute businessman, but that certainly does not mean—I love him. I listen to him on TV sometimes. I'm not a Kenneth Copeland groupie. I just—when I catch him on TV, it's always refreshing.

It just seems like he's sort of non-pretentious. I don't know, he's got wild eyes! He's real demonstrative. He's not conservative at all in his presentation. And I just like him. He's fun to listen to, and when he's fun to listen to, I really listen to him.

RANDY

The first time I went down there, it was me and Shalom and Hubie and my wife. That was about four years ago. It was awesome, especially being down there the first time, I think, was the most awesome. Just being with all them people who don't look a whole lot like the normal Christian, the everyday Christians, and how strong they were praising God.

Also seeing this thing was bigger than Indiana, what was going on. It also, there again, it reminded me of Paul, of how the Lord took Paul, he just blew people's minds with Paul. And that's how he does with bikers and street people who get saved. We're not just run-of-the-mill Christians, whatever that is.

A lot of people have talked about the fellowship in the campgrounds there and that seems to be the main attraction. What about the preaching from Kenneth Copeland and Jesse Duplantis?

Oh yeah. Yeah. Yeah, that's, Whew! The first time, I first started hearing Jesse, he got to turning me off a little bit. I was thinking he's a cocky little dude, you know. I don't know, without humility. Without getting humble, without having some kind of humility about you, there ain't a lick of honesty about it. Because without the humility, then you're standing—anyway, in my outlook—you're not standing in the right place with God. I placed myself before God too many years, you understand what I'm saying?

I think humility is a form of knowing your place. Well, anyway, I thought Jesse was kind of uppity and kind of cocky and stuff. Then, the very last year—no, it was the year before—I was thinking, I was watching Jesse, kind of huffing in my head, saying, This is cool, he's good, he's a talker, and stuff like that. And then all at once, it was just like, just as I was thinking this, he dropped to his knees and started crying. And it just did something for me.

I think in every one of us, man, if we don't show that, if we don't have that humility, it ain't hap-

pening. I just don't think it's happening. I think we got something that's blocking our view or something.

We were sitting around the campfire when we were down there last year, and you and Buck were talking. He said that he didn't have much use for them. He thought that they were all false prophets, and you said that you had wondered about that, too.

Yeah, I do that with everybody. But we're told to watch out for false prophets. I mean that's scriptural. Somebody better be checking me out as I'm giving the word. Not saying that the Lord's gonna lead us wrong, but we may lead ourselves wrong. My gosh, that happens all the time.

There's some things about him that I don't get into. I think they got a real heavy big money thing going, but I know we need money. Our group needs money. We're trying to get money together for stuff.

But I've never heard—there's a couple things that I've heard other people tell me about that they've heard him say, like Jesus going down into the depths of Hell and doing this, in the three days that he was, the three days of his resurrection. Well, I ain't read that anywhere in the word. But I've heard that's being professed.

That's part of it. Sometimes I just, I don't know, my spirit just leads me sometimes not to believe all of Kenneth's little stories that he tells. Not taking away from that word, but—but, naw, I think they come out of the Bible on the majority of stuff that they have. They come right out of it. And to tell you the truth, I've never heard Jesse say anything but stuff out of the Bible.

I think also there's a thing amongst—Buck, he's a very, kind of an old-time preacher, Buck is. And a lot of prospering that the Copeland Ministry is into, Buck has never been led to be into that real heavy monetarily prosperous kind of thing. Coming out of doing that in the name of God, you know?

I know my grandmother was like that. Very, No, we can't have this, and we can't do that, and we ain't gonna be able to have this because we ain't supposed to have too many things and material things. My dad used to tell us how she kept from having a whole lot of things when they were younger because of that belief. I'm just kind of breaking free from that now, about there's nothing wrong with having some stuff here as long as we don't place it before him. But he will help us prosper. But I think if the worldly monetary or the material prosperity starts to get too out of hand, I think that stuff starts being another God. That stuff starts getting in your way. There's so much snag. There are so many snags here.

There was only one Jesus that walked the earth, that none of us are going to be perfect.

SPARKY

He lives on a quiet road in the country with his wife, Meg, and their son Marcus. "It might not look like much, but the Lord gave it to me." His yard looks like many yards in southern Indiana, scattered with junked cars and motorcycle parts, and it looks over acres of woods and rolling meadow. Outside the garage where we are looking at motorcycles and motorcycle parts, neighbor kids ride their bikes and talk about the medications they are on for attention deficit disorder.

I grew up in a little town called Worthington. Kind of a troubled time, early '60s. Well, I got drafted in '70, so that ought to tell you something. I was in that time era. My dad's a biker, was a biker. My grandpa was a biker, and Dad was a biker. But my dad, he don't ride anymore. He got hurt pretty bad in a wreck. He was an alcoholic. He just rode with a bunch of guys.

I remember when I was young it made an impression on me. He got hurt on a motorcycle—I think it was an Atlas Norton. We lived in Connersville at the time, and I must have been about Marc's age, about six, and he didn't have any more motorcycles from that point on. And after that point on, he got drinking real heavy and probably using some stuff, too. He would come in and work my mom over. I had two adopted sisters, which were, in essence my cousins, living there, and he worked the womenfolk over, mainly.

Wouldn't say too much to me unless I did something wrong or mouthed him. He didn't allow nothing like that. He'd tell you one time, and then the next time, you know. He didn't believe in spanking. He'd just knock you through the wall.

I left home when I was—let's see—I was about sixteen. I got my first motorcycle when I was fourteen and started running around, trying to get a little gang together on bicycles, acting like bikers. By the time I was fourteen I got my first motorcycle, which was a real small motorcycle. Always would get *Easyrider* magazines, every bike magazine I could get, everything that I could learn about working. And there was an old man and old woman and a bunch of guys that rode together, older folks. They were older to me. They were about my dad's age, maybe a little younger. They was younger than my dad. And I'd hang around down there 'cause they'd wrench on motorcycles. They all rode Triumphs and Harleys. They partied a lot, too, but there didn't seem to be any abuse there like there was at my house.

I started working at a real early age. I had a paper route, mowed the older people's and the widow women's yards, and I went to school. I'd get up at three-thirty in the morning, run my paper route, get off, and go to school. Then I'd get off of school and go mop floors at a laundromat, and then I'd work at a gas station until, oh, about ten-thirty, then I'd go home.

When I wasn't doing that I'd hang around with the bikers. Kind of bike enthusiasts. I got real attached to this guy, and he taught me some real bad things. He was a drug dealer, a heavy-duty drug dealer. He didn't drink, but he did drugs real heavy. And drugs then, then a joint was like heroin is now. Real bad.

I come home one night, and I went to bed. My dad come in, and he'd been drinking, and he was screaming and yelling and busting things. And I got up and told him that he was acting like a—I said something bad to him. I said, "You're acting bad, and I'm tired of you doing it. And if you hit my mom again I'm gonna get a gun and blow you away." And he grabbed me, and he throwed me through the picture window. We had a big plate-glass window.

Our floor at the time—we was remodeling the house—my dad's gifted with being able to do anything he wanted to do, and he's a very good carpenter, and he was putting a floor in the house. Basically, what I'm saying is we lived on a dirt floor. This was about 19—, oh, it would have to be '66 or somewhere around in there.

I got on my little bike and rode off and started living down there. 'Course he come down, try to get me back. The law came down there and told me I would have to go home, and so they hid me out. And I stayed down there. Pretty soon, they met some other friends and got selling. I went ahead and went to school, and I'd go see Mom and go home when Dad wasn't there, pretty much. Got seeing my dad again, and Dad kind of straightened up a little bit, but I was already—I don't know, felt like I had a better home where I was. 'Cause I could do anything I wanted, basically.

And I was making money because they put me to selling pot. What they'd do, they'd let me go cross town when I was running my paper route and deliver to this guy, and they was running me back and forth, and I'd get paid good for it.

So there were enough people in Worthington, Indiana, in 1966 buying pot?

Yep, there was. Then they got me going to Jasonville. There was some bikers in Jasonville, Indiana. A bunch of them recently got busted. But anyway, I was running from Jasonville and back and forth.

They let me drive their car and stuff. Anyhow, by the time I was about sixteen I had my own car. A pretty nice one. I was making more money than most people working in factories at the time. I still kept my jobs, my other jobs that I had, but then I'd deal drugs, too.

There was a big bunch of us kids riding together. There was twelve of us running together, riding our motorcycles. Then you could get your license when you's fifteen and three months, I believe, motorcycle endorsement. And we all had our license and we was wearing colors on our back, trying to be bikers. I'll never forget, there was a whole big bunch of them pulled into Worthington one day at the bar. First time we ever seen like real bad bikers. Had West Coast plates on.

Two of 'em got in a fight out in the bar. We's actually chanting 'em on. That club—I'd rather not mention club names, okay?—that club ended up, a couple of 'em stayed there, and where I was staying they started wearing their colors. Colors meaning the patches on their backs, like this one that I've got now, which is a Christian patch.

By the time I was sixteen I was probating for a national club, a world—a big club. Things got worse, and I started not only selling drugs but sampling a few.

Met this girl. Okay, one of their, as they called 'em then, old ladies had a daughter, and she was about my age. We ended up getting married under club law. By the time I was eighteen she was pregnant and I got drafted. I went in the service, went to basic and went straight, pretty much, to Vietnam.

When I was in Vietnam I found better drugs. I started experimenting with LSD and started experimenting with heroin, opium. I spent my two-year term and was getting ready to come home, and we got captured. They took us to a POW camp, and three of us got away. Two of us had been wounded pretty good. Two of us made it out of it, and we got back in 1973.

How did you escape?

The first thing they do—I'd rather not go through the whole thing if you don't care. I'd really rather not. It's kind of disgusting. It really brings me down. For a long time when I came back, in 1973, I had a real chip on my shoulder, felt like the world owed me. I went through some real bad things. We just got away. I was just tough. I'm a little skinny guy and I always was, and I was always real wirey, and you could hurt me pretty bad and not keep me down.

What they'd do, pretty much, is they hobbled you. They break your feet and your toes. You've seen me barefoot before at the Boogie and stuff. What they do, they take a gun and they bust your toes. They did it to all of us. They take your shoes.

Well, we got away, and a couple of us got hit. And we got away and only got to a village. We got back and got to some ROK soldiers, which are Republic of Korea soldiers, in 1973.

And when I got back, I tried to look my wife up, see my daughter and my mom and my dad, and they wouldn't accept that that was my daughter.

Didn't the government tell your family that you were dead?

Yes. When I got back I tried to find my wife, and she had got a letter, after thirteen months, twelve months, saying that I was missing and dead, pretty much. My mom, too. I went up and knocked on the door, and my mom had a heart attack. She thought I was dead. I didn't even call home. You just get home as quick as you can.

I found my ex-wife, and she was getting ready to get married again. She was gonna drop the guy. When I got back I weighed about ninety-five pounds, and I knew that I had a habit, a full-fledged heroin habit. I was pretty much using needles pretty heavy-duty. Actually, it was opium, but opium's a little harder to get here so I switched to heroin.

Just really didn't want her anymore. I don't know what was going through my head. I told her to go ahead and marry the guy, and we went and we got the paperwork done. 'Course the annulment wasn't right. We got it where she could get married to the guy. They said, "Well, if you sign your daughter over to him and let him adopt her, then I won't try to get no child support from you, or bother you in any way and bother you again." So, because my parents wouldn't accept my daughter, they wouldn't accept my wife, and me and my dad, as soon as I got back, he didn't like Vietnam vets because they're all hippies and trash and so on and so forth.

It hurt me. I just pretty much ran. I left my daughter. Walked out on my daughter and my wife, just took the easy way out. Got running and went to Haight-Ashbury, and I went to California. I went back and forth a few times, and I got settled back in with the very same people, got dealing the very same way. When I came back I had real good connections, had real good connections on marijuana, hooch, pot, marijuana.

I could go down, I could go to Florida, and I had some people coming in on a boat, and I was getting it, taking, bringing it back to Indiana, and running. I was running big time back and forth, making a lot of money. In the black market while I was over there, too, while I was overseas. I come back with a pretty good chunk of money, American currency.

I had a new bike, new car, new four-wheel drive. I always was into hot rods. Just went nuts. Built me a hot rod, started just chasing all the women, and I met this woman. We got married, under club law, and she had a baby. Things got real bad again, and I packed my bags and I left her. Got a divorce and I just left. Left my boy.

Met this other woman, pretty much did the same thing. Packed my bags and left. Met this other woman, and we had three boys. We were together thirteen years. We dealt real heavy-duty, made our money pretty much that way. I had got a job when I got out of 'Nam in '73. I got the job that I got now, working for the telephone company in Indiana, so I stayed here.

What was the difference with this woman that you stayed with her for thirteen years?

[Long pause.] Uh, she liked everything I liked. She wouldn't tell me not to use or I was getting too messed up. She liked a lot of sex. She was a party woman, and she'd do whatever I wanted her to do. Things got real bad in thirteen years. I kept my job and we's making money, but I was running with the guys. If I wanted to bring somebody else she let me, and if she wanted to go with somebody else I'd let her. And we lived that way.

All the boys that we had were mine, and I knew it. I don't know really how it turned out that way, but it did. One thing led to another, and things got real bad, and I did pretty much the same thing. She sent me down after some cigarettes, and I just sent one of my buddies back to her to tell her that I wasn't coming back. I was tired of life that way, and I'm gonna change my life. Just, it was done.

We fought all the time. We would get in big fights, shoot at each other. I knew as long I was there we'd do it, and the kids was starting to grow up, and I thought that it was, it was all me doing it. I was under conviction then, but I didn't know it then 'cause I was still unsaved, of course.

So we split everything fifty-fifty. I had three drag cars. I drag-raced. I got the drag cars, she got the house. I had a lot of bills that I was gonna have to pay. She finally ended up losing the house. It was in my name, and I got stuck with that bill. So I was forced with needing more money. At that time, I had a pretty good habit, probably, I don't know, five or six hundred dollars a day. So I only had one option, and that's making money to pay everything and keeping my habit and all my desires that I wanted. I liked cars, I liked fancy women, I liked fancy houses, I liked fancy clothes, I liked fancy motorcycles.

So I started really heavy-duty dealing and really still using heavy-duty. After several years after that divorce—three—I built a little '65 Mustang up, and I mean it had a supercharger on it, and I'd go to town. I never was, I don't know, I'm not no handsome man, but I always had a way with women. And man, I mean I was running everything, chasing everything. I was dating high school girls. I was just sleeping with everything I could get to sleep with me.

And partying. I started riding with the club again. That was the thing with my thirteen-year marriage. My wife didn't like bikes. She was a partier, okay? She was an old flower child, basically. So I put my bike up, but when I got divorced I got my bike. I pulled it out, and I started riding it. Bought another bike, started running with the bunch. And I mean we were just running around and just trying to get in fights and just fought with other clubs. We started dealing guns, started stealing cars, started using real heavy.

Right here in Bloomington. Bloomington and Indianapolis and Vincennes and all the surrounding area. Got running with a bunch of heavy-duty people. Got me a pretty fat bank account. Got kind of tied in with people that knew what I was doing, prestigious people per se. Got me fixed up where I could buy law off. Got pretty much being the man, you know?

I got running the streets. I'd lived with a girl for a while, a woman. Actually, I was living with three women, and they all knew it. I was their sugar daddy, so to speak. One of 'em, occasionally I'd make money off of her or drugs or whatever it was. When my big man came down, you know, he supplied, and he'd pay me visits to make sure everything was okay.

Things just got real nasty and real bad. One of the guys got busted. They said I pointed fingers. There was some threats, and things just got real nasty. There was some shooting and some houses blowed up and some cars blowed up. My bike got torched, and some things happened, and I got back in again with another bunch and got dealing, and things kind of smoothed out.

I met this young lady. I met her brother and her brother—I wouldn't deal to the kids. I dealt to three people in Bloomington, and they would deal to kids. But I knew who they was dealing to, and they pretty much knew I was doing it but they couldn't prove it. I'd still go to town and hang out with the teenagers.

I got doing that. 'Course, when I first starting dealing, the people I was living with, they put me on the playground dealing joints and nickel bags back then.

I met this guy and I liked him. His name was Frank, and he was a young guy. He was running with a guy, and the Cooper guy I was interested in because his parents had a big farm, and he had a lot of money. So I got to selling them pretty much what they wanted. They'd pay too much for it. Frank seemed to have money, too.

Got tight with them, and one day he brought his cousin down, and me and her got running together and dating. Pretty soon one day I seen his little sister. She was about fifteen, maybe. To me, she's just the cutest thing I ever seen. Red-headed and freckle-faced and young and tender, and I thought, Boy, if I was younger. But I didn't try to bother her, and I don't know why I didn't but I didn't.

And I dated her cousin for a long time. And, of course, I had a car. I'd go down and impress all the young girls, all the young guys. We would drag race, street race, and I'd always win because I had the money to build a fast car. My bike was all chromed out, and I had it there. You know, the big shot.

Finally about a year went by, I kept seeing this little girl and just couldn't get her off my mind. Finally one day she come up and said, "Would you take me riding in your car?" I said, "Yeah, I'll take you riding." She jumped in my Mustang, and we took a ride. She said, "You take my cousin out. Why don't you take me out?" I said,

"I ain't getting arrested for nobody." I think she was about sixteen.

How old were you?

Let's see, there's twenty years' difference now. She's twenty-five now and I'm forty-five, -six, now, so what would that have made it? If she was sixteen, I'd've been what, thirty-six, thirty-seven?

She moved in with me, basically, right after that. She asked me how come I did what I did and how come I dated all those women and how come I did that. I told her that I did that because I didn't want to get hurt. And I did. That's why I did it. I didn't want to keep one, because I was afraid that I'd get hurt again. I didn't really want to admit it to anybody, but I admitted it to her. And she said, "I think I'm falling in love with you."

She ended up moving in with me. I went to her parents, and they okayed it. And I did it like I should've. That's why I didn't get arrested. And she didn't party or drink or nothing, though.

Then I got my kids back, but I didn't get my daughter. I got my boys. I'd get to see 'em every other weekend. Like I said, I had some people bought off, and there's no reason I shoulda got 'em, but because of money I got 'em.

She would actually watch my kids while I'd go out and party. When we moved in together, we had an agreement that she wouldn't mess around, I wouldn't mess around. We wasn't never gonna get married, and I told her I'd never marry her. But we'd be married under our terms, kind of like a club thing like I'd been married before. But not by law, because I didn't want to go through a divorce and lose my house and lose my car. Plus it hurt, and that was the main reason but I didn't want to admit that to anybody. I knew it deep in my heart.

Things went real good for a while. I slacked up on using a little bit. I got riding, and she liked to ride motorcycles. She'd like to jump on back and go with me. She'd go anywhere I wanted to go. She liked having doors open for her, she liked fancy clothes, she liked fancy cars. But when I'd party, she didn't want to be around it. She told me that very plainly. So I'd give her money to go shopping and give her a pretty good bunch of money and a car to drive. Usually, it was a pretty new car. She'd go stay at her mom's the weekend, and we'd have drunken brawls, and the club would come over. I'd call her when it was safe for her to come home, and we lived that way. We seemed to be happy for a long time.

And then I still had my habit. I hid it from her, I hid it from all my wives, I hid it from my employer. I never missed a day's work. A lot of people, when you say "heroin addict" they think of somebody floppin' in the gutter. I never missed a car payment, never missed a house payment, never missed a day's work, never got arrested. Only thing I ever got arrested from is fighting. Seventeen times, total. Assault and batteries. Assault and batteries and related things.

You bought your way out of all of those?

Pretty much. Pretty much, pretty much. Got good attorneys. There was a couple deals made a couple times, a couple buy-offs. My attorney knew somebody, and pretty much through the system—this one judge got tired of seeing me, and he knew what I was doing. Finally, he started putting pressure on me after time.

But same old story, I was still using. I got using real heavy again and running with a bunch of guys that was starting a new club. They was really wannabe bikers, and they was partiers more than anything, and they wanted me. I was supplying. I was running drugs for three of the big

clubs. So that kept me in drugs, you know what I'm saying? It kept me in money. And it was pretty underground, because they was discreet 'cause they were older, more seasoned. People like myself not like kids that'd go out and get busted and turn over on you. Because they knew me. I had a reputation, and I'd shoot you. I'd stab you and whatever it took.

I had some money, and I bought an interest in a car lot, and I made more money. I pretty much just had money to buy whatever drug I wanted. The reason I never drank is because of my dad. All the clubs I was in, the reason I had the women, I would always, in my eyes, treat 'em good. I never beat 'em up, I never shared 'em with other men if they didn't want to be shared. I never would beat 'em up. They always had a car to drive and a house to stay. I was always the one where all my brothers—like this place where we're setting now, there'd be people passed out all over the place. They'd be in the yard, they'd be in the house and ate my food. I supplied it all. It was like the hang-out, like the clubhouse.

Finally, I got running with these guys, and I got using real heavy-duty and drinking on top of it. Got using Xanaxes on top of everything else. And alcohol, real heavy-duty. What I would do, I would drink boiler-makers and eat Xanaxes, and then I was using what my body had to have. And the reason I did that was my drug of choice was no longer filling the void that I needed. It was no longer getting me high. It was something I had to have. And I wasn't getting my jollies off, so to speak. It took something pretty potent to get me off, so I started doing everything.

One particular night I went to the clubhouse, which there was a bunch of guys that called theirselves—well, I won't mention names. They hung around down at the tattoo place down there on Adams, and I got running with them guys. Got really using heavy. I got down there one night, they decided that I wasn't getting loose enough so they mickeyed my drink after I already did everything. I jumped on the bike, had words with 'em. We got in a fight, and I jumped on the bike, and I come home. I don't remember coming home.

One of 'em got worried about me 'cause he knew that I was really messed up, and he was one of the ones that mickeyed my drink. So he come out here. I shot him in the leg. My girlfriend come home, and I started beating on her. I tried to torch the house. She put it out. Torched the bike, torched the car that I'd bought her, which was a Trans Am. Beat her up so bad you couldn't tell who she was. 'Course the cops was out here all the time. They knew. She left.

'Course my buddy left me. It was a clean shot, went all the way through his leg, and he'd been shot before and he knew that it was a clean shot so he had her doctor it. She'd doctored people shot before.

They decided to come back, and when they came back I was laying on the floor with a gun to my head. I passed out, and I remember I was gonna kill myself. I wasn't breathing too good, and there was foam coming out of my mouth. The guy that I shot called 911. When they found out where I was they didn't send an ambulance, they just sent cops out.

The same cop that took me to jail several times came out. He threw me in the back of the car. He decided he'd just take me to jail. Usually, by the time we got up here to Little Cincinnati, which is a few miles away, I'd kick the cage out of the back of the car, kick the windows out the car, tried to choke him. I wasn't doing that, so he checked on me. He seen that I wasn't breathing at all, my lips was turning blue.

He knew I was dying, so he decided to radio up and get an ambulance coming and take off for the hospital, and they met me in Stanford. Didn't know it at the time. I found all this out afterward.

Well, they shocked me. They gave me defribulated—got my heart going and got me to the hospital. And I come through in the hospital, come up with a knife out of my boot, hurt a nurse pretty seriously. Tried to take a doctor out, and they got me back out and got me back down and got me strapped down. Put me in the psycho ward. Found out what all I was on.

I spent quite a bit of time there, and they put me in the detox. When I finally came down and come to my senses, where they unstrapped me—kept me strapped for several days—I knowed what I did. I knew everything I did. I knowed that I beat her up. That was like my rock bottom, the lowest thing I could do in my life, to me.

But it didn't affect me. It was like, well, Have to find me another woman, you know? I'll just pack my stuff. I'm kind of done with my job anyway. I know I'm gonna lose it now because I've been here a long time. They put me in the drug treatment center. They told me that my liver had quit.

For a long time I'd been sick every winter, like two or three years. And I'd been passing blood in my stool and when I urinated for a long time. And I'd vomit blood for a long time. And when you're using like that, you think it'll go away. And it'd go away for a while, you know, and then it'd come back. I knew I was sick. They said that my liver would just shrivel up to nothing. It wasn't purifying my blood and that's why I was sick all winter, like I had the flu. I actually thought I had AIDS.

I didn't have it, come to find out. When they put you in a place like that they give you a complete physical. When you're in a detox ward they do your vital signs every so many hours. They take care of you.

I'd been there about five days and I got a number to call. Couldn't get calls, but they'd take 'em and they'd give you numbers that you could call back. You could call out. I thought, Well, I'm gonna have to find me another woman. I know I've lost my job.

Well, finally I called into work, and it wasn't too bad. They acted like it'll be okay. I had insurance. I knew they'd pay for all of it. I was gonna get right out and use. I'd just take it with a grain of salt. Going through their stuff just to get out. I wouldn't talk to nobody because they would try to find out if I was gonna stay clean. I just wouldn't talk.

There was a woman in there, a girl in there I knew. We got pretty tight, pretty close. She had a desire. She wanted to quit. She was sick and tired of being sick and tired. And she'd always been with guys that beat on her, and I knew it. And I told her what I did. She couldn't believe it. That kind of touched my heart at the time.

Finally, I got this call, and I called it back. It was my girlfriend. I returned the call after a day. And I'll never forget what she said. I'll never forget it. I'll never forget it. It's really what changed my life. I didn't accept the Lord then, but I decided I was gonna get clean.

I got on the phone, and I called her, and she said, "You know what you did to me?" "Yeah." And she said, "You hurt me bad." I said, "Yeah, I know. I know what I did." She said, "Well, I'm gonna send some pictures to you, how beat up that you did me." I said, "You don't have to. I remember." And she said, "I love you, and I

want you to know that. But," she said, "I ain't living with you any longer and watching you kill yourself." She goes, "I know what you're doing now. It's out. I knew it before, but I didn't want to admit it." And she said, "When you had me down, beating on me," she said, "I looked in your eyes [holds back tears], and that wasn't you in there. That was something else." And she said the word *something*. And she said, "I don't know what it was, but it wasn't you."

And she said, "Through all your problems, you've always been just plumb sweet to me. I'll forgive you for that, but I can't stay with you and watch you kill yourself. And I'm not taking another beating again." And she said, "If you get clean, which I don't think you can from what they tell me, we might have a chance. But right now, as it stands, I don't want to be around you till you went through treatment." She goes, "I know that wasn't you. That's something else." And she said, "And I don't know what to do about it, but I want you to know that I love you."

That night I dreamed her words all night long. [Holds back tears.] And I decided that, you know, I just evaluated things, and it was wrong in my mind. But I remember thinking, Well, I'm not gonna do any better than a woman twenty-two years younger than me. She's a sweet kid, and she does love me for me. She don't love me for my car and my bike or for my drugs, 'cause she don't even do drugs. Why is she even with me? She has to love me for me. And I started evaluating things in my head. And I decided, Well, Sparkplug, if you ever wanted to get clean, now's your chance, because you've got people that's gonna pay for it. You're in the union, they can't fire you, you're gonna have your job back. You just might have a chance at life.

So I decided I was gonna get clean. So when I told 'em I accepted it, they started trying to see what kind of physical damage it did to me, and it was a big, long list. Looked like a Dead Sea scroll when they brought it out. And they told me I was gonna have to get in the methadone program, that I would never be able to live without something. And that I'd damaged my heart for life and that I'd damaged my liver and my kidneys.

If I cleaned my life up, I may have as long as five years on this earth. But if I didn't, they didn't look for me to live over three years and that was the bottom line. They wasn't gonna tell me that until I wanted to get clean. That didn't sound very good to me, because, like, two years difference? I got thinking about it, and we had that little boy that you just heard, coming in wanting a popsicle. I got thinking about dying alone, with nobody, getting old and dying with nobody. Or dying because I was faced with dying. And dying with nobody. I walked out on everybody that ever cared for me. I hadn't spoke to my parents for years. Walked out on them, had run from everything and everybody. And the reason that I did it, I didn't want to get hurt, and I had this big fence all up around me, and I knew I was gonna die alone. And that scared me.

For the first time in my life, I got thinking, I ain't got no brothers. They're my brothers, but none of them's come up here, and any time I've been in jail, my car's been wrecked, and I been locked down they ain't come around. It's been me having to get myself out. Sure, I got them out plenty of times. I got evaluating things.

My brain got working cause I'd been clean for a month almost. And my brain got working, you know? So I went to the treatment. I was in there like four months. I started going through some real heavy-duty withdrawals. I mean some of the most terrible things I ever been through. I been through some before, 'cause I tried to stay clean on my own several times. Nothing ever worked. I tried switching drugs around, 'cause I knew I had a problem but I thought it would go away.

I had a lot of physical problems. My teeth, I hadn't taken care of them, and I had abscessed teeth. I'd had bike wrecks and had broken bones, I didn't go to the hospital. I had people patch me up. I started feeling the hurts and pains when I started coming down off of everything. I was a mess. Finally, I got out, and I come back to this house. It was just a mess.

My girlfriend had called me, and I called her while I was in there the whole time. I wanted to see my little boy. She brought him over, and I got to see him. [Holds back more tears.] He was just a baby then. He always called me Daddy. He still does. Just come running up to me and hugged me. I got thinking about it, you know? I thought, Well, here's my only chance. I've always wanted somebody to wrench on bikes. That's my last chance I got.

My other boys was getting up to teenage years. They'd come around when they needed something, needed bailed out of jail or needing something. I thought, Well, what would it really be like to be a father? I got thinking about just life in general. Got thinking about all the rotten things I did to everybody, all the people that I hurt. I'd go to bed at night and wake up in a cold sweat, withdrawing, thinking about all the people's lives that I ruined.

I had started young kids off, smoking dope. Now they was dealing heavy-duty. This was all going through my mind as I was going through the withdrawals. I don't know, it just went hand in hand with it. And I was really having a real problem with alcohol, because you turn the TV on and it's there. Everywhere I went. When I got out, I got into this thing called Narcotics Anonymous, which is a very good program.

What were you going through physically at this time?

Well, I'd get up in the morning and have a desire to use, and my legs'd cramp, my arms would cramp, I'd feel like I had lockjaw, my bladder would let loose, my bowel would let loose, and I'd start vomiting. Sometimes I could crawl to the bathroom. Sometimes I'd make a mess where I was, in my pants, on the floor, just right there. I don't know how to explain it. It was horrible.

I know what was going on, but I couldn't make my body do nothing. It was just like your muscles would all ball up. You're hands and your toes would all go all different directions and your fingers would go all different directions, just like you was a derelict. It was awful. It was horrible. I'd go into little convulsions and pass out, not know what happened or how long I'd been there. Couple times I'd been there a real long time and knew it 'cause I knew what time it was.

My girlfriend came out one time when I was in that state, and I had stool in my pants, peed all over myself, and had vomit all over me. I was laying in the vomit. She decided to move back in to take care of me. [Holds back more tears.] She'd carry me to the bathroom, and she just literally took care of me.

I was missing a lot of work. And they was getting on me. At work they were like, Okay you went through detox, you're healed, you're okay. You know what I mean? They didn't understand. They was telling me I was gonna have this for the rest of my life.

Me and her got real close, closer than we'd ever been. She knew I was trying, and we just got a real tight relationship, which I needed. I got thinking about things, and I got telling her about my daughter. I needed to find her, and I needed to get ahold of my boys. And I started calling every night and talking to 'em, trying to talk to my ex-wife, trying to get things to where we could talk without trying to kill each other when we seen each other.

That didn't go too good, but my boys got coming over. All my buddies that hung around, they was still kinda hanging around. When I got clean they left one by one. See, that was my family. I walked out on my real family.

I was hurting. I was all alone, and they all walked off on me. I didn't have nobody but her, and it was like she's the only one who never walked out on me, except for one buddy. He was a guy I met in Calhoun, Georgia, 1974. He was a runner. Me and him shared needles together, we shared women together, we went back a long ways. He come from Georgia down here 'cause he got in trouble with the law, had to run. Come up here, and I set him up, okay? Before I got clean. And when I got clean, he kept coming around. He kept saying, "You know I really envy you for trying." He never did say, "You ain't gonna make it," he never would say "for staying clean."

And I went to NA, and I started riding my bike more than I ever rode. Always before, we'd clean our bikes up on Friday, all week, and we'd get 'em real nice for Friday, and we'd all do a couple lines of coke and drink and get all drugged up so we could go down to the bar, try to drink all the beer up. Kick our bikes for forty-five minutes 'cause we were real bikers. We didn't believe in electric starters. We'd go to the bar, and the ride was over. Then Monday we would get everybody's bike out of impound, everybody out of jail, do the same thing. It was our life. Bike didn't get really rode that much. When I got clean, I got riding a lot. I'd go to NA meetings and ride my bike.

There was people there that had a desire to stay clean, and I knew I wasn't around people that wanted to get dirty, wanted to use. The guys that hung around here, I wouldn't let 'em have nothing here anymore, so naturally they left. And the club I rode with, I put my colors down. I didn't tell 'em I was pulling out of the club or nothing, but I bought another vest and when I'd ride I wouldn't wear no colors on my back.

Did that create any problems for you?

Eventually it did. Finally, things got better for a while. Withdrawals kind of let up, things got real good. I'd have withdrawals, but I got to where I could control them with mass quantities of coffee, caffeine. I wouldn't take caffeine pills. I couldn't even take an aspirin 'cause I felt like I was using when I did, and I'd have a guilt thing. I was really trying to not use. So I wouldn't even take aspirin. And they gave me some drugs I was supposed to take and I quit those, for depression and things. And I quit all of 'em on my own. They recommend me not, but—I knowed the system wanted to keep me hooked just enough to—I had insurance.

It was the Lord then, but I didn't see it, giving me the knowledge to know that and the wisdom to know that. So I quit everything cold turkey. That's why I was so sick. I'd get up in the morning, fill up with coffee when I finally got the coffee to stay down. I'd get through the day. I got to where I could do that, and I was maintaining my job and working every day. I was getting up at five-thirty in the morning so I could be to work by eight o'clock. Sometimes I couldn't go.

Kind of got a little pattern going to where I'd be sick a lot of the weekends for some reason. I'd

ride a whole bunch and I'd go to meetings. In NA they taught you—it was a twelve-step program like AA but there there was no God—they told you of a higher power. I was searching for a higher power, and I got to where Harley-Davidson, of course, was my higher power, and the people of NA.

And a couple of them guys took me for some money, 'cause I still had some money at this time. They was kind of letting me down, basically, slowly. Things was getting kind of bad. My girlfriend, she wanted to ride with me, and I was afraid to take her with me on the bike 'cause I was afraid I'd go into my withdrawals and she'd be with me and I'd get her hurt. I'd already hurt her, and I didn't want to hurt her again.

Things started getting bad again with my withdrawals. And I started getting a desire that I wanted to go hurt somebody. I wanted to fight or I wanted to just beat on something. I went through a thing where I bought an old car, and I beat on it with a hammer, a sledge hammer, till I'd just pass out. I'd get so mad and frustrated and want to hurt somebody, anybody. Didn't make no difference who—just anybody. That's what I'd do. I didn't know what else to do, so that's what I did. I'd go through that.

Finally, one day, she said, "Why don't you buy me a motorcycle and teach me to ride so I can ride with you? Because you're off by yourself, and I know you're not using, but I just feel like I could help you if I was with you." She goes, "When you come back, you're not no better." One minute I'd come in and be okay with her, next minute I'd be crying and a nervous wreck, and the next minute I'd be rude to her, and the next minute I'd be lovey-dovey. She wasn't understanding it 'cause she'd never even used. I was telling her, at the same time, I was gonna be like that the rest of my life. She never said it to me, but I'm sure she was thinking, Can I live with him like this?

I didn't want to live any longer. I'll just put it the way it was. I got insurance in her name, so this house and everything would be paid for, and I pretty much made plans to—I'd always had race cars, and I always blasted up and down the road, fast as I could go. I was a wild man. Always had the fastest bike and the fastest car. Was a crazy man. I had that reputation of being a crazy man. Nobody would have never knowed the difference, and I knew it.

I got insurance. I thought it through a couple more months, and I taught her how to ride the bike. Things got a little better during that time. Once again, and then again, it's like a bike circle. My whole life. I had desire to want to leave her. I wanted to get back on the road. I had a real strong desire to use. The withdrawals was getting horrible once again, and they'd hit me. They'd be okay, and I'd think I'd be okay, then they'd just grab me and then just take me down so hard that I just didn't want to live any longer.

I'd get on the bike, and I'd ride a lot. I'd go to a meeting every night, NA meeting. Every night I'd go. On the weekends I'd want to ride. One particular Friday, we jumped on our motorcycle, and she says, "I want to get in traffic and drive." And she'd ride with me, and it was good. It was helping me, you know what I mean? It was good therapy, so to speak. We'd get a babysitter for my little boy, we'd jump on the bike, and I'd talk a lot about my boys and my family. I mentioned my daughter. I knew her name, what her name was changed to. And my wife is the same age as my daughter as it turns out. She was my girlfriend then, of course.

And I mentioned Kim's name, and she said, "Well, I know Kim Vaughn. I went to school

with her." I said, "Do you know how to find her?" She said, "No, I know how to find her mommy." So I found my daughter. She didn't want nothing to do with me and that hurt. I went to my ex-wife's house and beat the door. And it was good. Got some things behind me.

One particular Friday night, we jumped on our motorcycles. I'd been withdrawing real bad that day. I had a boy living with me that, he'd got in trouble with the law so his mom just come over here and dumped him pretty much. He was like fifteen, sixteen. No, he was sixteen, seventeen. Been in a lot of trouble with the law. Following my footsteps. I taught him karate. He was a black belt in karate. So am I. Just been in a lot of trouble. A chip off the old block. Running with a street gang, and she'd had it. She wasn't any better, but that was her way out. That kind of created problems. He didn't understand me getting clean, wasn't accepting it.

Things got real bad. That one particular Friday, I come home, I felt like I had the whole world on my shoulders. She said, "Let's go to town. I want to learn the traffic." So we took off, riding our bikes. We pulled into a gas station. Second Street there in Bloomington, Bloomfield Road, the Bigfoot. And we pulled in there. She's always got to have a Dr. Pepper everywhere she goes and a smoke. So she was smoking her cigarette and drinking her Dr. Pepper, and I was drinking coffee, trying to make sure that I was gonna be okay. I heard motorcycles roaring up. Looked up, here they come, pulling in, and it was my old brothers.

And they all pulled in there. They seen me there, and they come over, and they hugged me. They said, "Brother, we miss you. We love you, man. We miss you. We're going to Big Hoss's to party." That's just right down here, down the road. They said, "Why don't you just come on with us? We won't put nothing on you. We miss you, man. You know, we need our bikes wrenched on, and we miss you and we love you. We won't push nothing on you."

I wanted to go. I looked over there, and there she was with her hands on her hips, tapping her foot, looking at me like, Don't you go. And I knew if went I'd use. It hurt real bad. I was all alone. I didn't have nobody. People in NA was different than me 'cause they weren't bikers. It was different. They wasn't my breed. They didn't wear leather coats, and I couldn't talk bike trash to 'em. Just totally different.

Anyway, here they come, and I really wanted to go with 'em real bad. But I didn't. My girlfriend said, "Let's just go on uptown and ride." She said, "You handled that right. You know that, don't you?" Hugged me, just was real—like I said, took care of me.

She said, "Why don't we go downtown, so I can get in some heavy traffic and you can show me what to do. I need to get used to this." So we went right downtown. We went down Kirkwood. I didn't want to go because I—I didn't like anybody that was different than, that wasn't wearing leather and a biker. You can identify other bikers pretty easy. I didn't like the college kids, and I didn't like black people, and I didn't like white people, and I didn't like much of anybody. I been that way all my life.

We went down through there, and I seen a whole bunch of bikes, all lined up at People's Park where I used to meet a guy that sold drugs down there. I thought, Well, they're not gonna use here. They was wearing colors on their backs, a club. I couldn't identify the colors. And that was rare for me 'cause I knew all the clubs. So I just backed in. My girlfriend, she backs in her little bike. I got off, and I seen a guy I knowed a

long time. Name's Larry Mitchell. Seen him walking off. We called him Modo.

I thought, What's he got going on? Then I seen the "serving Jesus Christ" thing, and it didn't mean much to me. I seen a couple other guys that I'd knowed over the years, that I'd crossed paths with. He also had been a drug dealer, and me and him were rivals. I kind of stayed away from him.

But I got talking to some guys, got to talk bike talk. And while I was down there I felt real good! One of them started talking to me about Jesus, so I left. It was on a Friday night. I come home, and that week went by, and my boy that was staying there said, "Dad, this stuff's been showing up on the front porch when I come home from school." I made him get in school. And he said, "What do you want to do with it?" And it was stuff from churches.

That week, I'll never forget it, I went to Kmart and there was a hand-written Scriptures stuck on my windows of my car, in the door of my house, everywhere I went. And it was just like magic. That next Friday I went back down there, see if them guys was there. There they all was, lined up and down, so I backed my scoot in. My wife was with me. Talked to 'em, got real friendly with one of them. One of them had a '57 Panhead, just a gorgeous bike.

I walked up to Larry Mitchell, Modo, that night, and I said, "Larry, Modo, what kind of gimmick you got going on here?" He said, "Well, I'm pastor of a church now." I said, "Yeah, right!" He said, "This is real. Start hanging around and you'll see." And I remember walking off, thinking, Boy if I ever get religion, I sure as the h___ ain't gonna go to his church. 'Cause that dude's got something a-going. Look at him. He's smiling all the time. He's got something up his sleeve."

I got talking to this one guy. His name was Paul Clark, and he had this real boss-looking Pan-head, man. I mean it was gorgeous. All chromed out, all put back nostalgic, had big white sidewall tires on it, mudflaps, leather bags. He was real gentle with me. I know now that God just led me to him.

He mentioned a little bit about Jesus and then backed off. I got looking at his bike and seeing Jesus stuff all over it. And in my house, when I grew up, there was no Jesus Christ ever talked about. Only thing I ever heard about it, was I had a grandma, which I now believe she prayed for me then. She was Pentecostal. There was talk about how nutty, off the rocker, she was because she gave her money to the church and how bad religion was. That's all that I ever heard about religion.

That kind of come back to me. I thought about my grandma for some weird reason while this guy was talking to me. And that was weird, you know? We went home that night, and he called me on the phone, talked to me a couple times that week. Things got real good. And I went down there next Friday, and I found myself down there the next Friday and the next Friday. I didn't know what it was, but when I was with 'em I felt good. Finally, one day, they asked me to ride with them somewhere. And I did, and it was to church, and I stood outside and wouldn't go in. But it felt good.

Finally, Paul, he got talking to me, and he said, "Why don't you come to my church?" Some part of me wanted to become a part of them and part of the church, but I didn't think I could because I did so many bad things in my life. Finally, I told him, I said, "You don't want me around you, man. I'm a junkie." I just told him that, and I don't know why I said that. I just blurted it out. He put his hand on my shoulder

and he said, "Man, Jesus Christ will forgive you for it. He loves you, and I love you, too." And a tear come to his eye. And I thought, boy, that's weird. That guy's weird. He said, "Man, I been there." He said, "I know you're hurting. I feel it." He just kept his hand on my shoulder and kept talking to me. Made me feel real good.

He said, "Man, I don't care where you been or what you done." He said, "I just care about now and where you're going." He said, "I want you to come to church with me next Sunday." I said, "Okay," and I went to his church. My wife had been to churches before and I didn't know it, my girlfriend at the time. My little boy loved it and she loved it. I felt good there again, just like I did when I was with them.

I went there a couple Sundays. When I went in there, they give me a New Testament, and I got 'em laying right in there, still. Give us both one. I brought it home, throwed it down on this very table. 'Course this table was always just filled up with junk, trash all over the place. It's not the best now. It ain't no Taj Mahal or nothing, but it's home, and God's give it to us. It's clean, there ain't vomit in each corner.

We was still living that way, and I throwed it on the table. And I went to church with him a couple Sundays, and I kept going down there on Fridays. And I felt good. Finally, one day I got my bike, was gonna ride by myself on a Friday. I kicked it up. It was cold out. I put my leathers on, and I got about, oh, ten miles from here, my bike quit. Out of anger, I kicked the bike down and started jumping up and down on top of it, cussing it. All of a sudden a feeling come over me like in the summer, like when you raise up too quick, like I was gonna pass out, and I passed out.

When I did, I came through, the bike was setting upright, and there was words coming out I never heard before. I was praying, and I'd never prayed before. I went to the church, but I never kneeled down and prayed. Wasn't gonna do that 'cause that was sissified. Seeing them guys do it, Aw, that's sissy. For a man to kneel down like that.

I kicked the bike off, and it started right up. I didn't think a thing of it. Rode home, I thought, Man I'm losing—I'm gonna hurt my girlfriend. I'm gonna beat her up again. I'm losing my mind. And I called my sponsor in NA, and he said, "You're getting ready to relapse. You need to get into a rehab again." My psychiatrist had been trying to teach me how to cry, because to get rid of the feelings of wanting to hurt somebody and kill somebody and beat up on something, he said I needed to learn to let it out. And he was teaching me how to cry. And he never did teach me, by the way.

My psychiatrist was on vacation. They wouldn't help me. They kept putting me on hold, and I finally got mad, jumped in my car, which at the time was a '78 Ford Fairmont with a 460–24, full-cam, built-to-the-hilt, eight-point cage tubbed out with fourteen-inch ring coils under it, and I remember going to town as hard as it would go and getting mad and going into the emergency room and screaming and yelling until they got somebody out there.

They sent some cops down, escorted me out. They finally agreed to meet with me. But they wanted me out of there, basically, because I'd already raised enough Cain that they didn't want me there. So, he agreed to meet me down at Burger King. He met me down there, and I told him my story.

Now at the time this happened, I had a vision, a dream. And all it was was a bunch of faces, lights going down the road like a bunch of bikes.

There was faces in those lights, and my face was out front. I couldn't tell the rest of the faces except three faces behind me. And one of the faces that was behind me was this guy that was my rival, that was riding with the Unchained Gang. His name's Chico. And the other two, I seen their faces but I didn't know 'em.

I told this head shrink all that, what happened to me, and he looked at me just serious as a heart attack and said, "Man, you don't need to get locked down. You don't need to go to treatment. You need to see your preacher, your minister, your priest, whatever it is you believe in." I remember hitting the table real hard and said, "I don't believe in that shit!" And he looked up at me real calm and said, "Oh yes you do."

I jumped up and tried to turn the table over, and it was bolted down and wouldn't turn over. And I said, "You ain't gonna help me, are you?" And I jumped in the car, and I remember going as hard as I could go home. And I come home, my girlfriend was here waiting on me, and I was mad and told her what happened and I told her she needed to leave. I was going to hurt her. She wouldn't leave. She said, "I don't think you are." She said, "I want to stay here with you."

I was real rude to her that night, trying to make her leave, and she just came to me and just stayed right with me. I wouldn't have did it if I was her. I got up the next day and was sick. Had a withdrawal. I couldn't go to work that day. And I went through it pretty much all week. I mean the worst I'd ever went through. I got up, I remember, one day I was gonna go to work, and I got up, and I was trying to make coffee, and I was shaking. I had a little pit bull dog at the time, and there's a big dog fight out here at the back door, and I grabbed the door. Doorknob come off in my hand, I was trying to make coffee, I got between the two dogs, got dog-bit, come in to get the coffee, and the bottom fell out of the coffee pot. I mean, I had a real bad morning. I was just ready to kill somebody.

I walked out to start my car and let it warm up, and it wouldn't start. The battery was dead, and I tried to hook up jumper cables and hooked 'em up backwards and blowed the top out of the battery, and I looked up and there's a man standing there. And he hands me something, and it's from the church. I told him to get out of my face, I had stuff to do. He left.

I laid the thing down in the seat of my truck. I went through that week, and that thing stayed in the seat of the truck. I don't know why I didn't throw it away. I went through that week and was gonna get up and go to church, 'cause it always made me feel better. I couldn't go down there on Friday, with the guys riding. Couldn't go to church that day because I was too sick.

I got up at five-thirty in the morning on Sunday and was on my way back and forth, making coffee on Sunday. I was real sick, been sick all week, battling it all week. I was to kill myself that very next Wednesday. I already had planned to go ride with a couple of my old buddies, one of the ones who stayed hanging around, and it was gonna happen with them. It was gonna look like I lost my bike, and I was just gonna get in the way of a truck or a semi or something.

I was gonna go to church, because my little boy loved it so much and my wife was enjoying it. That guy that was so gentle with me, I had respect for him. Wanted to see him one more time, you know? I was kinda gonna let him know, but I couldn't, you know? I knew it.

On my way through to get coffee, I'd been vomiting everything out of my stomach and was filling back up on coffee. I come in through here, and that New Testament had somehow got uncovered and was laying there that very corner that your elbow's setting on. I remember thinking to myself, I want to see if this thing works. [Laughs.] And I walked in here and set on the toilet, got sick and vomited. I used to keep a five-gallon bucket in there to puke in while I was setting 'cause stuff would come out the other end, too. I went through all that.

When I had that vision when all those lights was like motorcycles roaring down the road, we roared into a drive-in theater. I ain't seen a drive-in theater in a long time. And on the screen was Romans 12. I didn't know what Romans 12 was, still didn't know at the time even though I'd been to church for several—well, a month. I wasn't seeking the Lord. I was seeking staying clean.

Anyhow, I went in there and I set down, and I opened the book up. I seen Romans 12, and that dream just popped back in my head. And I remember reading the very first Scripture, Romans 12:1. And it says, "I beseech you, brethren, if you use your body as a human sacrifice, holy, acceptable to the Lord, which is your reasonable service." And I remembered thinking, Boy, you ain't did that, has you, Sparkplug? And then I remember thinking, Boy, listen to you. You sound just like them Bible-thumpers you been hanging around with, man.

I went ahead and read the whole thing. And I remember thinking, Man, if everybody lived like this and did everything it says here and treated everybody the way they supposed to be treated, like it says here, and angered not anybody and treated their enemies with love, we wouldn't need no law. It'd be Heaven on earth! And I remember thinking again, Listen to you, man. You been around them guys too much. You're getting soft. I remember thinking this.

Remember I told you about, in NA they taught you about a higher power? I was looking for a higher power. I'd tried Buddha and I'd tried Harley-Davidson. My Harley-Davidson let me down. And the guys from NA let me down. When I needed 'em and called 'em they weren't there.

I read on to 13:1, Romans 13:1. It says, Romans 13:1 says, maybe not word for word 'cause I haven't got the Bible open, but it says, "Let every soul be subject to a higher power, but there's no higher power but that of God and which is ordained of God." I went to my knees, and the very same thing happened to me that happened down along the road. And I made so much noise that it woke my girlfriend up. She came in, my little boy, we all come in. She didn't know what I was saying. She knew what was going on 'cause she'd been a Christian before, but she'd never seen it happen in anybody.

I kinda come through, I said, "I'm sorry. Did I hurt you?" first thing I said. She said, "No. No," and looked at me kind of funny. Seen the New Testament, which is out in there, which I keep, 'cause I just like to keep it here. It's just something I like. I said "Let's go to church." She said, "Are we gonna go over to Crossroads?" I said, "No, we're gonna go to Modo Mitchell's church, the House of Prayer."

We went over there, and I used to park myself right in the very back of the church, so if the Spirit get on me or something I could get out of there in a hurry. And I'll never forget the day I got delivered totally from my withdrawals. It was Wednesday. We'd went there for like two months. Things got real good for a while and then things got bad once again.

I talked to Larry and Chico. Chico started teaching me how to bless my food, how to pray, and I started praying. But I wouldn't do it at the altar where everybody could see me. I'd say something like, Lord help me with this or help me with that. They weren't really prayers from the heart. They're just prayers from the mouth. Know what I'm saying? It wasn't really from the heart. I really wasn't understanding about saying from the heart.

I went to church one particular Wednesday, and my wife had got a job, and things really was looking good. We was hurting financially because I didn't make money with drugs anymore. I had all these things that I bought, had to pay for, because I didn't make forty thousand dollars a year on drugs. 'Course I didn't spend sixty thousand either. She got a job, so she's having to work on Wednesdays, and that's church night.

I got going to church. Pretty soon the club that I started riding with started sending guys over to rough me up, threaten to burn the house, threaten to do harm to my little boy. My daughter showed up, too, in that time frame, said that we needed to talk. She started coming around, accepting me. Finally, one night I was there—I'll never forget it—Larry Mitchell was speaking. I forget what he was speaking on, but he talked about, You could leave tonight, church, and then be gone that quick, how he had a friend, his name was Honeybee. I knew Honeybee, and he talked about him dying. Tears come to my eyes. I started crying. There was a little old girl setting next to me. She couldn't'a weighed a hundred pounds. I worked with her husband, her name was Stevenson. Last name.

She had a Kleenex. I looked at her and I said, "You got one of them Kleenexes? Where you getting them?" She goes, "Up there at the altar," and she just pushed me out in the aisle of the church, and I was right at the back of the House of Prayer. And everybody's looking at me. I'm like, "I'm out here, dummy, go up and get a Kleenex."

I started up that aisle, and I could actually feel two powers pulling at me. I don't know how to explain it. It was like I'd take two steps forward and something would just suck me back towards the door. There'd be lots of times I'd go out of the church, run out of the church. Something would touch me, and I'd get ready to—feel tears.

See, when you use drugs you lose—the only emotions I had was hate and lust. That was it. I had no other emotions. This emotion thing, I didn't understand it, because after that many years of using drugs I didn't have no emotions. I could cut a guy open with a knife and not have no remorse from it. I started up and started feeling these tears come to my eyes. Then I'd want to get out of there. I'd take two steps forward, and it felt like I was being just sucked backwards.

All these eyes on me, and I'm like, What's going on? And I'd take two steps forward, and it felt like I wanted to run out. I just felt these powers pulling at me. I was just gonna go get my Kleenex, turn around and leave, get back to my seat. I didn't even know why I was doing it.

I got up to the altar, and Chico was up there, grinning at me from ear to ear. And he's got kind of a funny smile, and he's grinning at me from ear to ear. And I went down on my knees, and I remember my first prayer. I said, "Lord, I don't know you very good. I know you made your deal, but if you just make me one more deal, Lord, and let these withdrawals let up where I can keep my coffee in me, where I could just get through the day, Lord, I'd read your book and I'd live for you the rest of my life." A feeling come over me, and I mean tears come out, snot. Chico was there hugging me, and

pretty soon I looked up and there's all kinds of people around me. I got up from the altar—I never did get my Kleenex, by the way—got back and got set down.

I got home that night, and I felt real good. I mean I never felt that good. It was just like all those tensions and all that hate that I had just was gone. It was like I felt like I weighed less. I don't know how to explain it. It was just great. It was fantastic. I was on my bike, and I remember just—all the way home and having a real good time. I come home, I pulled home, and there was a guy waiting on me from my old club.

His name was Jim Gabbard. Gabby, we called him. And he said, "You know why I'm here?" I said, "Yeah." He said, "Man, they're wanting you, man. They're wanting that mark off your arm." I said, "Yeah, I know." He looked at me. He said, "Man, I ain't gonna do that," and he rode off.

Anyway, I come in, and my wife was here. I thought, Man, I felt so good, I don't care what they do. It just released from me. I didn't worry about it. I come in, and I remember feeling like, I'm not gonna be sick tomorrow. It's over, it's gone. Then I'm like, It can't be. I got up the next morning. It was nine o'clock before I realized that I didn't get sick. I didn't even make no coffee that morning.

Went to work, everything was just great, didn't get sick. Come home that night, and I'm like, Well, I'll be sick tomorrow. My girlfriend looked at me. She goes, "You know," she said, "you look like you're feeling real good." She said, "You got a smile on your face." I said, "Yeah, I am real good." She goes, "I never have seen a smile quite like that. Is everything okay?" I said, "Everything's real good." She said, "Well, so and so called." I said, "Okay." Didn't think nothing of it. She just said something, you know. And I said, "You know what? The Lord's delivered me from those withdrawals I been having." And she said, "Aw, don't get your hopes up." She said, "I know all about the Bible, and I believe in God. It's okay to, but I don't know about that. I don't want you getting let down and hurt again." She goes, "I'm here for you, regardless." I said, "No, they're gone."

I was still sick. Had problems with rheumatism and arthritis, and I've had other problems. I was still having to be sick all the time, 'cause my liver wasn't cleaning my blood. I was real yellow-looking. I said, "It's gone."

A week went by, and I never had no more problems. Finally, I remember she said to me, "God's really been talking to you, hasn't he?" I said, "Yeah." Pretty soon, as the world would say, my conscience started talking to me, and God's just—he give me a Scripture, the very first Scripture that God ever really give me. I don't even know where it's at in there, but I just opened up the Bible. I promised him that I would read his book, so I'd read different things. I'd go to church, and they'd share things.

I read a thing that said, "Whether you live or whether you die, you belong to Jesus Christ, belong to God." And I thought Well, God, you got me. God, whatever happens, you let these withdrawals up, this is real, I want to know it. Things started just getting real good. My wife said I looked a lot different. My face was wrinkled. Man, I started changing. I started looking different. I had people come up to me, and they would tell me I looked twenty years younger than I did twenty years ago. People hadn't seen me.

Pretty soon I wasn't sick any more. I didn't urinate blood. It all started just disappearing. I started reading the word. I read another thing in

there that explained to me why all my friends left me. It said, "By losing your life, you will gain life more abundantly." God just told me one night, in my sleep, "You thought you had life, didn't you? Living the way you lived and trying to fill up on things that made you feel good? If you really want life and you want it more abundantly, follow my light. Follow me. Learn to live the way that I set forth for you to live." He just told me that first-handed. He just reached his hand just right out and said, "Grab ahold of me." Follow me is what he was saying. And I started reading the Bible and getting strong. Pretty soon he just really anointed me, and I started really getting strong. God just started blessing me more and more every day. Totally, just, within about five months' time, he just totally healed me. I started looking different. I started feeling different. My life turned around.

You must have gotten married at some point in there, right?

That was about the time we decided to get married. Gabby came back, a couple other guys came back with him, and they kept saying, "You look different, man. What did you do? You look different." I told Gabby, I said, "I know what you're seeing. I got saved, and you're seeing Jesus." And he goes, "Aw, my dad used to be a preacher. I don't buy that." And he said, "Where do you go to church at, then, if you found religion?" I said, "I been going over to the House of Prayer." He goes, "I heard about that church! I ought to check that out one of these days." I said, "Well, I'm going tonight," and I was getting baptized that night. That was the night that Gabby got saved.

I went and got baptized, and Larry started speaking. I looked over there, and there was Jim and his girlfriend down on their knees. Same thing happened to him happened to me. It was great.

I got baptized, and we decided we couldn't live—it wasn't proper under God to live the way we was living. So we was gonna get married. My wife agreed to it. I thought, Well, what the heck. I'm gonna invite all my kids and my mom and my dad, 'cause they wouldn't accept my daughter. My daughter'd been coming around. Probably none of 'em will come, but I'm just gonna do it, and if there's just a big fight at my wedding, there's just gonna be a big fight at my wedding. I'm really gonna put it in God's hands.

All along, you know, they teach you to put it in God's hands and let God handle it. Stop trying to do it on your own. And I thought, Well, Lord, you got this mess. You know my heart. You know I'd like to have a family. You know what I'm concerned about, Lord. It's all yours.

The day I got married, we's setting in there. My mom and dad showed up. It was weird. Dad come up, shook hands with me. My dad was never a touchy person. He's saved now, by the way. My mom come in, and she hugged me and cried and hugged me and cried. Dad come over, was trying to make up and I knew it. I basically told him that I loved him and he didn't have to make up, that we both had our faults. It had been silliness. He agreed. I remember looking at him, thinking, He looks old. God started laying stuff on my heart.

Pretty soon my daughter walks in. This is the daughter they'd never accept. Somebody said, "Are you the matron of honor?" She goes, "No, I'm the daughter." And she looks quite like me. And they'd never seen her. And my dad looked over at her and fell out of his chair. And my mom went running over to her, and they just clicked off.

Well, from that time to now, we go over and have family reunions together. My boys are still—one of 'em's got out of jail, the penitentiary, and he's getting ready to go back. But one of 'em's been going to church, and one of 'em's saved, and the other one's real close. I got all my kids back. All my children are back.

You've got the one boy in Florida, right?

The one boy that don't want nothing to do with me. Yet. But he's going to because God's gonna do it. And I believe that. He was the one from the one marriage I was married under law. And I went down to Daytona. I wanted to see him. I got to see him, but I didn't get to speak to him. I did get to see what he looks like. It felt good. I just know God's gonna handle it.

My family's back together. As a matter of fact, this weekend we're having a grand opening of a store that my dad built for the family. He had hardware stores all his life, when he retired. I go over there quite a bit. My kids—oh, the Lord's just answered every one of my prayers. There was one night, it was so funny: I'd been praying that all my kids would be underneath my roof for one night. I just wanted to have like a big family reunion, and just all my kids.

Just sentimental?

Yeah, just wanted to feel what it'd be like. Kind of like the Waltons or something, I don't know. Just something, some silly little thing that deep in my heart I wanted. I remember coming home one night. I'd been to church. My daughter calls me and says she's living with a guy. Said, "I left my boyfriend." And my grandkids—I had grandkids. I'll never forget the first day my grandson called me Grandpa. I think I cried for two hours.

She called me up. I said, "Well, I'm going to church. Come on in, the house is yours." My boy was getting ready to get out of prison. This is right before we went to Daytona. My other boys decided that they wanted to be here because their brother was getting out of the pen. So he was to be there the next day. I come in from church the next night, and the other boys decided they was gonna stay here. All three of my sons, my daughter, and my grandkids. And my wife's here, pulling her hair out, about to go crazy. And of course my little boy I got now, and the grandkids and him's just running through the house. There, they was all there, and I walked in here and I looked around: Well, they're all staying. They decided they're gonna stay here, and Brad's not got nowhere to stay. Where're we gonna put all these people? I said, "Well, we'll put some of 'em in there. We got bunk beds. The kids can sleep in—we got sleeping bags. We're bikers, we got plenty of sleeping bags. We'll put 'em all down."

"I'll find somewhere tomorrow." I said, "Honey, don't worry about it." "How are we gonna feed all these people?" And we didn't have a whole lot of grub in the house. I'm like, "I don't know. Something'll come up, honey." "What are we gonna do?"

I looked at her and I remember saying to her, I said, "Meg, I prayed for this." She looked at me and said, "You did what?" I said, "I prayed for this. I prayed that all my kids'd be underneath the roof of my house again. She looked at me and said, "You'd better watch what you pray for from now on" and just went about her business. And everything worked out perfectly. They spent a night here, decided they—my boys didn't want to go by my rules of the house, which was not okay but okay. And my daughter, now, has got her a job, and she's moved out, getting her own

place and got her own car now. She's over here a lot, more than I care for her to be sometimes but I love her. We're getting ready to have a grand opening of a hardware store that my dad built for the family, this weekend.

That was my dad's dream. A dream that he'd had all along that I didn't know nothing about. Turns out that he's about as soft as I am. I see now that he went through a lot of the same things that I went through. My dad actually give me a hug for the first time about a year and a half ago.

My life's just totally changed. Oh, I still have my problems, I still have my battles. But I have nothing like I used to have. I don't have near the battles I used to have.

It seems like you and Meg have remarkably honest communication.

Oh, we do. The day we got married, we came home. We was so tired. That same night they wanted us to speak in church, and we did. We come home that night, and we could feel such a difference. And we'd been married with each other all that time and was tight, but we come home, and we both remember talking about what a difference we felt, how it felt different. We felt, actually, as the Bible says, Become one flesh. We have felt that, and we still feel that. When she's hurting, I'm hurting. When I'm hurting, she's hurting. And we pray for it together. We pray together, Lord help me understand her, her understand me. Pull this family together, Lord. I've prayed that prayer with her since I've went to the altar and got delivered. And when we got married there was such an anointing and such a closeness, and it's never let up.

We just had our second anniversary, and it was kind of a strange anniversary. We's broke, didn't have any money. I took the day off work, she took a day off work. We rode our motorcycles together, and we went and got haircuts for our anniversary.

We went to a guy, his wife's having a drug problem and they told him to prepare for her to die. They told her the same thing they told me. We went over there for our anniversary and talked to them. God just led us over there. Once again, we come home, and God give us that closeness, same closeness he give us our wedding night.

Is it difficult to speak that honestly?

Not any more. There was a time when it was. There was a time when I wouldn't tell you—I'm a man, and a man gets hurt just like anybody does. They show emotions differently. God showed me about myself. My emotions would come out in anger. I would want to beat something. When I was hurt I would want to hurt something. God's taught me to know my real self and know that I'm hurt. The only way to get rid of it is to ask him to take care of it.

If there's something I can do, Lord, give me knowledge and wisdom to know what to do to take care of it. If there's not, let me know it, Lord, and take it away. And he does. I can't explain how the Spirit does what it does, how God does what he does. And I can't explain why he made me so strong in him so quick. I have no idea why. All I know is it's not me. There's nothing I can do. It's God, and I give God all the glory.

There's no good thing in me. If it was up to me, man, I'd be robbing your wallet right now. I know you know it deep down, it's God. And I don't know how he does it, why he did it for me, why he's blessing me like that, a person that lived the way and sinned the way that I do. I know that he's already forgiven me for all of it.

The night I got baptized and I come up out of that water, and they told me that all my sins was behind me, cast into the sea of forgiveness, that I could have a new life and I'd be a new person, I was excited and I am still excited. Because every day he gives me something new. Oh, I know the world looks at me, and there's still people that look at me as he's the same old biker. There he is with a woman, twenty years younger than him, same age as his—I know people look at me like that, but I know that God knows God put us together. I don't know why he put her and me together.

The brother that she's got has now got MS, is bedridden, can't get out of a wheelchair. Her dad is, too. She has battles about that, why God don't heal them. And I can't explain that.

And Meg is manic-depressive, right?

Yes.

Is that a struggle?

Not any more. Not any more. She has her times, you know, her woman times, that she gets down. But God uses me to lift her up, and God uses her to lift me up anytime I have bad times. And we're there for each other. It's God. I don't know how to explain it. It's like, when she's hurting, God lets me know she's hurting, and I get there for her. Even if I got to go out of my way to baby her and it's silly. She's a real special person. She's real special.

To see her, to talk to her, you'd think she's just rougher than—tougher than nails, and she's not. And you think I am, too, at times, when you see me out working on the bike. I go ninety mile an hour, and you know that this year I carried all the water for the Boogie. But God lets me know when she's hurting. I just know how to push her buttons both ways. It goes both ways.

I don't know how to explain it. God uses me. I pray for her when she goes through her bad moments with her family. The devil tries to drag her down. And God lets me know that it's him and when it's him. He also lets me know when it's just worldly things. He gives me words to say, just the right words.

The world does it—as the word says, "You will live in tribulation." We have a lot of tribulation. I wasn't in a methadone program. They come and tried to take our little boy away because if I wasn't in the program, then I was using, according to the world. I wasn't. They drug-tested me and took blood out of me every month for two years and messed with us, and the welfare was down our throats, and they messed with us heavy-duty for two years. And that was heavy tribulation. It was hard.

We relied on God, and we kept praying about it, and finally one day, the caseworker, the very caseworker that give us trouble, she's saved. God touched her heart, and now it's dropped. We don't have any trouble. We're family. That's my little boy in there.

How much do you talk about your past or your present with him?

Unless he comes to me and asks me, we don't talk about it. There's times that he remembered me drinking "yucko beers," he calls it. He remembered me. He remembers. He'll mention it. And I'll say, "Yeah, daddy used to do that, but Daddy's not the same person as he used to be, and Daddy don't do it anymore. Jesus is forgiving."

Is he aware of things like heroin?

No, he's only six years old. But he knows beer. There's a different way of life, and he remembers some of the old bikers. They used to set him on

their lap, and we'd eat hot peppers, and he'd eat hot peppers with us. They wouldn't give him beer. Just because they lived in the world, they weren't bad people. They were the same as me. They were lost. There was one guy called Chief that—I don't know where he's at now but I pray for him and I love him—that he was a big old rough guy, and that little boy could sit on his lap, and that guy would melt. And even though I was in the world, I seen that then. And he'd shot people and killed people and he was a big old rough guy and he had tattoos all over him and lots of parts of his body pierced and did anything that there was to do, and that little boy'd sit in his lap. And you'd better not ever say anything bad about that little boy.

He maybe wouldn't handle it right, but you could see the goodness. You could really feel it and see it. And he remembers him, and he remembers people setting, eating hot peppers. And he mentions it sometimes.

As he gets older, will you talk frankly about that world and your past with him?

Unless God tells me to, no. If God tells me I need to tell him, for a reason. I just rely on God. For everything. I had my life. Forty years I run my own life, and it was such a mess. I had my body to where it was just a mess. I was dead spiritually. I didn't have life. I was getting closer and closer to death, carnal death, and I was already spiritually dead. If God tells me to do it, I will.

He's told me no. He's told me to put my past behind me and go forward. Told me to put my hands on the plow and go straight forward is what the Lord told me to do. And not look back and not worry about it because he'd already forgiven me. And that's exactly what I do.

Oh, yeah, old Satan comes up and says—he'll put somebody in my way to remind me of things

I done. And make me feel not worthy. And I'm not worthy! It's by the blood of Jesus, and I know that. The price has already been bought and paid. God showed me that and told me that. I've only be saved three and a half years, and he's given me the Bible in doses. You know, they say that you start supping milk, well, he give me barrels of milk real quick. I don't know why. I know why: He's got a need for me. He knows where I'm supposed to be. He put me where he wanted me to be.

I went through battles, and I still do. Yes, there's times I look at a pretty woman, and I have to get down on my knees and fight like a man. Remember how I told you I wasn't gonna be a sissy and get on my knees? Well, now I consider that fighting like a man. Let me tell you what: I thought I was tough before packing a .38 and carrying knives all over me. You really want to be tough, you go to the Boogie and tell people about Jesus. You can do that, you're tough. And God showed me that.

And there've been times when I got weak, and the Lord showed me that I got to stay in fellowship with other Christians. I got to stay firmly rooted. I've got to stay in the word, I've got to stay in constant prayer. He's give me such blessings. To see one of my big old brothers get down on his knees, and all his sins get cast in the sea of forgiveness and his life change, and him to have what I have, whew! That is more riches than I've ever had. There's no hot rod, there's no motorcycles, there's no house, there's no fur coat, there's no leather coat worth that. And I mean that from the heart.

People that I hurt—I told you I used to go to bed and it hurt me, the people that I hurt. One of the boys that bought the bike—I just sold the Rainmaker—he come over here to buy a motorcycle, he gets saved! That's one of the ones that I—I'm one of the ones that ruined his life. I'm one of the ones that started him smoking dope. My kid run with him, he went to prison with my kid. He's out, my kid's still in there. God's not done with my kid yet. Whatever God's will is is fine with me. That boy, I can see it. I can feel it. God's gonna make him a warrior. He's gonna be riding right along beside me

My past, and I told you, and I been through a lot of other things that I haven't told you. God reached his hand down, and he pulled me out of a mess, and he give me life when I was done give up. And that's the only reason I want this story out is so that it will glorify God. If it's for any other reason, then you're doing it for the wrong reason. And if it's to glorify God, to let people hear the story of the gospel of hope and peace, that's why I want it out. It's because it's true and it's real, and I can't explain it all, and I don't know how it's all done, but it is real. It's not faking. I'm not getting paid for this or getting profit for this in any other way other than I want God to be glorified. That's all I got to say.

THE WORLD

It is a five-minute walk from the reception desk to the back of the plant where Chico works, assembling cam boxes for elevators. To pass the time, the human resources manager tells me some statistics about the company.

We stop for a moment at a table where a dozen workers are taking a break. They complain to the human resources manager that when the company held the drawing for the fire extinguisher somebody from the front office won and it seems like that was always the case. People on the line never win the fire extinguisher or the fire alarm or any of the drawings. Others talk about finishing last night's golf game early enough to have time for extra beer.

I recognize a familiar face. He smiles, says hello, and we shake hands. Mike is the greeting usher at the House of Prayer and was the first to welcome me there as well. He tells me he has worked here for nearly twenty-eight years.

Chico has worked here for fifteen. "I thank him for . . . all the things that he's done for us. He's provided me with a good job." For the most part, the members of the gang work in factories, or as truck drivers and clerical workers or in similar occupations. Some like their work; some do not. For many, their jobs are only a portion of the conflict of living in a world from which they feel profoundly alienated yet in which they still must participate.

Perhaps as a consolation for enduring this conflict, perhaps as a means of survival in it, the bikers' faith does not require waiting until death to receive their rewards. They manage and prosper in this world, largely by a flowing abundance of blessings from God. In church it is often expressed as an enticement, a small taste of what is to come after the Rapture.

Chico at work on an assembly line.

John at work as an elementary school custodian.

Gabby at work, hauling a load of gypsum.

Gabby blessing his food at a truck stop.

Nancy at work in her father's insurance agency.

In addition to being the spiritual leader of the group, Pastor Larry is also the best mechanic in the bunch. It is not unusual for the congregation to wait in line to talk with him after services, as is the case in any church. Only about half will discuss spiritual matters, however. The other half asks about tires or hydraulics.

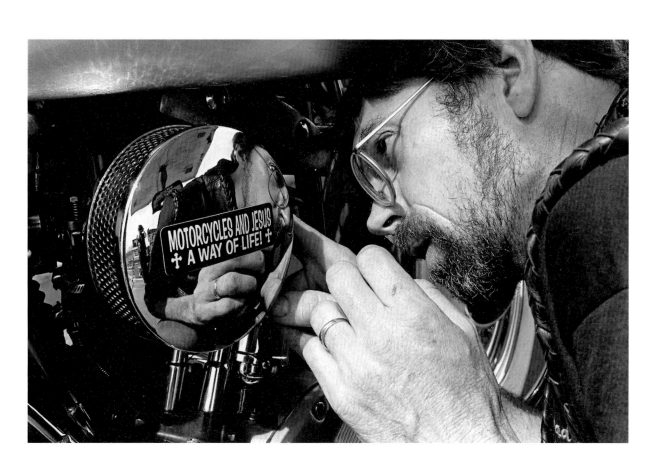

Sparky working on his bike.

Sparky at home with his son, Marcus.

Sparky and Marcus.

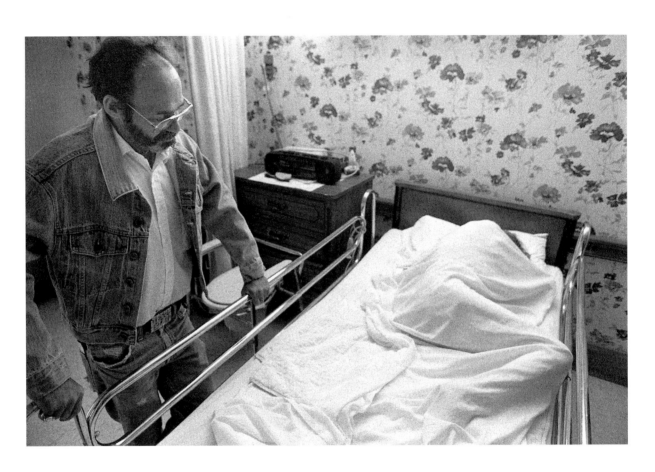

Paul visits his father in the Alzheimer's ward of the nursing home.

PAUL

I've been through a rough time for the past long time. Quite a while. But it's mainly been analyzing the words that I speak and being held accountable for the words that I speak. Going through some hard times because of the words that I speak.

Give me an example.

Fears that I have, I've had to walk through. Things that I have said before that I had pretty well conquered in the area of a fear or something. Or even a character deficiency. I've had to walk through and make decisions, and usually I make the wrong one. From a pure character to an impure decision.

So these would be problems that you had some time ago, and then you made a decision and you thought you came out the other side?

I've made a lot of decisions, many of which I feel like have been not led by the Spirit but led by the flesh, led by impure motives or lack of boldness. Just, I don't know, all I can say is what I told the Unchained Gang one time a couple weeks ago—maybe you were there—I said I've been through a really rough year. It was pretty rough, but I have so grown closer to the Lord in the midst of it. It's like, I don't know, it's almost like a fire. A purifying fire. Even though I'm not pure yet.

And I know, I realize, I'm an impure vessel. I realize there are lots of things that need changed in me yet. But I've also recognized that God still loves me, even in the midst of my insecurity, the midst of my bungling. His will for my life, he still loves me. Just to rest in the fact that God still loves me, who has sinned against him even

after I've been a Christian. Willfully sinned against him.

This isn't the first time that's happened, is it?

Maybe not the first time, but . . .

You've told me before about you had a period where you were living with a woman.

Yeah. That was one case, yes.

What was going on then?

I had been a Christian about six years. I was serving the Lord fervently, going into the jails, preaching the Gospel anywhere I could. And I went through what the world would call a nervous breakdown, emotional breakdown. I would call it backsliding, 'cause I went and bought twelve beers, six beers, I don't know, maybe twelve. And I was drinking and driving back roads, crazy and out of control. What happened, I don't know. Just dropped on me.

And I ended up in jail—and this is after I'd ministered in jails—and I ended up in the mental health center over here at the hospital, stress center. And I was diagnosed paranoid schizophrenic.

It's like a big chunk of my faith had a big hole knocked in it. See, the word talks about we have a shield of faith. It talks about armor that the soldier of God has, the helmet of salvation, the breastplate of righteousness, loins girded with truth, feet shod with the preparation of the gospel of peace, and the shield of faith, where with we're able to stop all the fiery darts of Satan.

Well, my shield of faith had a great big hole in it because of this. I felt like God should have kept me from what happened, but he never. I didn't realize how much was my part to do and how much was his part to do. There's things in the Bible, promises, that have requirements attached to them. He will if we do. There's just a lot of those things in the Bible that have not only consequences but requirements.

In what way did you not live up to your part of it?

Well, without faith it's impossible to please God. It's scriptural. Bible says that. It says, "He who comes to him must believe that he is rewarder of those who diligently seek him." On those two Scriptures rests almost the whole, the whole basis of Christianity. On one you have to believe that God is. And you have to believe that he wants the best for you and that the word is true. That he rewards, maybe not in this life, maybe in this life, but he does have rewards for those who diligently seek him.

I lost track of those things. I got to looking at now. And whenever I backslid I was listening to lies. See, a lot of people don't realize how Satan manifests himself to Christians, and that's through the mind, through thoughts. The world would say, Well, it's natural to have impure thoughts. Well, it may be natural, but it's not supernatural.

I believe that these thoughts come from demonic forces. If you listen to the lies long enough you start believing them, because they're subtle. They're lies that would say to you, for instance, You couldn't be a Christian because you couldn't live the life. You just couldn't stand the legalistic control over your life. That's a lie, because you could. God didn't make anybody who's not able to.

What were the lies you were hearing?

One of them was that God hadn't answered my prayers about my wife. See, I'd been divorced

ever since I been a Christian. This is six years ago. I'd prayed for her for six years. I'd prayed for a reunion of my marriage for six years. I'd prayed for my farm back, my home in the country. And none of these things happened.

Then the thoughts that came was, See, God's not listening to you. God doesn't care. You might as well forget serving God. He's not gonna hear your prayers. And if you buy into the lies, then you're an open target for anything else to come through that shield.

What else came through?

Oh, nicotine did. The main thing that hurt was the faith itself was damaged. Without faith—and I'm not meaning just mouthing faith, I'm talking about faith that's walked out. I'm talking about faith that's lived—without faith, nothing of God works. Nothing. Without faith, the word of God is God's word and that he designed it to be the guidelines for a person's life. Without faith, nothing of God works, because it's just the way it is.

My faith had a tremendous flaw in it. And all of the studying and seeking God and prayer was constructive. It was construction for my faith. God is so loving that he will allow you to get into situations where you must have faith, where you don't have anything but faith.

What was that point for you?

There's been several. Many. See, I've had this fear of dogs for a long time. Ever since—oh, I was on my motorcycle one time at a friend's house, Gene Kelly. We was setting there, talking about the Lord. I got on my motorcycle to leave, and the dog clamped onto my leg and put teeth marks on both sides of my calf. That was just one instance. I had this thing about dogs, and it bothered me. And I'm not completely victorious over it yet.

I was hunting a house a while back. It was somebody that would give some clothes to somebody that I was supposed to take somewhere, and I couldn't find their house. And I saw this house and I thought it was it, but there were two big dogs in the yard. I mean big dogs. And it was before daylight. It was like five o'clock in the morning or so. And I felt like I was prayed up and I was ready to face whatever God had for me that day. And I got out of the truck in that drive, and those two dogs came running out, and I got out of the truck, and I walked up to the door, and I knocked on the door. Something said to me, "Fear not, for if you do, you're dead." That's just what I heard at that time.

Well, that's not like me, 'cause I'm timid. It's not bragging, either. It's the fact that it's just an area of growth that I walked through at that particular time in my life. That's only one time. Given the same situation again, I don't know how I would react. I don't know if I would have the boldness to walk through it again. But for that time, God used it as a growth tool in my life.

There've been a lot of little things. There's been times when I've walked through impending death situations. I mean in my mind. They were mental, I'll admit. They were probably imagination, but to me they were as real as you and I sitting here.

What kind of situations?

Well, once I was going on a field call at work. I work at Crane. You know about what Crane does? They store ammunition. Okay, I was going on a field call. As soon as I started to get in the truck, something said, "If you get in this truck, you'll never live through it." I mean it was that

clear and that vivid in my mind. And I said, "I'm a child of God. I'm going anyway." So I got in the truck, and I drove out there. Well, all the time it got more intense: "Don't go, don't go. If you go, you're a dead man."

I got out there, and it was a bunker, and it was way out in the boonies, and there was a team of men standing out. The forklift was broke down inside the ammunition bunker, and it was full of bombs or projectiles or something pretty explosive. High explosives, anyway. I started down from the pathway, and something said, "It'll blow to pieces before you get out of there." 'Cause I was the only one there. All the other people were way back, back away from it.

This thing was so intense and so overwhelming, I just started singing "Peace in the Valley." [Sings, "There will be peace in the valley for me some day."] And I walked on up to the bunker, and I walked in. There was a forklift that was broke down, had a blown hose. I couldn't fix it there. It was one of those cases that had to be taken in. So I walked back out, knowing that it was going to have to be taken in. Got in my truck and left.

It seems like, telling it, that it was a real minor thing. But you don't know the mental. The things I went through just—and that's not an isolated case.

Where did that voice come from?

I'd say it had to be demonic. Because it was a lie. It never materialized, see? God's not the father of lies. Satan is the father of lies. He's a liar and the father of it, Jesus said.

I think that we can judge some of our thoughts in the thought life by whether they come to pass or not. To learn to discern where they're coming from. See, in the Old Testament, a prophet of

God was never wrong. That was one of the requirements of a prophet of God: He was never wrong. That's how they knew he was a prophet.

The Lord has shown me a lot about mercy and grace the past year. The times when I've failed to be bold, to share Jesus with somebody, to do the things that I probably should have known to do, by the word. I'm recognizing that he has mercy and grace.

In forgiving you for not having done that?

And he's shown me, like in almost every book in the Bible, that Paul wrote, he writes in about the first or second verse in the first chapter of each book, "Grace, mercy, and peace from God the Father and the Lord Jesus Christ." He was a man who had persecuted the church, and he had done a lot of things wrong, to Christians. And I think this man knew about grace, and he knew about mercy, and he knew about peace because he'd walked through it.

I'm learning more about grace and mercy. I mean, I'm not super-spiritual. I'm just somebody who's trying to serve the Lord as best I can. I have fears within and fears without. I'm not ready to walk into a lion's den. If God leads me there, I guess I have to go. There's no other choice.

It seems like the intercessors' convention in Atlanta really affected you a lot.

It was good. It was a time, but even though I was going through stuff down there, too, in my mind. I fasted almost the whole time I was down there, just because of the mind games, being with strange people who I knew from the church but I didn't really know. But I really got some deliverance there.

I believe I came close to realizing what the New Testament talked about when it talks about—in the Upper Room they were of one accord. In the Upper Room, before the Holy Spirit was poured out, they said they were of one accord. The 120, or however many was there, were of one accord. That means they were of one mind. They were of one attitude.

And down at that Intercessors 500 in Atlanta, it was like the whole group, the whole five hundred or however many were there, was of one accord in praise and worship, in communing with God.

And that's different from what you experience in church?

It's like turning up the intensity a hundred times. That's what it amounts to. And I think part of it is because if you get 290 some people in there, which is about an average Sunday service, you're going to have 150 of 'em that maybe don't—ain't really on fire for Jesus, who are really wanting everything God's got for them. So if you've got 150 in a service of 290, you've got a few that really want to enter into God's presence, who really want to worship God. And they can carry it. They can rest in God's presence.

God'll be there anyway. I'm just saying the intensity, I guess you could call it, of his presence is not as great because of the one accord, I think. They're not of one accord. It's like, you could put five people together and be praising the Lord, and if one of 'em don't even know the Lord, it may affect the others somewhat. It's like a damper's been placed on the—well, it's the same way at a church service. It's not to say that you need to isolate churches and make 'em all Christian. I'm not saying that, because they are to be outreaches for the unbelievers. But it's nice sometimes to be in complete accord, where everybody is just leaving everything behind and pressing into fellowship with Christ.

What can you take from that experience once you come back to Indiana? How is your life different from having had that experience?

I think it's caused me to be more of an intercessor for other people. And I think it's given me a more intimate relationship with the Father. It's like I yielded down there some things that I had held locked up inside, that I would just not let go of, that I just—you probably want to know what things.

If you want to tell me.

Well, just probably in the area of that faith. A damaged shield of faith that had never really truly been repaired. Faith cometh by hearing and hearing by the word of God. So the word of God can repair damaged faith, but I think down there it got a more complete overhaul. It was like something was birthed in me. The Holy Spirit was birthed. It was like I gave birth. I gave birth to a new spirit-man that came out of me to commune with the Father.

In September, Randy told me that he saw you on your motorcycle, that you were taking a leave of absence from work to go be a missionary.

Yeah, I had thought about doing that. I really felt like I wanted to just go spread the gospel and go and go and go. And I was ready to go.

You had your motorcycle all packed?

Yeah. And I stopped at the mission, and that, I guess, was a mistake if that's what God wanted me to do. I don't know what happened. It just seemed—I was ready. I mean I was eager to. I

don't know why I stopped, but I did. I have to trust—I wanted to go to Texas, too, but I don't know why things just don't, you know, didn't come about. It wasn't so much that I was fearful. I don't know. Circumstances didn't come together for it.

What happened at the mission?

We had church service that morning. I don't know if Gene talked me out of it or if I talked myself out of it. I don't really know what happened.

But after church you just decided not to go?

Yeah. Yeah.

Do you think that was the right thing to do?

Not really, 'cause I was planning on seeing Randy at Texas.

What did you go through, then, after you decided not to go?

I don't know. It's been a terrible struggle with my job all year, too. Had I went that day, I don't know if I was—well, I had told them I wanted a thirty-day leave of absence without pay, to just see what God was doing. I didn't have any money. It would have been a complete total leap of faith, other than credit cards.

That's another thing the Lord's been teaching me: trust. If God calls it, God pays for it. And if he don't call it, we pay for it.

How has he shown you that?

Things that I needed to go to, I had the money for. Right now, I'm in a situation where I don't know if I'm in God's will or not. I'm on sick leave, pending a disability retirement. And I don't know if I'm in God's will or if I'm in my flesh or what I'm doing.

That's hard for you, I imagine.

Well, one guy that works there is not a believer, he says it's a cop-out.

What does he mean by that?

Taking the easy way out.

I know, but out of what?

Out of working. And it does seem to be the easy way out, but there are—I don't know. I'm not gonna—I don't know. I figure if God doesn't want me to take it, it won't be approved.

So this is something you've applied for, then?

Well, I've told 'em to apply for it. I haven't applied for it yet.

But you instigated it?

Yeah.

And this is based on the diagnosis of . . .

Two doctors.

For paranoid schizophrenia?

[Nods yes.]

What do you think of that diagnosis?

I think it's spiritual. I always have thought it was spiritual.

Meaning what?

Meaning that it's a spiritual problem not a psychological problem.

Lack of faith, you mean?

Yeah. To me, paranoid schizophrenia reduces down to fear. What's one of the symptoms of paranoid schizophrenia is a conspiracy to do harm to you. Or good to you, either one. But what is that? That narrows down to fear, that somebody would want to do—some group, some large group of people—would want to do me harm.

As a Christian, who cares? See, that should be the attitude. Even if you do feel like that's happening, what difference should it make? To a Christian? And I'm not grown through all of the things about that that I believe.

Do you think there is a psychological foundation to that, though? Even if that's true, it shouldn't matter to a Christian?

I think even if you feel like there is a conspiracy, it shouldn't matter. However, I can see how it could cause tremendous stress over a long period of time, to feel like this conspiracy's going on and on and on and on and on and on and on.

Do you feel like that?

I have. For a year.

And that conspiracy's the devil?

Well, I'm not convinced. I'll just say conspiracy. The Bible says all things work together for good to them that love the Lord, who are called according to his purpose. So I have to look at it. Maybe God's using it to do some work inside of me, to change me, in the areas that I need changed and weaknesses that I have in my body, in my flesh.

See, a lot of people don't realize what Christianity's all about. God has shown me the whole purpose of God's Christianity is that we be conformed into the image of Christ. So that everybody who professes Jesus Christ is an example of Jesus Christ. Now everybody you meet is gonna be in a place because God is an individual God. He works individually with each person. And the things that this Christian over here has got victory over, this one over here hasn't. But this one over here has come through some things that this one hasn't. So God's in the process of forming both of them into the Christ likeness.

The only way you can be formed into Christ likeness is for the flesh, the me part, my rights, my will, my desires, my, my anything, to be destroyed, so that it's not my will but thy will.

The Lord's Prayer: Matthew, aw, I forget where it's at, but anyway, it says, "Thy will be done on earth as it is in Heaven." Thy will be done. That means not my will but thy will. And Jesus prayed that in the Garden at Gethsemane before the Crucifixion. Not my will, but thy will. If it be possible, let this cup pass from me, but nevertheless not my will but thy will, see? So he gave up his own will for the will of the Father. And that's what God wants for us, too. But sometimes it takes us a lifetime to get there.

Do you talk about things like this with your doctors?
Yeah.

What do they think of it?

Well, last time I told 'em that I thought I was hearing from God, they sent me to the stress center. I didn't understand it. But I know I preached while I was there, and there were a few people that were touched by the power of God. I don't know. It was just another episode in my life.

Did they give you medication or anything? Do you take medication now?

Haphazardly. That's one thing, paranoid-schizophrenics don't take medication very good, from what I've heard. I'll tell you the main reason I take it, and it's really simple: I could sleep. That's it. I tried to tell my doctor. I said if you give me a good sleeping pill it'd probably do me as much good as all this psychological medication you been giving me.

So you don't notice a difference?

Not that much. The symptoms still—you know. I guess it helps, but . . .

Have you claimed a healing?

Yeah. I thought I was walking in it. But I know, too, that God doesn't heal everything. But I know that he never puts more on us than we can bear. And I know that Paul had a thorn in his flesh—and I don't know what it was—that God didn't heal. Nobody knows what it was, they just know that he had one. God told him he was putting it there. Or it was Paul said in one of his writings, it was put there to keep him from being exalted above measure after all the things that God had revealed to him that he not be prideful.

I don't know. We don't understand all the things of God. I believe God is a healer, and I'll still believe God is a healer. And I believe I'm gonna walk in divine health. Someday. I believe that we can lay hands on the sick and they'll recover. Maybe not all of them. That won't stop me from praying for people. I don't understand all that God does, but I know that God has shown me some things in the spiritual world that some others have never experienced or even know about.

Like?

Like the fact that he will not override a will—your will, my will, a Christian's will, any will. He will direct and he will bring people across your path to direct you and push you in an area, but it's still your will. It's up to you to decide. Will you do this or thus? Will you follow Jesus or not? He will not override that. That's free choice that God gives everyone. We're free moral agents. I used to think, when I was praying for my wife, I knew that he would not override a will, but it was made real clear to me when I have made wrong decisions in my Christian walk that were outside of God's will. He leaves me to make wrong decisions, I guess so I'll learn, I don't know. So I'll learn to make right decisions.

There must have been times where he's surprised you with unexpected rewards.

Yeah, yeah, he has. Many times. Every time I sing it's a blessing. He's let me sing and gave me a talent for music, hundreds of songs in my mind. Just a memory for 'em. I don't know, I can't remember your name, but I've got thirty songs in this tape box that I can sing all the words of all the songs.

How did you know you'd been anointed that way?

That's a good question. I think I first noticed it when the Lord allowed me into the holy of holies, in praise and worship. The holy of holies in the temple, or in the tabernacle of Moses. It was the holiest of all. And inside the holiest of all, only the high priests went once a year, only with a blood sacrifice. Inside of that was the Arc of the Covenant, which resided the presence of Almighty God. On top of it was the mercy seat, [on] which blood was sprinkled for the atonement of the people of Israel once a year. It was

so holy that no sin could dwell there. The high priest went in with bells around his skirt and a rope around his foot, and if he died while he was in there and they quit hearing the bells they pulled him out under the thing. It was that holy.

When Jesus died on the cross, the curtain between the holiest and the holiest of all, the holy of holies, was rent from top to bottom. It was a drape, they say. I've heard it's four inches thick. That was torn from top to bottom, signifying that God did it and man never. Not from bottom to top but top to bottom. Opening up the holy of holies for the congregation to fellowship with God, in the place, because Jesus was the high priest. Jesus, with his own blood, sanctified the holiest of all and made it to where the congregation could come in.

Well, whenever I used to praise and worship I would close my eyes, and I would just be transported. I could just visualize the Arc of the Covenant, even though I can't tell you what it looked like, just that it was gold. And that I was in the presence of God, and that I was singing these songs to God. Not about God, to God. In the process of singing these songs to God, his anointing came through like a snowball. The anointing came through, and I felt the anointing, and I felt more in God's presence and the anointing came through.

That's one of the reasons I stay away from the medication. It stifles that free-flowing into the spirit realm. I don't want to trust in feelings. I know feelings cannot be trusted. Emotions are not trustworthy. Emotions are of the flesh. We need to trust in the fact that the spirit-man is in control, and that God's word is true, and if we don't feel something that doesn't mean that God's not there. It's nice to experience that presence with the most high.

I've got to tell you, Paul—and I hope this doesn't embarrass you—your command of Scriptures and your knowledge of Scriptures is really amazing. Do you just read all the time? Where does that knowledge come from?

I read a lot.

Just the Bible, or do you read commentaries, too?

I read commentaries; I read the Bible; I read books that are laced with Scripture. I read studies, I listen to preaching on TV, I read magazines. I get three or four magazines from different preachers.

When you say commentaries, do you mean like the Confessions of St. Augustine or Billy Graham?

I've read *The City of God* of St. Augustine. I've not read the Confessions of St. Augustine. I've been told that I need to.

Why is that?

Because I have a poor self-image. And he had a poor self-image. But anyway, I've never read it. I've got a Bible commentary by somebody, I can't even think of his name. I read it. And I read several translations of the Bible, too.

Do you read in Greek or Hebrew?

I've got a interlinear Greek New Testament. I don't read Greek. I do have a Strong's Concordance, which has a Hebrew/Greek dictionary in it, and I use it some but not extensively. Most of it's just things I've picked up here and there.

From what you've told me about your life before you were saved, I can't imagine you were very bookish then. Is that right?

No. No.

A lot of people have told me that when they were saved that one of the hard things was that they had never read before, and suddenly they had to start reading the Bible. And that was hard to just have the discipline to read. You seem to really have taken to it.

I think whenever the Holy Spirit come to live within you, you get thirsty. You get thirsty for the word. It's like the word is the road map. It's like you can get to Heaven without it, but you can't be conformed into what God wants you to be without it. It's like the molding tool that the potter uses to conform you into what he wants you to be.

There's people who have lived Christian lives, and the Holy Spirit convicts them of things that are wrong inside of them without very much of the word. Especially in foreign countries where they can't get very much of the word. They cling to a page. But the Lord has also shown me that a vast knowledge of the Scripture is no good without putting it into your feet and your hands.

You said that you get a lot of that from hearing the word, though. What kind of process do you go through when you're trying to grow in the Lord?

Allowing the word to be alive in your life.

I know you hate it when I get specific, but give me an example.

Okay, the word says, "Be ye doers of the Word, not hearers only." Says that in James. Well, that means—Jesus said one time, "By this shall all men know that you're my disciples, if you have love one for another."

Okay, now, the first Scripture I quoted said, "Be ye doers of the Word, not hearers only." Jesus said, "By this shall ye know that you're my disciples, if you have love one for another." If I walk into church and I'm bitter at half the people in there for this or that, that's not having love for one for another. So if I don't walk in this Scripture that I know—now, I'm not talking about Scripture that you don't know, or you've never read, or you don't know anything about, or you didn't even know that was in there. I'm talking about what you do know. It says, "By this shall ye know that you're my disciples, if you have love one for another." I need to walk in love among the believers.

So you'll just remember that passage and then . . .

And try to walk in it. It goes a little deeper than that. God'll even connect that to First Corinthians 13, which is the love chapter. Tells what God's idea about love is. Love does not hold grudges. Love is not self-seeking. Love is not arrogant or high-minded. I forget all the things it says. First Corinthians, thirteenth chapter gives all the attributes of love.

The passage they always read at weddings.

Well, they do sometime, yeah. But I think it's more important than that. Any family man ought to read it about once a week to his wife. And his wife ought to listen, and they ought to apply it. Because it's agape love is what it's talking about. That's the God kind of love.

You work with a lot of non-Christians. You must take that covenant into the workplace with you.

I'd say my workplace testimony is probably the poorest that I have.

Why is that?

'Cause I don't like mechanicin'. It's all I've ever done. It's all I've ever been trained in. It's all I know. And I don't like it.

You're a heavy equipment mechanic?

Well, forklifts, basically. But I have talent in it. God has blessed me with it, and I should be thankful for it, but I'm not. I'd say of all the places that I have a poor testimony is at work.

Do they stifle you there?

No, not that much. They have tried to.

They tell you, "Don't talk about Jesus at work"?

No, they don't tell me that. It's been pretty free, pretty open.

Do they argue with you?

No. No. I just sing most of the time. They hear the gospel through music. Whenever the radio's not playing country, I'm singing. When I was going through some real rough times when I was working for the army side in production, it's like whenever the pressure would come on harder, I'd sing louder. It seemed like the more they'd throw at me or that Satan would throw at me, I'd sing louder. I don't know if they appreciate it or not. 'Course I didn't really care. And I'm still here, so I survived. They didn't work me to death.

What's your life like at home?

Not very good. I've got a father who's in the Alzheimer's unit of the Hospitality House. I've got a mother who's partially disabled with a stroke and heart surgery.

And you live with her?

[Nods yes.]

So you have to take care of them?

Well, they take care of my dad at the Hospitality House. I go down and see him once in a while. I used to see him a lot. It just got to be too emotionally draining, so about once or twice a week I see him maybe. Maybe two or three times a week. I used to see him every day.

There for a while, I was just seeing him on Tuesday night when we had church service down there. I help out down there with the guy that has church service on Tuesday night.

Are your folks believers?

Yeah, I don't understand my dad. I've prayed for him, and I've prayed for him, and I've prayed for him. I've prayed for the Lord to touch him and heal him or take him home, either one, I don't care. And nothing changes.

But I can't make myself God. If I do that, I'm back on the wrong side of—First Commandment says, "Thou shalt have no other gods before me." That's the most frequently broken commandment. That's the one that I make myself god above Almighty God. It means I choose to do what I know God says is wrong. And I make myself a god, over him. We make a lot of gods. Sex used to be my god.

And that got you in some trouble?

Yeah. Got me venereal disease, it got me beat up a time or two, it got me married to a real young girl. It just got to be too big a thing in my life. It was what I lived for, basically. It's why I got married, which was the wrong reason.

You just had the one marriage?

Uh huh. Bible has a lot to say about marriage, too. Good stuff. Marriage is ordained by God. It's beautiful. It's one of the most holy institutions there is. Even, it's so holy that God calls us, the church, the bride of Christ. The marriage relationship is so holy on earth that he even compares the heavenly relationship to it. The intimacy that a bride has with a husband, God wants us to have with him. There's just a lot of similarities between a bride and a husband and a marriage relationship.

That's why Satan fights so hard to destroy it, to pervert it, to twist it, you know? 'Cause it is. Look at it logically: You break the marriage, you break the tax structure, you break the economy, you break the nation, you don't send missionaries out any more, the churches are disintegrating. See what you've done if you destroy one factor in our society?

You think you'll get married again?

Yeah, I think so. Maybe to the same one, maybe not.

She's not saved, is she?

[Shakes head no.]

So you're praying for her to be saved?

I told her I wanted to talk to her. Had some things to say. Haven't maybe got the nerve yet to do it. [Laughs.]

Is she willing to talk to you?

Yeah, she's pretty hostile. She went though a lot.

You were drinking a lot?

Yeah, and we had some other problems, too. See, I always have been a person with a pretty low self-image. And I know it says in the Bible when we become saved all things become new. "Old things are passed away: behold, all things become new." But one thing that did not become new in me was my self-image being so low. It's being changed, but it's still, I'm not, you know. But I'm coming to the place where anything good in me is Christ, and anything that's not is something that's not been changed.

And that poor self-image was carried through a lot of my marriage. It manifested itself in jealousy. I looked in the mirror, and I saw a shrimp who was five-foot, three-inches tall, who was not all that handsome and good-looking, married to this beautiful, queenlike creature. And what did she see in me? And if I was her, I'd probably be cheating on me, because I would've were the situation reversed.

Being as I approached the relationship with that attitude of jealousy, that she was probably cheating on me 'cause I had such a poor—it caused lots of problems. Lots of problems. Jealousy is a destroyer. Trust is a builder.

Would you marry her again if she weren't saved?

If she weren't saved? [Very long pause.] I don't know. The Bible says, "Be ye not unequally yoked together with unbelievers." [Another long pause.] I don't think so. I don't know. I still love her. That part of me still works, but I don't know if could. The Holy Spirit would have to convict me.

I've seen it work backwards. Many women who fall for an unsaved man, who think, "I'm gonna get him saved after we get married," and it never works. They always, the godly one is pulled away. I mean, not always, but many times the godly one is pulled away from his faith into whatever lifestyle the other one has. I don't think I'm that weak that that would happen, but you know. I also know what the Scripture says, too, so . . . so I don't know.

It's kind of an unfair question. But you haven't been dating anyone in the church?

No, took one motorcycle riding once, and I dated one other lady. Took her to coffee once. She got married on me. I was kinda hoping that something might get going there.

She was a Christian?

[Nods yes.]

I'm not opposed to dating. It's like I've not been totally released yet, in fifteen years.

From your old ways?

From my old wife. Released free, feeling divorced. Because a long time ago the Lord kind of quickened in my spirit for me—not for anybody else, this is not for anybody else but just for me—when she remarried, that would be a closed door. And I have Scripture to back that up. That was something that I felt like the Lord spoke into my spirit, and she never has remarried. I don't know.

I've also come to the point where I'm willing to be whatever God wants me to be. If he wants me to spend the rest of my life celibate, I'm ready to do that, too. Not willingly. It would be kicking and scratching all the way, but if that's God's will, that's God's will. He will bless what he calls. He calls something like that, he'll give me the strength to go through it.

Does it worry you that that would be a stumbling block?

Yes it does. Well, it's like a—it's like a shadow. It's kind of over you, but Lord, please don't ask that. [Laughs.]

But when we say Jesus is lord, it means—the word *lord*, did you ever look it up or hear anybody explain what it means? It means master, ruler, king, full authority. It means full authority in my life.

It says in Romans 10, 9 and 10, if we confess with our mouth and believe in our heart that Jesus is lord, we shall be saved. Now it don't say confess that he is God, confess that he is almighty. 'Course those things have to be in there, too. But confess that he is lord. That means that he has full authority in my life, see?

When I confess that he has full authority in my life, then he can start changing me into what he wants me to be. And so many people, I feel like, are walking in the area of, they've accepted him as savior and not lord. My sins are forgiven. I'm justified before God but not enough to obey him, see?

So what was that point for you?

When I truly got saved, I feel like.

Yeah, but did you hit bottom before that?

I had moved out on my wife, moved out of the house. Left her and a nine-year-old daughter at home and started staying in the bars, living in a motel. And I'd done this about two or three weeks, and my wife came down to the bar where I was at one Saturday night and told me that is this what I wanted? And I said, "I don't know what I want; I'm still thinking." And she said, "Well, I've made my decision. I'm filing for divorce." She left, and I stayed at the bar and drank till about three A.M., when it closed. It was the Bassaloon.

The next day, I never slept any that night. I's too torn up about my marriage broke up and I still loved her. And it was chaos. I was mentally a wreck. I needed somebody to talk to, bad. So I went to the mental health center, and I didn't find anybody to talk to there. I may have been in the wrong place, I don't know. I was still drunk from drinking all night. Hadn't had any sleep,

and it was five or six o'clock in the morning, or seven. Finally I ended up going out, I thought of a friend of mine who used to be a drug dealer, who was a good friend you could talk to, you know? He lived at the commune at Needmore, out past that.

So I started driving. I ended up driving out Nashville Road, and I got way out there, where you have to really know the roads to cross across to Needmore. And I didn't know all those county roads in Brown County. I was in the pits. I was looking for trees to crash my truck into. I was, I was, I was a basket case. And I happened to think, he told me of a church he was going to. I didn't know what kind of a church it was. Last time I seen him he was a drug dealer.

But he did mention this church that he was going to. So I pulled into the driveway on Yellowwood Road, and I walked up. I set there for a while. Finally, I walked up to the door and said, "I'm not afraid of any church. I've been in a lot of churches. I was raised in church, you know?" When I opened the door to that church, it was like all this hurt and all this garbage and all this pain just came out. I was in tears, I couldn't talk, I couldn't do anything. And this friend of mine came back, and he said, "So what's the trouble?" And I couldn't talk, I was just too, I was just too, I was, I was out of it. All I could do was cry.

And he said, "You know what you need?" I said, "What?" And he said, "You need to be right up at that altar." And I said, "You're right, I need to be right up at that altar," and I went up to that altar. And while I was kneeling there, I didn't say, "Lord, you're my savior," 'cause I already knew that he died for my sins. I'd heard that since I was a little kid. But I'd never really made him lord. And I said, "I've been in charge of my life for thirty-seven years. From now on, if there's anything you can do, if there's any way you can use it, it belongs to you. You can have it."

There were some of the other elders of the church come up and prayed with me. When I got up from that altar, I was a different person. I still was divorced, or getting divorced. I still had a lot of hang-ons of the flesh. I hadn't been transformed by the renewing of my mind, you know? I wasn't perfect in any way, shape, or form. I had a lot of fear, a lot of other things.

Throwed my cigarettes out the window of the truck on my way over to my friend's house that night, that afternoon. Never drank any after that, never wanted any. I went through some hard times. I was even beat up in my own front yard. Not beat up but knocked down by my wife's boyfriend in my front yard, which I, Lord, I don't understand this. But God knows. He knows what I needed to make me into what he wanted me to be. He knew just how much pressure to add and when to release the pressure, when to bless me, when to—and he's still doin' it. He's still doin' it.

Just the other day, I was really going through a hard time. Satan was really battlin' with me. I was starting to drive a little radical, and it was really messing with my head. It was Tuesday night, and we had a church service. I loaded my mom up, and I took her down. She goes to church with my dad. We get him out of the Alzheimer's unit and take him to church. I got there about six o'clock. We know a lot of the people down there, and I was still—all this churnin' in my mind. This is only last week or Tuesday of this week.

I got a bunch of people in there, and I just started singing. I opened my tape box and started singing. By the time church time came, seven o'clock, I had sung about four songs or so, and all my oppression had lifted. Gone. And I was ready to have church. I don't why I allowed myself to get into that shape, why I couldn't sing myself or pray myself out of it. I couldn't, and that's what it took. Since then I been fine. Not fine but existin', blessed.

I know it's getting late, but if you don't mind, I'd like to ask you one more question. You obviously have been through a lot of hard stuff in your life. The Bible has obviously helped you get through that. I don't know if you have one, but what is your favorite or what are some of your favorite passages, that you really find strength in?

Oh, lot of 'em about fear. The first Scripture song that I ever learned was Isaiah 43. See, I sing a lot out of the Bible, too. Some of the songs—I used to have about eighty different Scripture songs that were word for word out of King James. One of 'em I learned was Isaiah 43, verse 2 and 3. Says, "Fear not: for I have redeemed thee, I have called thee by thy name; thou art mine. When thou passeth through the water, I will be with thee; through the rivers they shall not overflow thee: Neither shall the flame kindle upon me. When thou walkest through the fire, though shall not be burned. Neither shall the flame kindle upon thee. For I am the Lord thy God."

That was the first song that I really can remember learning, and it's where Satan hit me the hardest: in fear. Something that I should have known and should know because I have that Scripture, that's an area that I get hit in. Another one is, I think in Second Timothy, 2 or 4. It says, "A good soldier does not entangle himself with the cares of this world."

Another one, there's just so many. The Twenty-third Psalm is a good one. "The Lord is my shepherd; I shall not want. He maketh me to lie down in green pastures: He leadeth me beside the still waters." You break that down, you know, "The Lord is my shepherd." A shepherd takes care of the sheep, but he also disciplines them, he also guides 'em. He leads them to green pastures where they can feed, in the word, the word of God, where they can feed. He leads 'em beside the still waters. Sheep can't get near rushing water. If it's splashing, it'll get in their fur and it'll pull 'em under. So they got to be real still water where they drink. There's some spiritual connotations to that, too.

"He anointest my head with oil." Priests were anointed with oil. Aaron was anointed with oil. We're made priests and kings. "He anointed my head with oil. My cup runneth over. He prepares the table before me in the presence of mine enemies. Surely goodness and mercy shall follow me all the days of my life." That's not all of it, but that's a lot of it.

To me, Jesus had a garden at Gethsemane, when he came to the absolute bottom. When he came, the flesh had to die totally. I believe David did when he wrote the Twenty-third Psalm—if he wrote it. I'm not positive he did—whoever wrote it, you know, was in a garden of Gethsemane situation, where they knew that their dependence was totally upon God. I've been there lots of times, many times this past year. Without God, I'm nothing. If God anoints it, it blesses. And if there's any of me in it, it'll probably be messed up.

In October 1997, several members of the gang went to Washington, D.C., to participate in Stand in the Gap, the Promise Keepers' gathering on the Mall.

Stand in the Gap.

Members of the Unchained Gang pray with fellow Christians on the Mall during Stand in the Gap.

The Unchained Gang holds a prayer circle before leaving the Promise Keepers' gathering.

NANCY AND SHALOM

I would like to start just by opening up in a wide and general way and ask you to talk about sexism in the world biker gangs that you've experienced and how that carries over into the Christian world. What's the same? What's different? What's worse? What's better? Is that too general?

Nancy: No. There is, as you mentioned, there is still sexism carried over, but in different ways. When we were in the world, in the bikers' world, the sexism was much more—what's the word I'm looking for? Just open.

Shalom: Mm hmm.

Nancy: It was very open.

Shalom: It was very degrading.

Nancy: Very degrading, very master-slave type of thing. And very accepted. It was just an acceptable thing. It wasn't thought of to not be acceptable.

Shalom: All women work, all men don't.

Nancy: The women work. Usually the men don't, and if they do it's a poor excuse of working. It gets 'em by. Master-slave.

Shalom: The nickname for woman is a filthy word beginning with *c,* and she's never really called anything else. That was the whole biker-world thing.

There was a certain amount of protection. And I say that because I think part of the Christian stuff is some kind of paternalism, protection, deal. In the one-percent world, women have responsibilities, and that's bring in the money, never reveal what's going on to anyone. I've seen women get treated badly, I mean physically badly. In the Christian world, there's still a pretty big separation between men and women, although . . .

Nancy: Men being the superior.

Shalom: Yeah, although I'm very proud of the Unchained Gang in that they did elect a women officer.

You?

Shalom: Yeah. It was me, but that's not—just that they did.

Nancy: But you fought for that.

Shalom: I didn't even know I was gonna be nominated, though.

Nancy: No, I just mean you have fought for your place. She has taken the blunt end of a lot of just making the way for other women to be even where they are because she just—her persistence.

Shalom: Or stupidity. [Both laugh.]

Nancy: Well, there's a fine line between a lot of things.

Shalom: Absolute mental numbness. I feel like in the Christian world, again you have protection, and for the most part—see, I can't actually say, "Well, all the Christians are like this or all the one-percenters are like this." There's some guys in the Christian world who come from a one-percent background and actually expect more realistic things of a women than some of them who've been married for ninety-seven years to the same woman and expect her to be cute.

It's as widely diverse as that. It's as diverse as all the people. But in just a general sense, I think that the Unchained Gang has come way up, and I'm really proud of the strides they've made. There are some more motorcycle groups now around town. Freedom Riders has equal patching for women, and I'm not even sure, I think New Jerusalem does. So it's happening.

That would never happen in a one-percent world. Never. She gets a patch, but it's a property patch. In the Christian world and in the Un-chained Gang it says property, but a woman can have a patch without being attached to a man. So it still says property, and the reason they do that, they say, is so they don't anger the one-percenter world, which is who we're supposed to be ministering to.

Nancy: I disagree just a little bit with that: A woman can be in this club without a man. It's not an easy thing.

Shalom: Boy, howdy.

Nancy: You can, but it is not easy. It took Terry six years?

Shalom: Eight years.

Nancy: Eight? Eight years, to get a patch with-out having a man attached to her. Myself, I stood back and watched—I still don't have a patch, keep in mind. I've more or less distanced myself. I have other things that need to be prior-itized right now than to work on that, but I know that I watched men get patches—that were single men—that there was no more reason to put a patch on them than me as far as I'm con-cerned. But they were men. I do know that when I was prospecting and hanging around and riding and being with the club a good deal, I did not get invited to the PJ and Tammy get-togeth-ers, I didn't get invited to—in fact, I never got a call, ever, until Al Cox came into my life and was interested and showed interest in the club. Then all of a sudden [makes trumpet fanfare sound]. Hey! We have this meeting out in Nashville. Oh yes, the one I've been hearing about for a year? I've been hearing about this for a year. I'm now married, I'm invited? I was never invited, ever, until I was married.

Shalom: Yeah.

Nancy: You can. She [Shalom] did it, Terry did it. Did any other woman do it?

Shalom: Cindy.

Nancy: Cindy?

Shalom: From Lawrence County.

Nancy: Well she—that was a while before, wasn't it?

Shalom: She actually, literally, came in a day or two before I did. She actually got her full patch before I did. I was supposed to get mine first, and I can't remember why I didn't. I think it had to do with that pesky smoking. [Nancy laughs.] I really do think it was something to do with smoking, but I'm not sure.

Nancy: There again, in her case, and in Terry's, there you've got women whose children are raised so they could full-time. Cindy did the jail ministry full-time.

Shalom: And had a staunch sponsor and support-er in XL.*

Nancy: That's what I was gonna say. Wasn't she somehow attached to him? And he's just very—was there, getting the job done. But what a fight. And to me, that is sexism. The fact that, okay, if you're older, if you're forty or older and your kids are grown, and you can give us 100 percent of your time—you see where I'm going with that. If you . . .

Shalom: Are not a threat.

Nancy: Are not a threat to the other men's wives, and if you can give 100 percent of your time, there are women—and I feel this, I'm gon-na say it. I'm not being immodest or whatever. It's a fact that I noticed. I have been a junkie, I have been a prostitute, I have been a thief. Ev-erything you can name, I've been there. And if there's somebody at the Boogie that needs some-one to talk to, like Shalom, I think you can see it

---

* A biker in the Greene County chapter.

in a person's eyes. When you're talking to someone about something you're going through . . .

Shalom: You know.

Nancy: You know if they know what you're talking about. The fact that I have had teenage girls, I've been a single parent and had to work three jobs up until two years ago, when I started at IU for the student loans. Then I worked two jobs and went to school and still was in church every time the doors opened, with my children, trying. The fact that they will not accept you hardly, unless—that, to me, it was their loss. The Bean Blossom Boogie decision.

Shalom: At a national level.

Nancy: At a national level, the Unchained made the decision that single women cannot attend events such as the Bean Blossom Boogie. Excuse me, but I've been to the Boogie eight years when I was in the world, and Christ stood by my side. What makes them think that Christ isn't gonna stand by my side, that I could go to the Boogie this year, without a man attached to me?

To me, there has been—What is that called?—hypocrisy, in that Joe Weaver sat in a meeting here at Sunrise* and spoke of how God is so good. God protects his wife. He doesn't have to worry about her. They were in a very bad neighborhood. He told this story: They were in a very, very bad neighborhood, all black and Hispanic, in some bigger city. And they were ministering, and they went inside someplace, and Joe's wife realized the men needed to just speak to Joe and told him she would take a walk. Well he made the comment to her, you know, "It's not a very good neighborhood." And she told him, "Christ is with me. God is with me. I'm not worried." And she took her walk, and she had not a problem.

_____
* Shalom's counseling service, where for a while the Unchained Gang's monthly meetings were held.

Well, when I was in the world, I happened to be a believer, and any time I was in that situation I knew the same thing. I didn't verbalize it because I would have been deemed crazy. To me, why is Joe Weaver's wife, why does she have God with her and . . .

Shalom: We don't? Well, I'm married now.

Nancy: Yeah, you're married now, but before you were married, same thing. I have a problem with that. It's sexism. The men literally said to us that they did not need us to put them in that situation where they would feel like they couldn't get the ministering done that they need to do because they were too busy protecting us. Well, I just don't see that. I've never needed protection before.

Shalom: Well, another thing I see is the attitude of: My beloved wife is too precious to be here among the dirt and the puke and the beer.

Nancy: Right. Right. Right. Yeah, some of the men don't allow their wives to go to like that. Frankly, myself, if single women can't go, why can single men? There's naked ladies all over that place. Naked women. More naked women than there are naked men. To me there's more women that need help there than there are men.

Shalom: You bet. You bet. I was sitting there this year, and we had a separate canopy because we had our little entourage of other people with us, me and Gabby. So we had a tent right there on the corner by Checkpoint Charlie.

There was this woman in church about—I'm not gonna time it—six or seven months ago, who stood up every service and your heart just went out to her. She was just so miserable, and she'd praise God, and she'd praise, and then she'd cry. Her life was just unmanageable. She'd broken up with her boyfriend, which was a real serious, long-time relationship. Said she'd been away from Christ and just wanted to be back, and she became this every-time-the-door-opened church person. I was called about giving her a job here and all that kind of stuff. And I'm sitting there in our canopy, it was late afternoon, early evening, still light. I was just looking at the corner 'cause there's a corner there right in front of that tent, you know? And here she comes on the back of a bike, stark naked.

Nancy: Oh!

Shalom: And she like saw my face. She was really rowdy, coming around the corner, and then she saw my face, and she got this just—I don't know—like a real sad look on her face. And I couldn't find her. I couldn't find where she went. But my point here is not one of the men could have ministered to that woman.

Nancy: No.

Shalom: Neither could an earth woman. It would absolutely have to be someone from that world.

An earth woman, meaning?

Shalom: Like plain people.

Nancy: Non-alcoholic, non-biker.

Is part of that that the men are not recognizing those women's needs or that the protection overrides everything else?

Shalom: No, I don't think they even pay attention, because they set up this rule thing, that it's dangerous to minister to a woman.

Nancy: And it is.

Shalom: And it is. Yeah, quite frankly, like I won't have a one-on-one relationship with a male client. I mean I do like if they want to come in my office and chat or whatever, but as far as doing long-term, one-on-one therapy, Gar-

many* does it. I don't do it. Certainly, transition is a—well, what happens is they take all their needs, and all their wants, and all the [women] they ever loved and—it's "transference" is the word I'm looking for. It's just a dangerous thing to do. But I also see some of: The only important people to witness to are men. I don't even think it's conscious. Do you, Nancy?

Nancy: I don't think they're malicious.

Shalom: I don't think they wake up in the morning and selectively pray for people.

Nancy: Or dis women.

Shalom: Yeah, right!

Nancy: No, it's not malicious, but it's not correct either. Just like—well, I don't even know—but it is not malicious, but it is not correct. And it needs to be corrected.

Are they open to correction when it's suggested?

Nancy: Not very.

Shalom: The ones that are stuck there are pretty stuck there. I need to really say that it's not everybody.

Nancy: No.

Shalom: It's just that the ones that are stuck make it very painful for single women.

Nancy: And I also see—and not all of them, but there are a few of them—that shirk responsibility to their family, to their wives, to their children, through this ministry. It's usually the ones that you hear that are married with little kids, and you hear them bragging and boasting at the meetings . . .

Shalom: About all they've done for the gang!

Nancy: "I haven't missed a ride! I haven't missed a ride!" And they're proud of that.

---

* Shalom's business partner, Jim Garmany.

Shalom: And "if I can do it, you can do it."

Nancy: Yeah. Well, I don't have a wife.

Shalom: No, but I'm looking for one. [Laughs.]

Nancy: I said that once to Larry Mitchell. "You know what I need is a wife," and he was like, "You don't mean that literally, right?" But it is, it's frustrating to me, because there was a time when I wanted to do this, and I made as many of the rides as I could. And listening to the men, you know, I make every ride, and knowing, from hanging around with their wives, the . . .

Shalom: Reason they made every ride. [Laughs.]

Nancy: Right. Their marriage is on the rocks. Their marriage isn't doing good, their children are neglected of their time. One guy had the brains to pull me off to the side, finally, and say, "I see what you're trying to do here, what you're fighting for, but you don't need to make every time the church opens its doors. You're working three jobs, you've got two kids, how can you possibly be giving them the time they need if you're trying to make all these meetings? Don't kill yourself doing this." I had been thinking about it anyway. To me, though, I watched, and, yeah, if you're a single man you can be doing things that you're not supposed to be doing and still get a patch.

Shalom: Boys will be boys.

Nancy: Yeah, boys will be boys. And get a patch on your back.

What kind of things?

Nancy: Having sex with women outside of marriage-type things.

Shalom: Again, this is not pervasive through the whole bunch, but . . .

Nancy: Well, I don't know. It slips through. You look at it. The single men, or even the married men that aren't doing quite what we get reprimanded for, and they're doing it, and they get their patches, and they get preferential treatment. Whether there are those who disagree with it, it seems like the ones that are stuck, like you said, where they're at, they seem to be the ones that that's the way it goes.

Shalom: I had a guy tell me one time that—I forget, they got married when they were sixteen, seventeen years old—and I had him tell me that his wife didn't need any male friends because she had him, and he didn't ever need any female friends because he had her. And at the time it angered me, because of my personal situation that I was in at that time. And now it makes me so sad to even say those words, so sad that this man has missed so much of life, so many good things. Things that would've enriched both of them.

Nancy: And that was his law.

Shalom: I don't know if it was his law. See, I was raised in the Methodist church in Spencer, but at like twelve or thirteen years old I was out of there, and I never came back to church until I'm in that church,* so I really don't know what other churches' doctrines and rules and all that stuff. It may be from his church, but I couldn't hang with that church if that was one of their rules.

Nancy: So, there is still sexism, but the difference is tremendous. The degrading type of sexism that we did live in to the sexism we put up with now.

Shalom: It's almost like pedestalism now. I know that's probably not a word. [Laughs.]

Nancy: It's more a hierarchy, and women are lower on the hierarchy and then the men. And they, somehow, twist that God made them to be our protectors, and, to me, God is my protector.

---

* The House of Prayer.

If he uses a man once in a while to do that, that's fantastic, but he's used women, too. I have had more women protect me than I've ever had men.

Shalom: Had them protect you from men. [Both laugh.]

Nancy: That's right.

When you were living in the degradation, what was your take on that at the time? Were you aware of it? How did feel?

Nancy: At first, I don't know about you, you said you were from a good family.

Shalom: A good family, but everybody died except my mom.

Nancy: I remember like it was yesterday when I first—I had dealt with biker clubs out in New Mexico from dealing to them. I knew the president. He invited me to parties every once in a while, and I would go for an hour at the beginning of the party, and then it'd be getting too wild and I'd leave. And I saw he had several wives, old ladies, whatever. I saw how that stuff went, and I remember thinking, God, I could never do that. And then when I got into it myself, I do remember the first time that I was told I couldn't go to the Boogie because they were making it a bachelor run. [Both laugh.] And I laughed! 'Cause Wheezer himself couldn't tell me this. His buddies came to the house to let me know. They're like, "Have you not told her yet?" "Well . . . ," and I rebelled at first, a little bit. [Both laugh.] I picked up my girlfriend, said, I'm gonna pay your way, you're gonna go with me. And we went in the car, and we went to the Boogie anyway. Stayed all weekend. Came home, I'd made my point.

That was three months into the relationship, and about three months later from that, from being

where we go, the bars you go to when you're with these people, with the bikers and stuff. The Greene County Picnic, the Boogie, the parties that we attended, when the Diablos show up, people like that, I fell into the protection part of it fairly easy. Where I had really hated the statement "property of," I latched onto it with everything I had.

Shalom: 'Cause that is your protection.

Nancy: I remember being at the Greene County Picnic, and a single girlfriend of mine, she rode a bike, and she came in, and the Diablos were there, and there were some there from California. Or Nomads, whatever. They took her bike. They just took it. And she came over to our camp, and she said, "What am I gonna do?" and was crying and whining, and I said, "Well, you best just sit right here and stay in the camp."

They were at a war, so to speak, with somebody. I can't remember the full circumstance, but I remember we didn't leave. Women didn't leave our campsite to go the bathroom without a man. And where I had fought that thought, that was my first time, you know, my transition, into holding onto that thought. It was more, I see how this works now. It's not a degrading thing to be property of, it's actually a status quo.

Shalom: Yeah, in the one-percent world you don't go to some kind of a board meeting and debate upon whether women get this or women get that. That's not the way it goes. At war people die, and at war women get stolen, raped, killed, beaten, badly beaten. Women might have information that the other side wants and will just be tortured until that happens. The protective patch, at that point, I was always grateful for.

The gang that I was with for eleven years was extremely high-profile all over the United States and at war with another extremely high-profile, all-over-the-United-States motorcycle gang. I can't remember that it ever, ever occurred to me once that I should have a full patch. That would have just been utterly ridiculous. If I had a full patch . . .

Nancy: That never occurred to me either.

Shalom: No, there isn't even an if. I can't imagine such a thing.

Nancy: But what did occur to me was the rebellious part at first.

Shalom: Well, but see, that was a private thing, almost, between you and him.

Nancy: Yeah. Him saying I was his old lady that whole . . .

Shalom: Like what you were saying, part of that's private and some of it isn't. The part that isn't is where I was the most grateful for the protective patch.

Nancy: I think when I first met Wheezer, too, I had just split up with Russell, the father of my children, so I was very, I'm not anybody's, I'm not anybody's. I've been somebody's since I was fifteen years old. I'm not anybody's. And it took me about six months to get out of that.

I distinctly remember the first few times where I came to an understanding with where their—and we were talking about the degration that women put up with. There's different levels, too. Myself, I did not belong to a club who shared their women.

Shalom: No. As a matter of fact, it was the unpatched women that would come into camp once in a while.

Nancy: Right, the turn-outs. But there are one-percent clubs that their women, like the president of the Dead Men in New Mexico, he would trade women with other presidents and give his

woman to someone for a week as a gift, a bonus, whatever. That, see, I would have never—he made them have sex with dogs at parties, you know, for entertainment. Stuff like that. So there's different levels that different groups have. So you can choose.

Shalom: Once again, it depends on who you're hooked up with. You can be treated like trash out here not connected with nobody, too.

Going back to the Christian world now, how did it change for you when you got married?

Shalom: Well, I got to go to the Boogie. [Both laugh.]

Well now, you were at the Boogie before you were married.

Shalom: Every year.

Nancy: So was I last year, but I think I'm the reason that they—because that guy, that married guy who didn't tell me he was married, took me for a ride on his motorcycle and then attached himself.

Shalom: Oh, attached himself strongly.

This was a Christian?

Shalom: Well, that'd be hard to call.

Nancy: His brother was a Christian. It was in our camp. When he rode in with his brother, I didn't see a ring on his finger, I didn't see a woman with him, and I asked him to give me a ride somewhere.

Shalom: To get your bike, wasn't it?

Nancy: Money, from my dad, here in Bloomington. I had only been riding for two days, so it was like, "Would you give me a ride?" And he did, and we stopped to get something to eat, and that man just started I-love-you type of stuff. Of course, at that point you know you're looking at someone who's not quite got all their marbles for whatever reason, be it a permanent thing or just for that moment.

All I know is he called and called and called. She had to find someone big and burly to tell him not to call me anymore. To me, I looked at that, and I'm thinking, Okay, it was that man attaching himself to me. We had a single man that we'd put a patch on his back who was attaching himself to women in the church, almost in that same manner. Very, very obstructively doing this and wound up with a patch on his back within two months.

Shalom: They took his patch, though.

Nancy: Yes, and then gave it back to him for a while. Have they taken it from him permanently? I've seen him with it on since then. They took it from him for a little while. Then he did get it back, and I think he's still got it. I don't know if he ever handed it in himself. But to me, there's sexism.

Shalom: Well, the rule should be: No single people at the Boogie.

Nancy: Period.

Shalom: Or it should be: Everybody welcome to the Boogie. But to say no single women to the Boogie . . .

Nancy: Right. I think it should be everybody. If you're going to let married men go to a place like that, where there is temptation all around, I'd rather have a single man there than a married man with temptation.

Shalom: Well, then that would point to married women can go without their husbands.

Nancy: Right. And I wonder what they would think of that.

Things must have changed for you other than just being able to go to the Boogie.

[Shalom laughs.]

I know you were joking, but how did things change? Especially because your most recent marriage*— maybe the one before that, too—has been an issue of some controversy in the community.

Shalom: Oh, buddy! My most recent—the one before that really wasn't. This one has been quite a bit of controversy.

Compare and contrast.

Shalom: I can't. There is none. The first one was, like, not a real marriage, and I seemed to be the last to know that. Everybody else did know it, kinda. I don't have any anger, fear, hurt, nothing in my body or heart that I feel toward that marriage. It was just kind of like air or something.

This marriage, I've noticed, well, number one, almost everybody likes him. One thing you need to know is that Christian motorcycle clubs, in general, do not necessarily consist of ex-bikers. As a matter of fact, very, very few have been bikers. My husband happens to be one who has been a biker. I'm a woman, but I've been in a one-percent gang for years. My sponsor, Larry Joe,** was a biker.

Nancy: So they accept . . .

Shalom: Well, that's just about it. Although people like him a lot, they tend to not exactly know what to do with or how to take him. But I feel friendlied upon now more than before. I'm not sure how much of that was me and how much of it was them. I was sitting here the other day

_____

* To Gabby.

** Pastor Larry.

thinking about how I never got invited to any of their homes, and then I heard this voice, and it was like, "Did you ever invite them to your home?" [Laughs.]

There's only been one woman, and this is out of both chapters, because when I became a full-patch member there was only one chapter, so this is out of the whole shebang, there's only been one woman out of all those men who has ever actually spoken that I was after her man or something like that—which I wasn't at all. So I didn't see the jealousy thing. But now it's like people do call us, we do get invited.

Nancy: A lot more than you did before.

Shalom: Well, I can't say a lot more, but more. Because I wasn't hardly invited at all before. But I'm saying the reason that we're not invited all the time, I think, is because of our mutual or separate one-percent background. He tends to make people's hearts kind of like get a little shock of startled or fear or whatever, and you know he's not like that.

Nancy: I don't see that, but I can see where some would that had never been in biker clubs.

Shalom: So that's another area: the biker thing.

Nancy: I saw a huge, huge difference from single to married. I just did. The six weeks I was married. [Laughs.] I probably got invited to more than the whole three and a half years I prospected. I did get invited to more.

Shalom: Yeah, I guess me, too, 'cause I've been invited to a birthday party, to a couple of dinners.

Nancy: Whether your man is a little scary to some of 'em or whatever or not, it's him that's the reason that you two get invited. It just is.

Shalom: When I was told about no women at the Boogie, you could just see my hair start to go—and my sponsor said, "No, that's unmarried women." And I can remember thinking, "Oh, okay" and walking off. And it didn't hit me till like a week later. "Wait a minute!" [Laughs.]

Nancy: Larry's good. He's good.

Shalom: Oh, he said it with such comfort.

Was there a difference in the way people treated you and the way they treated Gabby on the controversial nature of your union?

Shalom: I honestly don't know, because although Gabby and I had been pretty close friends for I'd say a year, I was not around him in any serious sorts of things with the gang. Where we became friends was on runs. My position in the gang had me also positioned at the back of the pack every time, because I was to be watching for any problems and all that. And Gabby always rode at the back of the pack beside me or behind me. He just always did. So we got to be pretty close friends and really talked to each other about personal things and all that. So we were friends, but I never was around him in that way. He was a probate.

I'm talking about once you got together and were living together, that kicked up a lot of dust in the gang, were each of you treated differently?

Nancy: Can I ask you something?

Shalom: Well, sure.

Nancy: Did they do to him what they did to you? Did they call a meeting and three men sit around, like that day they did that to you?

Shalom: There were three days they did that to me.

Nancy: I know. I didn't know that. But I know that they did her harsh.

Shalom: I tend to think part of that, though, is that I was a six-year veteran, full patch, vice president, and Gabby was a probate. I want to think that. [Laughs.]

Nancy: Yeah?

Shalom: I'm not sure. How would I ever know?

You're a little more skeptical that it wasn't just the difference in patch status?

Nancy: I'm a lot more skeptical. I think there was a little bit of that, but I think they used it. That just goes along the same lines of the Pete thing and the Nancy thing.

Which is what?

Nancy: Like I said, with me, that guy attaching himself to me and getting very weird about it, Pete was the one, literally attacking women at church. And the way they did him as opposed to the way they did me was so different. The woman gets—I mean it's almost like women scare these men.

Let me interrupt for a second. When you say Pete was literally attacking women, what does that mean?

Nancy: He raped me. But I didn't tell anybody for a couple weeks because I mulled it around in my mind. Did I deserve that? Did I ask for that? I went to Indianapolis, I stayed out too late. And then I got to thinking, Are you stupid, Nance? The guy put drugs in your—he bought, what he did, he came down here every night from Indianapolis, where he lives. Every night.

Shalom: To rub your feet.

Nancy: To rub my feet when I got home from my third job. I was working three jobs a day. And I actually had asked him as nicely as I could

to please not come down during the weeks. I just told him, I know you mean well. You want to fix my kids dinner, you want to buy pizzas, you want to be there when I get home and rub my feet. How can you argue with that stuff? He knew that. That was manipulating. And I was so tired, but I wasn't stupid because I've been there before. I've had a lot of relationships, and I know manipulation.

I tried very hard to be composed about it. I asked him nicely, "Please, I know you mean well" and all this stuff. "I can't handle it. I need to just come home. My kids have pot pies. They've been doing this for years. And I don't need my feet rubbed."

Well, he kept doing it. He quit for a couple of days, and then he went back into that pattern. And the next thing I knew he was saying, "I come down here all the time. I come down here all the time. You should come up to Indianapolis once in a while."

So, it was a Friday or Saturday night, and I trucked up there. I get up at five-thirty every morning. By nine o'clock I was usually dead. So I told him we need to have dinner rather early before I go brain-dead. One thing led to another. He had fifty things to do when I got there. "Oh, I just have to do this, I just have to do that." We didn't get to this dinner place till eight o'clock. And I was tired, and I started getting mad.

I don't think I even finished my dinner, and I told him, "We're out of here. It's nine o'clock. My head hurts I'm so tired." He took me back to his place, and I remember he just kept, "Well, I bought this sparkling"—what's that?—Welch's grape, you know, instead of champagne, it's in that champagne bottle—"I bought this!" "Okay.

I'll have one glass with you, and I have got to go, because I am starting to see double."

Well, I drank that glass of grape juice, and I was seeing double. I know the difference between being exhausted and being drugged. I had been exhausted for a long two years. That kind of seeing double you can get focused. I couldn't after drinking that grape juice. After two weeks of thinking about it, I thought, you know, he went in the kitchen. He didn't bring it out and pour it, he poured it in there. I've had this done before. I'm not stupid. I know when I'm drugged.

I know that I told him after drinking that drink, I could not drive. I said, "I'm going to sleep in my car." He assured me I could sleep on his couch. He would not bother me. I distinctly remembered him going up the stairs. I woke up at two-thirty in the morning, he was in me. So that is rape. I told someone about it two weeks later.

Someone in the church?

Nancy: Yeah. And nothing was ever done. He was spoken to. He was told, Leave me alone. That's what was done. And he didn't do that. I called several times this same person, crying. "He came here, he was crying. I made him leave. Somebody's gotta help me here." Two months later they put a patch on his back. Because you know what he did? That one person got on him. Never told anybody else. That one person got on him.

And that made me think, Well, somehow you think that was somehow partly my fault. And it was not. And the more and more I've gone over it, now, that was not. But I look at that and I think, What he did was he took that next two months, and he literally glued himself to this club.

And he's done the same or similar thing to other women?

Nancy: And then afterwards, after he got his patch, he was all over her. The roses, the balloons.

Shalom: Oh that's right, I forgot about that.

Nancy: He does it in a way that is very manipulating because it's very . . .

Shalom: Sparkling.

Nancy: Yeah, how can you go to somebody and say, "You've got to stop him! He's buying me roses and he's taking me out to eat! [Shalom laughs] And he's rubbing my feet!"? And you're going, This sounds stupid. And in the back of your mind you're always thinking, Who are they gonna believe? My stupid butt, who's only been sober, maybe, I was sober seven months when I met him. But then it started happening to other women. And they—you know, it takes you a couple months before you start feeling the manipulation of it, the closed walls of it. It's consuming.

Another woman called me, and when she conferred with me, then we conferred with someone else he started in on. We got to where anyone he attacked, we were there.

But you see where the women handled that? The women handled that. The men act like men. They cannot—and I'm being sexist here. I shouldn't say it—but to me, men are wimpy when it comes to dealing with other men. Oh, they can deal with their women. They dealt with her, they dealt with me. But let them deal with their men, they wimp out.

Shalom: In the world, that's called honor among thieves. [Laughs.] I don't know what it's called here.

Nancy: Bonding. Male bonding. [Both laugh.]

What sort of effect has the woman's movement and conventional feminism had on you?

Shalom: It's who I am.

I've heard a lot of women in the church and in the gang sort of poo-poo feminism or try to distance themselves from it.

Shalom: Well, the first thing to say is that our rule book is the Bible. So, as far as I'm concerned for my life, for me to be only woman-power oriented or the other side of that is the one person who is so stuck in nothingness or in everything for women, but the everything just happens to be him. To me, that's both ends of the continuum, and either one's wrong, biblically. The Bible says that the husband should love his wife like his church. Would he confine his church to only him? That would certainly defeat the whole thing.

Nancy: There is not an equality, but there should be.

Shalom: I was in college and worked at the Office for Women's Affairs, which is an extremely militant, feminist kind of deal. I didn't go there because of that. I was in a work-study position. They hired me. I had on a green army shirt, khaki pants, no bra, certainly no make up. My hair was much bigger than it is now. It was just everywhere. And I typed thirty-four words a minute with eleven errors, and they hired me.

I was there for a whole lot of IU women's issues and radical women supporting women and all that and got excited about it. I went on a lot of the Take Back the Night and all that kind of stuff and loved it. Had my daughter and my mom involved in it, which I thought was kind of cool.

So at one point I was extremely militant. I've mellowed out, and I pretty much love where I'm at. Like Nancy has talked about in some other areas, I just know in a general area that if I'm in some real trouble that requires a get-together that's gonna produce power and well-thought-out strategy, it's gonna be four or five women. This world today's not about who has the biggest arms, it's about who has the slickest strategy for the most part. So it would be women that I would gather together with.

There are two or three men in my life who could easily fit in that circle, but two or three out of a hundred and fifty's not very good odds. [Laughs.] I guess some people still look at me as a feminist. I don't look at me as a feminist. I look at me as an individualist, that each individual is who they are and who they work to be and who they aspire to be. And it doesn't matter who you are, if you're a man or a woman. I respect what you achieve and what you want and how hard you're willing to work to get it, your behavior along the way. And I today have some respect for myself, because I don't see how I could be a King's kid and not love me. So I'm a lot mellower today.

I used to just be plain mean about it. I got transferred from there over to the School of Education, and one of the professors told me that the very first thing he heard when they were talking about me coming into that office—that office had nine professors—he said, one of the very first things he was told by the Head Fred hiring person in the School of Education was, "For God's sakes, don't ask her to make coffee." [Both laugh.] And I wouldn't have. If they'd asked me to make coffee, oh!

Nancy: They'd've been wearing it.

Shalom: Oh, there wouldn't have been any. I used to always laugh and say that when I got a business of my own that my secretary would be a male with great legs. [Laughs.]

Nancy (who used to be Shalom's secretary): Hey!

Shalom: And that I didn't care if he could type. [Laughs.]

Nancy: Thirty-five words a minute.

Eleven mistakes.

Shalom: And I used to talk about that all the time with those professors, because we really all got to be pretty tight. And I have had three or four male secretaries.

Great legs?

Shalom: Well, not bad. [Laughs.] But even then, there's still a difference between then and now. It's been like a maturation thing, maybe, or just where to find my happiness. I don't have that horrible anger most of the time. For a long time I was just angry. I can get angry, but for the most part I'm pretty happy with who I've kind of turned out to be or who I'm becoming. I guess the background that that militant time gave me was a very well-founded knowledge of all that we are capable of. There's just a lot of power in women. And I'm sure there must be in men, but I don't need to try to be a man or attached at the armpit to a man in order to feel power. We have our own.

Nancy: My concept of feminism that I shun from—'cause I'll be one of those ones talking about, Feminism? Excuse me, no part of that. To me, those women, in a partial way, are relieving men of some responsibilities that I feel men have. I see their side of it. I was raised and told there was nothing I couldn't do, nothing I

couldn't have, nothing I couldn't be. But I don't want that to relieve the man from his responsibility to me, which I see as—I don't want anything from anybody that I don't give. If I give it, then that's what I expect, is basically what I give. And even, sometimes, I don't even expect that.

You're talking about abstract qualities like respect and consideration or tangible things?

Shalom: Or about dishes?

Nancy: I was just about to get there. To me, if my male counterpart goes out and works a twelve-hour day and I don't, I'm gonna have those dishes done, and I'm gonna have that laundry done, and he's gonna have a hot meal on the table, and I don't mind doing that one bit. On the other hand, if I go out and work that twelve-hour day and he does not, then I expect—I don't expect him to get everything done I do.

Shalom: I don't want anybody to do my laundry.

Nancy: Exactly. But I'm energetic, she's energetic, she knows what I'm talking about. We tend to do a lot. We don't expect everybody to be that way. But I do expect some consideration, the way I would consider him. I would expect him to not have a mess for me to have to come home to, if he'd take me to dinner if he can't cook it. Just the aspects you were talking about, the consideration and that kind of thing.

And I don't feel, personally, that the majority of the Christian bikers are there yet. And I think the ones that are are overpowered by the ones that are not. That's where I'm at with it. I see one we all know and love saying to me and you, anything he says to us he says to the club, but his stuff gets shot down by the ones who are saying, "I make every run, and I've got kids and bills!" And I'm thinking I could be a little forceful with it and say, Well, I know—but instead I figure, be Christlike. Back off and let God deal with it. And he will.

And how has he done that?

Nancy: I don't know, he just always does. And it's not always in my time.

Shalom: Or not in the same way that we would have it.

Nancy: Or in the same way that I would do it. I just had this conversation with a girlfriend of mine the other day who was feeling pretty low, and I told her, I said, "You know, I've lived just enough life now—I just turned thirty-five—and I just now lived enough life that I can substantiate that hypothesis, that God takes care of it. Maybe not within a year, maybe not the way either one of us might think." I'm always up for giving him suggestions! "This is one thing you could do." I've seen him use some things that I've thought of, and then I've seen him come up with much better . . .

Shalom: With me, he's come up with things that were nowhere near anything I'd thought of, just to let me know that he's in charge.

I also wanted to say a while ago when I said about the power from women, is that I fully recognize that's God's power through us. Some rather chauvinistic ways of thinking whoever it is doing that, almost assumes that God won't give women power. [Laughs.] That power, his power, that his power can't work as well or as strongly through women, and that's not true at all.

Nancy: I'll tell you a Christian man: Kenneth Copeland. There's a man that recognizes his wife and God's power working through his wife. He is not intimidated one bit about what his wife can do or what God can do through his wife. I

just don't see Kenneth Copeland ever telling Gloria . . .

Shalom: "You stay in here. I'm going out here to the Eagle Mountain Rally."

Nancy: Yeah. "You stay in here, Sweetheart. I don't think you can handle—" I can see him saying, "Go get 'em, Gloria. You, and God be with you."

Shalom: It's real old hat now, but I used to love that saying thing they had on a T-shirt and stuff: A woman's place is in the senate. Or in the house or the senate. I thought that was cool. I think Kenneth would just be proud of Gloria if she ran for president.

Nancy: I do, too. I would like to see the Christian bikers be able to overcome some of their—I really feel that they're insecure when it comes to women. I feel like they've always had the superiority thing going, and without that it's almost, kind of, I feel sorry for them, because they're almost scared of it. It's an unknown territory to them, some of them, and I feel sorry for them

One of things I've heard mentioned a lot in a lot of different contexts is that the man is the head of the household, spiritually and otherwise. And I've heard different interpretations of that Scripture. What are yours?

Shalom: I can tell you that my husband's and my interpretation is pretty much we both make our own decisions, we talk about things, but, ultimately, our lives are so separate, as far as I have a business here to run, he's an over-the-road truck driver, so what's he gonna do? Call me up from Wisconsin, ask me if he can go to Frisch's to eat? We pretty much just do our own thing. We talk to each other two or three times a day, but—and we've agreed on this, and I believe it to be biblical—that if there is a major decision that we actually cannot agree upon, biblically he would be the override.

So that's our agreement, and we're both very comfortable with that. As a matter of fact, it's a comfort to me to not be the last word on everything. I've been the last word on everything in life most of my life. In a way, it's kind of a comfort. But I've got it made. We don't play those stupid little games in our family. We just don't go there. Not even my son goes there. I'm full-grown with a mature and somewhat usable brain. I'm perfectly capable of making decisions and taking risks and doing transactions and business sorts of things without benefit of, "Oh honey, I just can't think. Can you come think for me?" I don't need it. And he doesn't have any desire to do that. So I think we're based biblically, and we're both happy.

Nancy: I had, in my short marriage to Al Cox, we had a problem with that. He was rather mean.

Shalom: Yeah, you couldn't trust his decisions were for your benefit.

Nancy: I couldn't trust that at all after we married. He kept yelling that Scripture, that man is the boss. God says. Or that man is the head of the household was his word. Well, I talked him into finally going to our pastor's house, having had told our pastor what I was going through, and our pastor put it to him this way: That Scripture does not say man is boss. It says he is the head of the household, which, interpreted, means the household is your responsibility. If you and your wife aren't agreeing, there's also a Scripture somewhere that says she is your helper, your helpmate, meaning consider her.

He said "head of household" means exactly that: You are responsible. If the two of you are not getting along, are not coming to terms, you're

the one responsible for resolving. Not meaning that you totally have to give in to her every time, but, in other words, it's not saying you are the boss, but you are responsible for being mature, and if there's a head-butting like this, he said, where there's no giving, you need to be the one to give a little. It's your responsibility to trust in God and give it to God when the two of you can't.

So he put it more to him that way. I see it that way, but like her, too, if there's a major, you know, that we can't click on—now if it's something I absolutely can't bend on, if my husband was asking me to do something that I knew was wrong, I wouldn't do it. But if it was just neither one of us seemed to be right and neither one of us seemed to be wrong, I'd say, "Fine, we'll do it your way."

Shalom: Yeah, but that's not really happened, has it?

Nancy: No.

Shalom: See, I can't see it really happening with us, either, because we would find enough information by which to make an informed decision, so I really can't see him ever saying, "I am the man! And this is it!" [Both laugh.] I can't see that ever happening, but we set that up that way. Another time that I have learned from one-percent gangs is that one advantage of never doubting that the man has the final word is at war.

Nancy: Mm hmm.

Shalom: Because it can save your life. If you're programmed to where you hear your old man: duck, shoot, run, hide, whatever it is . . .

Nancy: And you do it . . .

Shalom: And you do it without thinking, you're going to still be alive.

Nancy: Yeah.

Shalom: If you stand to question him, you could probably have a bullet through you head before the question's over. So that's not a real iffy, debatable kind of thing. That's the way it is out there is the one-percent world. It was then, and it is today. There are wars going on. There are very serious—people are getting killed. Clubs are being taken over.

Nancy: And the men are usually informed, because they have their little meetings that the women don't get to go to. So that's why you learn to do whatever he says. If I were at that meeting, I wouldn't need him to tell me what to do. [Both laugh.]

Some of what I've said sounds like I'm really down. But I'm really not. I think they do fantastic work. I do think there's still that area with the women that the men need some work on.

Shalom: And I wanted to say, too, that part of my mellowing over this last almost year now has been that the gang to which I belong did everything actually biblically, in that one person, my pastor, came to me, and my behavior continued. And then three of them came to me, and my behavior continued. And then it got really serious, and six or seven of them came to me. That part was biblically correct, although it hurt me, it infuriated me, it crushed me, but I had—I was wrong in what I was doing. All of that is exactly biblical. And today, throughout all this time without wearing my patch—I get it back in December—I have grown so much I can't tell you, to know I don't really need that patch on my back for people to see Jesus in my eye.

As a matter of fact, it seems to have worked better. I'll be places, and people just come up to me. And it's been a real growing experience. The part I was so angered about were the auxiliary things, the gossip about things that never happened. "Oh, I was there and saw 'em," when they weren't, because we weren't. That kind of stuff. It really, really bothered me. It doesn't bother me as much today. I've actually reached the point where I can pray for these people. Their lives must be so unexciting that they have to draw their excitement off of mine. But you're gonna find that not just in Christian motorcycles, you're gonna find that anywhere.

Randy and Gracie, Al and Nancy at the House
of Prayer.

Beth, who attends church at the House of Prayer, telling of her troubles with alcoholism as she explains why she would like to be a hang-around.

Gabby holding his then-wife's hand at an Unchained Gang meeting. They were divorced soon after.

REDEMPTION

"How many churches do we have represented here tonight?" Pastor Larry asked the visiting congregations at the House of Prayer's camp meeting. He held up one finger. It was a trick question. "He's coming back for one bride." They remind themselves and one another of this tenet often. It helps to maintain cohesiveness and harmony amid growth, factionalism, and disagreements.

In the two years that I worked on this project, a number of changes occurred in the group. Larry Mitchell completed his sixth year as president of the Unchained Gang and, citing other commitments and a shortage of time, did not seek reelection. The group elected as his successor Larry Gwaltney, a man whose soft-spoken honesty, integrity, faith, and humility have earned him the respect of others in the ministry.

There were also some new members, people serious about serving God and ministering to bikers, although most, like Larry Gwaltney, did not have outlaw biker pasts. Some left the Monroe County Chapter, first for Greene County and later for another Christian biker outfit, Bondslaves. Many left the House of Prayer for other churches, some for personal reasons, some who felt God led them elsewhere.

Randy left both the church and the Unchained Gang to start another motorcycle ministry, the Freedom Riders. It is still a young organization, sometimes at odds with the Unchained Gang, sometimes in fellowship.

The Eagle Mountain Motorcycle Rally was not held in 1998, and its future was still to be determined. According to a spokesman at Kenneth Copeland Ministries, "the Lord spoke to Brother Copeland" and told him not to have the rally that year. The spokesman denied that a motorcy-cle accident that killed two people at the rally the year before had any bearing on the decision.

Nancy did marry Russell, her ex-husband and the father of her children. Harley married a woman from the church. Gabby and Shalom both remarried and divorced—and then married each other.

———

Extreme as Christian bikers may be, they are all people who pulled back from going too far. They didn't die by the side of the road, and now they are growing older, settling down, and making sense of who they are in terms of who they once were.

I never checked anyone's criminal records or made an attempt to confirm their stories from the outlaw days. Some of that information is a matter of public record; some of it is impossible to verify. I always had the sense, though, that the atonement they sought was not only for the sins they committed but also for the sins they failed to commit. Both are difficult to reconcile.

Pastor Larry conducts a wedding.

The wedding party.

Dustin and Chico look on.

*Chico and Becky offer congratulations to the
bride and groom.*

RANDY

I was looking for a partnership, I was looking for brothers. I was looking for a closeness, you know, and I thought I seen that in the Unchained Gang. And it was like that. And it still is to a degree, but as always, the more people that come in, the more personalities we got in there. Some things started changing, started having some difficulties with a few people.

One thing was the size. And I don't know, I just think that it's kind of like the difference between a great big church and a small church. It's like there's a little more of a warm feeling in a small church. I'm not saying that I wanted that to remain a small church, but I wanted the small church feeling to be there, you know what I'm saying?

And I'm not saying that ain't amongst a few, but the crowd started changing. I don't know. To tell you the truth, I just think the Lord wanted me to do something else. We branched off over here, we have a Bible study up on the Hill,* we're planning on having a building up here on the Hill somewhere. It's going fine, it's going good, and I think that's just where the Lord wanted us to go.

SHALOM

I get subpoenaed to court a lot. To testify either for the defense or the prosecution, whichever way it goes. I don't think I've ever, ever, ever gone to court that the irony of me being an expert witness and the judge depending upon my truth, I never get over that. I'm not freaked out, I'm not even uncomfortable, there's just always this little—the irony.

It's almost like, if they really knew who they were . . . [laughs]. I've been real out front with my background all the way along. They all do know. They know from whence I came. So it's not like I can ever get caught up in the secrets of my past, because my past is an open book. I can't get caught in it anymore. All I can do is use it to go forward.

Still, it's just that feeling, that little-bitty feeling that comes in sometimes, oh, if they knew who I really was [laughs], and then I remember that I'm not anymore. It feels strange. I'm often called upon to dress up and go to meetings and do marketing sorts of things, do community sorts of things. I was on the advisory board at the work release center, the advisory board at the juvenile detention center, the Governor's Task Force for a Drug-Free Indiana, local coordinating councils. I was on the local coordinating council in Lawrence County, Greene County, Owen County, and Monroe County.

So in my life, there's been many times when I've had to be at least socially acceptable and in good clothes and that sort of thing. I don't like that, but I do it okay. I attribute my ability to do it okay to my experience at IU, to be honest with you. The mathematics education department adopted me.

It's like a Pygmalion's syndrome. [Laughs.] I think I was an experiment. They knew. I was always honest. Too honest. I was brutally honest. As a matter of fact, I've discovered in later years that that's how I kept people off of me: I'll be so honest that I'll scare you. You won't want to come near me, and then I don't have to deal with any of the rest of it. And they just said, "Come on anyway."

I was there about three years. Those guys just— just—I can't find the words to describe what

---

* Pigeon Hill, on Bloomington's west side, is traditionally the poorest part of town.

happened. They knew—I mean, when I started working there, I would come in in horrible blue jeans and camouflage jackets, and I was like the secretary and administrative assistant and all that. It's like they gradually, gradually, gradually taught me things. And I really do attribute my ability—with what ease I do have to move through those circles, I attribute that to them. Great guys.

CHICO

I been in jail a few times, but I ain't never been in prison.

'Cause you were lucky?

I was lucky. I was lucky. No, take that back, luck don't even come into it. I think the Lord had a hand on me back then. I really do. I spent two tours in 'Nam. I lost some good buddies there [holds back tears]. I've had people get killed on both sides and me not have a scratch on me.

And I still don't know exactly what it all is, but this is all part of it. There's no such thing as luck. I used to think there was, but I don't believe in luck anymore. The Lord's got a plan for each and every one of us, and he gives us a chance to fulfill that plan he has for us. He don't make us do anything, but he gives us the choice. You go two ways, you serve the Lord or you serve the devil. There's no fence-riding, there's no in-between. You're either on one side or the other.

It's like in the Bible, it says, "Be hot or be cold because if you're lukewarm I'll spew you right out of my mouth." That's the way it is. There is no lukewarm. You're either hot or you're cold. You're either for the Lord or you're against him. That's all there is to it. He's a loving God, but

he's a jealous God. He loves us all in spite of ourselves. It's like being in 'Nam, things that happened there.

Since I been riding with the gang, the Unchained—over in Illinois, me and Bugsy, passing candy back and forth on motorcycles. I'd hold a piece of candy out, and he'd ride up beside me and get it. We run sixty-five, seventy miles an hour. We done that all the way to Illinois. Went up there to an ABATE function. On the way back, we's doing the same thing.

Well, I held a piece of candy out. I still don't know whether he hit my handlebars with his hand or his handlebars hit mine. Anyhow, we came together. Like I said, we's riding sixty-five, seventy mile an hour. Of course, he was laying into me and I was laying into him to try to keep the bikes up.

Finally, he cracked the throttle and broke away. When he did, I started going down. I was drifting toward the guardrail. On the other side of that guardrail wasn't nothing but a big old dropoff. I remember the first thing come to mind, I said, "Oh God, all over a piece of candy." And it was just like the bike just set right straight up, and I drifted away from the guardrail. And there was guys behind me said, "Chico, you were down so low on the ground, to the highway, it was just like you could see the meat peeling up off your shoulder." Grizzly, a guy that was riding with us, said, "Man, you must've been strong to pull that bike back up." I said, "Strong? To pull that bike up, I'd've had to put a foot down. I didn't do it. The Lord straightened that bike up."

This conversation took place after we got on down the road a ways at a convenience store, and we got to looking, and I'd been down so low when Bugsy busted away I had his tire prints across the top of my front fender. I was already too low to bring that bike back up. I'd already gone past the point of gravity. I should've been down.

It never really shook me up till after I got back home. I pulled the bike in the shed and walked around there, took rubbing compound and rubbed the tracks right out of the front fender. I stepped up here into the kitchen, and my knees just buckled, and I went down to the floor. All I could do was cry and praise the Lord and thank him. 'Cause the Lord saved my life that day.

RANDY

Do you ever have any survivor guilt, like people talk about from Vietnam?

Well, [pause] yeah, I guess I do have. I look and I know that there's some people that do make it and there's some people that don't. I don't know, I quit trying to figure that out a long time ago.

You hear all the time, Well, God must have something in mind. And I know that God had something in mind for me. And he still does. And I think that that's pretty much the bottom line. I just think some people are stronger than others. Or God has, I don't know . . .

So this is God's way. It's God's thing, which is not man's way. We just can't understand that.

SHALOM

I was coming out of a pretty abusive sort of relationship. I knew that week before I left* that that was not gonna work out at all.

_____
* For Eagle Mountain.

He didn't hit me, but one night my son—and this was when it was over—one night my son was in his bedroom with Randy's guitar, which is a heavy electric guitar, and was about yea far from coming out to hit Larry* in the head with it because he knew that Larry was getting ready to hit me. It didn't happen.

I knew I had to go. He did not ask me not to go. He did not really want to be really around me at all. What he really wanted was my paycheck. He never contributed in any way financially to the household at all. He finally got a job, gave me two hundred dollars, which is like a portion of his first week's pay. They held out federal and all that. And I never saw another penny from him at all, period. So all he really cared about from me was money, and the least he could see of me the better off that was.

His parting words to me were would I go buy him cigarettes—which I preferred were never smoked in the house and they always were—and would I go buy him coffee before I left? He was trying to put a hitch on my truck, and I thought, Well, this is cool, he's being helpful. And then he gave me a nice, official, written-out bill for thirty-six dollars.

So I feel like I know that marriage is not disposable. I know that. And I've really gone through a lot of self-examination. When I went to Texas, I was pretty sure we were getting divorced. I at least knew that we weren't going to be living together. I was not going to live like that. I fought too long and too hard to have freedom in my life. I mean true inner freedom. I'm not gonna be afraid in my own house.

The man drank on our wedding day, which became my secret as well as his because I never told

_____
* Her husband from a brief marriage before Gabby, not Larry Mitchell.

anybody. Sometimes I laugh and say, "If I'm gonna be involved in a drunken mess, it's gonna be because I'm drinking." I'm not gonna fight as hard as I fought for as long as I fought to be clean and sober just to live in that. Although I don't want to pretend that he drank everyday. He didn't.

There's a difference between being dry and being sober. They talk about white-knuckle sobriety, where you're just, ggnnrrr—you're just miserable. Through working a program, self-investigation, and some trust, just getting better, you know, a certain amount of serenity and peace, goes along with sobriety. He didn't have that at all. What he had was just an awful lot of anger and meanness. Just plain meanness. So I just knew I wasn't gonna live like that. I thought when I went to Texas that I would probably live alone the rest of my life.

RANDY

We got to talking about it, and I said, "I'm just going to go ahead and start another group," so we started the Freedom Riders. And there's eleven, twelve, thirteen, fourteen now, something like that—I don't know—people in it. It's going pretty good, but there again, here we go, we got people involved, and there's problems going on. But I guess there always will be that.

PASTOR LARRY

How do you feel when people leave the church? I'm thinking of Chico, he's going to a different church now, the Freedom Riders splitting off from the gang. What does that do to you?

Makes me sad, makes me sick. I know there's been people that's left here in the will of God,

but there's been a lot of people that's left here that's been out of the will of God. What do you do? You can't keep 'em. I can't put chains on 'em. I can't shackle 'em. I just go ahead and try to love 'em. Just like Chico, we've known each other all of our life. I know his heart's here. His wife didn't want to be here. Her mom and sister goes to the Life church. I'm glad he's still in church. I'm glad he's walking.

God'll use him. God is using him. But it would've been nice if he'd stayed. I know that a lot of churches, a lot of people like Chico and the gang—the leather and all that stuff, blue jeans—they don't want to project that image from their churches. So it's gonna be a little bit tougher.

What about the Freedom Riders?

That whole thing is rebellion. That whole thing is rebellion. God's not in it at all. It's a stench in God's nostrils, and he's just about ready to slam the book on it.

Randy left here mad. He left here just really upset, really mad. He needs to obey God. He needs to humble himself. He needs to get pride out of the picture. All he's trying to do now is compete with the Unchained Gang. He thinks that we're legalist because we are accountable, we are responsible for one another. We want a ministry.

It's like I told Shalom the other day, I said, "I came from being a hardcore biker, and whenever somebody comes into the Kingdom of God and really gets saved, man, I mean I'm just busting buttons. I mean I think it's wonderful." I mean, we're in the business of making Christians out of bikers not bikers out of Christians.

So when people are out here living in sin, in the name of freedom, in the name of God, wearing a Christian patch, people out here on the sidewalk, they're not reading our patches. I mean they're not differentiating Freedom Riders from the Unchained Gang. Plus, they went off and made their rockers the same as ours.

So here they are out there—I'm not even wearing my patch. I told her, I said, "I'm ashamed to even wear my patch. Because I'm afraid that people will think that I'm one of them." Because people knows that they're, half of 'em's living in sin. God's not gonna bless that. He's not gonna bless that.

The new age movement is so strong today, and it's trying to suck Christians down in there. You can love—I mean, new age is just starting in the '60s. You know, if you can't be with the one you love, love the one you're with. And it's in the name of love.

And we ought to love one another. That's God's principal, too. But if you don't have truth, it ain't real love. It ain't. And that's what I preached to them. You got to have truth first. Truth is your foundation. Then you pile love on top of that. And it's got to be that way.

You can't, in the name of freedom and in the name of God—we're not free to sin, we're free to overcome sin. We're free to be triumphant and to have power. Randy's encouraging these babies that hasn't got—they're on a pacifier, and he's patting them on the back in the name of freedom. He's calling us legalists, saying that we're legalistic. Well, if holiness is legalistic, so be it. But we're not.

People can come in here and tell that we're not legalist at all. You can't give people the license to sin. And he's gonna be held responsible. The Bible says, "If you offend"—Jesus was doing the talking—he said, "If you offend one of these little ones"—and he's talking about a little convert, a little child—he said, "If you offend one of

these, it would have been better that a millstone would have been wrapped around your neck and you'd have been cast in the bottom of the sea." Now, that's pretty strong words for Jesus.

And that's where Randy's at. And I've begged him. I've begged him. He's heading for a world of hurt. And God loves him, but the wages of sin is death. And I hate it. You know, what do you do? And that's where I'm at as a pastor, loving these people, trying—you know, you see these people birthed into the Kingdom of God, then all of a sudden, down the pike, you see the devil get his stinking fingers in here and work around people. Pride gets in the way, and then you see things happen, and you just—but we go on. The survivors will go ahead.

The Unchained Gang's went through a tough year, but I'm encouraged again, and we'll be here when they're not. We'll be around, because we've been through this stuff before. 'Cause our foundation's in truth.

You talk a lot about these being the final days. What do you see as the signs that indicate to you that these are the final days?

The main thing, Jesus said, "No man will know the day or the hour." We know that. A lot of people try to pinpoint it as far as dates and stuff, but the biggest thing, the biggest thing is, is that he says, "As you see the budding of the fig tree"—'course the fig tree's Israel—keep your eyes on Israel. Of course, we know that Israel became a nation in 1948, and that's the budding of the fig tree.

We've been in the last days. 'Course they preached it in the New Testament. And Paul was talking about it. So these last two thousand years, from Christ till now, have been the last days, but now we're seeing the budding of the fig tree. We're seeing the dry bones of Ezekiel take place, where all the Jews from all over the earth have just got this drawing back to Israel. We see Israel coming together again.

The Egyptians, the Arab nation, found out that Israel is a power to be reckoned with [laughs] because over the, what was it? The Seven-Day War? Six- or Seven-Day War, I can't remember how many days, but there wasn't even a war to it. It was about like us fighting the Gulf War. I mean it was over. Boom. God just closed the book on that one.

So that's what we're watching. And we're watching now, gosh, the ten toes of Nebuchadnezzar's dream. The dream of Nebuchadnezzar and Daniel interpreting that dream. We're seeing the European Common Market come together as the ten toes, the final empire, the kingdom that will rule the one world government. 'Course that's all that Bush talked about in the Gulf War, is the one world government. And they're hoping that'll be in place by the year 2000.

So here we got the European Common Market, we got—oh, I'm trying to think of what organization stood up, and they said, "Whether it be man or a demon, we want somebody to rise up now and take his place."

Where was this?

I'm trying to think who made that statement. I've got it written down.

Take whose place?

It's the Antichrist. They're wanting a man to rise up now and take his place.

And so, with the formation, with the—giving away the Golan Heights and other strategic places, Israel's left herself kind of exposed, and she's gonna have to make a treaty with some-

body. Whenever Russia or whoever it is, is gonna come down their throat. It's still pretty much in prophecy that Russia's gonna be the one.

You keep up with all this through the newspaper?

I used to, but I'm just—Whenever I got saved, that's one of those fifteen books. I got really big into prophecy. I studied it and had tapes on it. Then after a while, I got to thinking. I don't know, God just changed me on it. Just said, "Get out there and get souls. Get out there and get people in the Kingdom. Don't worry about this stuff."

So, I really felt good about that. So now, as a pastor, we're talking about it and teaching it, so now I've got to get back into this again, try to get my head on straight so that we can get all this stuff sorted out as nearest we can.

Does the millennium play a factor?

Yeah. I believe it. That's the revelation of Jesus Christ. He's gonna come back, and that was part of Nebuchadnezzar's dream, too, and Daniel's interpretation of that dream, that finally, that we know the Battle of Armageddon's gonna take place. Jesus is gonna come back, and he's gonna wipe 'em all out. He's gonna set up his kingdom that will be forever.

And that'll be around the year 2000?

By all points. That's what our calendar is dictating to us.

*This might sound kind of off the wall, but what's your take on the comet people in California?**

I talked about that a little bit Sunday, and that's just so crazy.

---

* This interview took place shortly after the Heaven's Gate mass suicide.

Do you think that is an indicator of anything?

Yeah, it says that one of the signs in the last days, we're gonna see stuff in the heavens. We're gonna see different things. I believe that the landing on the moon and all the spaceships and the airplanes, I believe it all stands for something. But Jesus, he warned us four times in Matthew 24: Don't be deceived, even when many man says, Lo, here is Christ or there is Christ, don't be runnin' off. Don't be goin'—you keep your eye on the fig tree.

So the people in California who killed themselves were all deceived?

Yeah, it was just nothing. They were all deceived. Jim Jones, the same way. I've met people that got saved under Jim Jones's ministry, when he was preaching the truth. But he left the church, just like Randy.

CHICO

Becky helps me all the time. There's a Scripture or something, we can sit down and we can discuss it, what it means to us, to each other. She's helped me a lot. She's helped me a whole lot.

We're going through a rough time right now, Becky, that is. Found out she's got colon cancer. She just got a phone call today from the doctor to tell us that it had spread. It was in her uterus, and it had spread to the lymph nodes.

We're going with that right now, but that's a lie from the devil. We're just standing against it. It's not true. 'Cause the Lord's gonna—no, the Lord has healed her. She just hasn't received verification of it yet, but the Lord has already healed her.

We'll wait until we see the surgeon tomorrow, and then we're supposed to go in and talk to one of the other doctors Thursday. They said they want to get her in just as soon as they can to the hospital.

Everything's gonna be alright. The Lord's not going to take her from me. We've got too much work to do. We got too much to do.

Like what?

There's a lot more souls out there to lead to the Lord. We got a ministry of our own to take care of. We got kids to feed on Kirkwood. We got too many things to do. The Lord's not going to leave either one of us here by ourselves. We're going to do it together.

You keep praying all the time, gotta keep that faith. I was at a church Sunday night, and they was an evangelist there, over in Unionville. The preacher there had told him about what was going on with Becky and I. They were calling up people to be prayed for, and he asked me to come up. I went up, and he said, "We're gonna pray for Becky's healing," and I said, "No you're not."

He looked at me kind of funny and said "Huh?" I said, "You're not going to pray for her healing. She's already been healed. I'm not gonna slack off from that, back off from that a bit. I'm saying she's already being healed, and I'm standing on the Lord's word. Anything that we speak, we speak into happening. The Lord tells us that."

He looked at me, and he kind of grinned, and he said, "Yeah," he said, "I'll go with that one." He said, "That's the way you ought to pray. That's right."

Later, talking in the truck . . .

She said something the other day that just blew me away. She said, "Either way I win. If they operate and the Lord heals me, I win. If he calls me home, I'm done with all this junk, and I win."

I set on the couch for a minute. Then I just had to go into the bathroom, lock the door, and set down. And I just bawled. I said, "Lord, I know this is selfish of me but don't take her away from me. Lord, don't take her away from me."

RANDY

Larry and some of the people over at the House of Prayer thought that we were blatantly living in sin and there was a lot of things going on anti-word, anti-biblical, anti-Jesus. I'm not saying—we was dealing with problems. We dealt with some adultery in our midst, and we dealt with some different things. And that's why I went over to talk to Larry. I said, "We're dealing with it just like you do. We're handling it. We're dealing with it." And I think he got peace over that. I went over and talked to him, and I think it's kind of set his mind that we weren't just playing a game, we weren't smearing the Lord's name. Because Jesus is on our back, just like it is theirs. It's on our patch. I don't want it to shame. That's really what it came down to.

So I think that's pretty much taken care of, hopefully. It is on our part. There for a while we was bad-mouthing them, they's bad-mouthing us, and it was ridiculous. At the same time this stuff's coming out of your mouth you know that it shouldn't be coming out.

It's just a lot better. Matter of fact, tomorrow night at the House of Prayer, they have the blessing of the bikes, and I'm gonna be going to that.

SHALOM

Before I had come up to the church, the closest experience I'd ever had to this sort of a group was Narcotics Anonymous, which a close friend was in. There, personal responsibility is such a big issue. It is in the Unchained Gang and Christianity, too, but I was, at first, struck when I started spending time with everybody—I don't want to say this the wrong way, but what at that time I perceived as an evasion of personal responsibility, of handing responsibility up to God, people not acknowledging responsibility for the actions that they had taken, doing violence to other people, and so on. And I think it was you who said something that really made me understand that in a different context, which was saying that without God forgiving you, you couldn't have forgiven yourself enough to move on.

In a lot of areas of my life, I think of things in the Christian way and then I compare it over to the therapeutic way, which sometimes is a Christian way, sometimes not. But it's like two separate programs that can come together. I think about the authority that we have to be under and how most of us buck authority. To hand things up to God can be a complete cop-out. Because God gives us the ability to make a decision, and we're supposed to be responsible, we're supposed to be models, we're supposed to be witnesses, we're supposed to demonstrate him.

We can't just say, "Well, the devil made me do it," or "Hey, don't talk to me, talk to God." [Laughs.] Addicts tend to say, ten years after they're clean and sober, "Hey, you knew I was an addict when you picked me up." What's that about? Take some responsibility in your life.

I see those as being very closely alike. The forgiveness of something—I told you a little bit of what my life's been like. If you've been drug-addicted, if you've been in the "real" biker world, and possibly just been a whatever-normal-might-be kind of person, you don't come to to-day without having something in your past that you need forgiveness for. Unless you have no conscience, no morals, no standards. There's something in your past that you come to terms with, that you need to deal with and not carry around any more. It's old baggage.

RANDY

I think it's the same thing about with anything: If you can identify with it, if you're on the road of recovery and you see somebody gomming up the way you did, there's compassion involved there. But it's got to be the Lord, man, 'cause I tell you, Satan's got ahold of this world, man. He's got ahold of this world. And it's got to be the Lord's strength, 'cause I ain't got it to fight that chump. None of us do.

CHICO

I don't care about remembering a lot of the stuff that happened when I was in Vietnam. There's a lot of it I remember that I wish I didn't. I tell you what, if I could be remembered for any-thing, I think I would just like for people to re-member me as a man of God, a Christian, some-body that the Lord used. That's it right there, just to be remembered that I loved the Lord and that I walked with the Lord.

People say that I helped lead some people to the Lord. And I think that's an accomplishment that's above and beyond all others, because that's

what it's all about. If I do things that please the Lord, then that's all I want to do. That's all I want to do.

You don't feel that way about the army?

No. I learned a lot while I was there. But all I saw was death and destruction. I don't see any glory in that. Look at all the lives that were lost. And what did we get? No, I want to be remem-bered as a man that walked with the Lord, that loved the Lord. That's it.

POSTSCRIPT

During my time with the Unchained Gang, friends and acquaintances who had been curious about the group took the opportunity to ask about them. One of the most frequently asked questions was, "Are they crazy?" The gang's answer to that is, of course, "Yep! Crazy for Jesus!" Another question to consider is, Are crazy people entitled to believe in God?

Years ago I asked a therapist friend to explain the difference between psychotic and neurotic. He gave me a thorough and clinical definition of psychosis having to do with the truly profound gap between the internal personal reality and a larger consensual social reality.

And what about neurotic? "That's you and me, babe," he told me, trying to make sense of a world that doesn't make sense. How do you make sense of your grandfather getting you drunk at the age of three? Or turning twenty in a POW camp? Or coming home to find your parents giving away your belongings a week before your wife remarries because everyone who knows you thinks you're dead? Or the death of a child? Or the death of a parent? Or how do you try to make sense of surviving when everyone around you, on the streets, in the jungle, on the highway, died?

Christian bikers, for all of their controversial beliefs, dramatic worship, and uncommon aesthetics, are searching for fulfillment of the most basic human needs: love, structure, and spirituality, the same as anyone else. These are things that give meaning to a life.

AFTERWORD

Colleen McDannell

In Rich Remsberg's introduction to *Riders for God*, he writes that the Ellettsville House of Prayer, the church that most of the Unchained Gang attend, "has the hallmarks of a Pentecostal church." Later in the interviews Remsberg pushes Pastor Larry to try to place the church within a specific tradition: "There's a lot of terms," Remsberg says with a certain air of exasperation, "Pentecostal, fundamentalist, born-again, charismatic, full gospel, Spirit-filled, evangelical." Pastor Larry tries to explain the differences between the terms, but it seems that his heart isn't into clarifying definitions. "We're a church out of the Book of Acts," he finally concludes. Pastor Larry and the members of the Unchained Gang are so intimately involved with their faith that they have little interest in sorting out where their community lies within the larger world of Christianity. By situating the Unchained Gang within American religious history, however, outsiders can better understand the values, beliefs, and practices of these Christians.

Sociologists of religion have noticed that religions vacillate between periods of intense fervor and calmer, more routinized, moments. The fire, the enthusiasm, that motivate religious innovation must periodically be rekindled. Reform movements within Christianity, from the earliest Gnostic communities of the Middle East to the most recent incarnations of Fundamentalism, seek to recapture a lost, "true" Christianity.

Sometimes these reform movements come from within the educated classes. More often, they bubble up from the grass roots and involve people not normally considered religious "experts"—women, the poor, and the uneducated. When these people become involved in renovating an established religious system, they often express renewed faith through vibrant rituals and heroic statements of commitment.

Three reforming trends within Christianity are evident in the religion of the Unchained Gang. First, on a very basic level, Pastor Larry, Chico, Randy, and Nancy are all children of the Protestant Reformation. As with Martin Luther, they hold that one must have a personal, intimate, and intense relationship with Jesus in order to realize salvation. Second, the faith of the Unchained Gang reflects the innovations of early-twentieth-century Fundamentalism and Pentecostalism. In contrast with liberal Protestantism, these Christians assert the reality of the supernatural, the importance of experiencing the divine through the body, the bifurcation of reality into good and evil, and the imminent Second Coming. Third, the Unchained Gang has adopted much of the spirit of the Jesus movement of the 1970s. They are a small part of a diverse Protestant subculture that includes Christian elementary schools, Christian psychotherapists, and Christian rock music. Unlike earlier fundamentalists and Pentecostal Christians who rejected consumer culture, Christians seek to modify mass culture to fit their religious needs.

Early in *Riders for God,* Pastor Larry describes a vision that changed his life. He was in a bad state: His life had been threatened, drugs and alcohol were ruining his health and making him paranoid, and a good buddy had just died of a stroke from using too much marijuana. On January 28 he couldn't sleep: "I was in there on my back," he recalls, "and I had a vision. God gave me this vision." In the vision was a huge set of scales. On the one on the left was Larry's life of drugs, alcohol, gangs, and death. On the right scale was Larry's life with God, which included peace, joy, and eternal life. "And when the scale dropped," he explains, "it was like all of a sudden my whole thinking was different. It was like everything had ahold of me for years of my life had to turn loose for a while."

When Pastor Larry observes that "all of a sudden my whole thinking was different" because God had reached out and touched his life, he echoes the attitudes of the sixteenth-century Protestant Reformation. For both the Protestant reformer and Pastor Larry, people are powerless to move from a state of death (sin) to a state of life (grace). Martin Luther argued that neither receiving the Catholic sacraments nor upholding doctrinal truth can mend the split between people and God. Only God's direct intervention can still the anxiety we feel deep within our souls. "I knew that my life was being destroyed," preaches Pastor Larry in his sermon "Valley of Decision." "And it seemed like that I was on the highway to Hell. . . . My accelerator was stuck. There was no brakes on the vehicle and seemed like I just couldn't stop. I was out of control. But I thank God for his mercy, that he got me stopped. He got me stopped." Although the terrors that plagued sixteenth-century Christians were cer-

tainly different from those that attack Chico, Randy, Nancy, and Shalom, these people all recognize that salvation can occur only through God's mercy and individual faith.

Narrating this shift in thinking, this personal experience of conversion, is a major aspect of Protestant religious life. In their diaries, Puritans agonized over the state of their souls; at camp meetings, nineteenth-century revivalists preached the need for a new birth. Likewise, much of the power in *Riders for God* resides in the stories of men and women transforming lives of pain, anger, fear, and violence into lives filled with hope, healing, and faith. Conversion narratives, whether told by new members or remembered by the well-established faithful, help keep the Christian faith real and maintain the intensity of belief. Although members insist that one should not dwell on past failings because God has forgiven all, they use the memories of their painful past lives as evidence of God's saving presence.

If faith is to retain its spiritual intensity, then Christians must devise strategies to keep it "on the edge." Religion easily becomes routinized when it associates with the comforts of home, the security of government, and the pleasures of entertainment. The stories of the Unchained Gang are stories of extremes—of violence, of addiction, of death, and of rebirth into a life with Jesus. Their recitation of conversion stories, ventures into prisons and free-for-all biker meets, and attendance at revival meetings continue the desire of many American Protestants to imbue religion with a hard, gritty intensity. In the past, Protestants argued with slave-holders, witnessed to streetwise prostitutes, fought to close saloons, and traveled to far-away lands to spread the Christian message. Protestants entered dangerous or unfamiliar situations because they wanted to bring the message of Jesus to all people *and* because it was in these situations that their own faith would be tested and hardened. Keeping "on fire for Jesus," although not an easy task, is essential for maintaining the Protestant spirit of personal faith.

Throughout much of Christian history, the power of religion has been experienced by what people perceive to be direct contact with the supernatural. By the beginning of the twentieth century, however, many of the educated in Europe and America were questioning the desire—and even the ability—of God to break through into the world and assert his will in everyday life. Modernist Protestants who increasingly controlled the seminaries, ran the government, and established the colleges, stressed the ethical dimensions of the Bible and preferred scientific explanations for nature. In response to the demystifying tendencies of these Protestants came a reformation by fundamentalists. Fundamentalists preached the reality of the supernatural and rejected the modernist acceptance of biblical criticism, changing gender roles, situational ethics, and American consumer culture.

The Unchained Gang shares many traits with those reformers we now call fundamentalist and Pentecostal Protestants. Christian bikers, for instance, have visions and dreams that help them understand the present and predict the future. For them, the devil and demons are not merely symbols of psychological states but real entities that manipulate and intimidate people. God is praised in unknown languages, not only in church but also riding along the highway. Gang members "know" things before they happen, and they listen to prophetic messages given to them by other gifted Christians. Horrible accidents are avoided through the specific and intimate involvement of God. This is not to say that the Unchained Gang rejects modern technology or

psychology. Like many contemporary Christians, they see the world as a whole piece of cloth, with sophisticated medical techniques as much of God as faith healing. The miraculous can and does break into modern life.

As early as 1801 at the revivals in Cane Ridge, Kentucky, people shrieked, cried, danced, and fell into trances when they felt the power of the Holy Spirit. By the mid-nineteenth century, some Protestants argued that only a second experience after conversion, called "sanctification," would eradicate a deep-seated sinfulness in humans. Other believers in the 1880s and 1890s taught that Jesus through his atonement had made physical as well as spiritual healing possible. As the twentieth century arrived, people flocked to churches named "fire-baptized," "holiness," or "Pentecostal." As in fundamentalist churches, they heard the Bible preached with clarity and enthusiasm. In addition, however, Spirit-filled Christians praised God in strange languages, predicted the future, cast out devils, and healed the sick by touch, as the disciples had done following the resurrection of Jesus. Singing hymns and accompanied by drums and guitars, Pentecostal Christians witnessed New Testament miracles in modern times.

Early-twentieth-century Pentecostal and holiness congregations continued the traditions of Methodists and Baptists by prohibiting drinking, dancing, and even movie-going. Women were not to wear makeup, short skirts, or flashy jewelry. These were "the legalistic Pentecostal churches" that Pastor Larry knew of from his childhood. As more and more Americans spent their leisure time in such idle pursuits, members of conservative Protestant congregations stood out even more on the cultural landscape. Legalistic Pentecostal churches drew sharp boundaries between their congregations and much of what was going on in American society.

Pentecostal churches also distinguish themselves from other Protestant congregations by encouraging members to experience Jesus' saving grace through their bodies. For them, piety may be expressed through quiet reflection, but more often it comes through motion, touching, hearing, feeling, and seeing. When Chico accepted Christ, he "got numb from the top of my head to the bottom of my feet." By the time he got up from the altar, his shirt and pants were "wringing wet from sweat." When Mary experienced the power of prayer, "I felt this cool little puff of air . . . and the next thing I knew I was over backwards and there was nobody to catch me." Men hug, cry, and touch each other, freed from the threat of being labeled queer. Rich Remsberg's photographs dramatically illustrate the physical and sensual nature of the Unchained Gang's faith. Hands, fingers, and arms that are painted, ringed, and tattooed fill the photographs. Bodies are portrayed in every conceivable shape: mutilated, obese, bulked-out, pierced, and bare. And they are in constant motion. Bodies lay on the floor, hug, hold back tears, and grasp. It is through the immediacy of the body that these Spirit-filled Christians experience the divine.

The intensity of the bodily experiences of the Unchained Gang is matched by the intensity of their convictions. Throughout *Riders for God* we are presented a binary world of lost versus found, life versus death, Heaven versus Hell, and alcoholic versus clean. Like other fundamentalist and Pentecostal Protestants, the Unchained Gang knows that God has created an orderly world full of meaning. It is Satan who makes the world appear to be disordered, lacking in rules, and having no absolutes. People need to choose either good or evil; there are no shades of gray. "You go two ways, you serve the Lord or you serve the devil," Chico explains, "There's no fence-

riding, there's no in-between. You're either on one side or the other." Even in the afterlife, there is no middle ground. In "The Valley of Decision," Pastor Larry remembers that when Porky was killed, Randy wanted to pray for him. "You know, a lot of people believe that there's an in-between place, that there's this place called Purgatory. You'll not find it in your Bible," he preaches, "Porky already made his decision. And he made his decision by not accepting Jesus Christ into his heart and into his life." Pastor Larry, as with other fundamentalists, takes his Bible seriously: "Then shall he say also unto them on the left hand, 'Depart from me, ye cursed, into everlasting fire, prepared for the devil and his angels.'"

Pentecostal and fundamentalist Protestants use military rhetoric to describe both the intensity of their personal struggles and the cosmic battles that will be fought at the end of time. Taking their clues from the Book of Revelation, they feel that in the last days Jesus will return to "rapture" believers away from the world. Those left will undergo a terrible tribulation and then become the subjects of the Antichrist. A final battle will take place at Armageddon, and, as Pastor Larry puts it, "there's gonna be a lot of blood spilled there." Satan will be defeated, and the millennium will begin. Fundamentalist Protestants and Pastor Larry feel that these battles will begin very soon. "We are at the end of the age," he reflects in his sermon, "standing at the threshold of the tribulation period, and many, many people are still standing in the valley of decision, not able to make up their minds." By focusing on the violence of the last days, when "blood and dead bodies [are] stacked up to the bridle of a horse," the Unchained Gang joins other fundamentalist Christians who anxiously await the Second Coming.

Fundamentalism and Pentecostalism were reform movements within American Protestantism. In the 1970s, those conservative traditions themselves experienced a spiritual renewal. Young people, influenced by the counterculture of the 1960s, sought to encounter the reality of Jesus outside of an institutional church structure. Like the Unchained Gang, many of them had been involved in drugs and lived a meaningless existence on the streets. When these "Jesus freaks" discovered God, they knew that he demanded more from them than an hour each Sunday morning. They understood their conversions to entail the total realignment of their lives. For Jesus movement reformers, Christianity was not merely a private set of beliefs orchestrated by an institutional church. Christianity needed to be integrated into every aspect of living.

The Jesus movement involved more than transforming hippies into Christians. It caused the blossoming of a Christian subculture. Jesus freaks opened Christian bookstores. They invented Christian slogans and started companies that put those slogans on jewelry, T-shirts, coffee mugs, and posters. As they married and had children, they pulled those children out of public schools and began private Christian academies. When they wanted to vacation, they went on Christian cruises. When they became depressed, they went to Christian therapists. Unlike Pastor Larry's legalistic Pentecostals, these Christians did not flee from modern culture. They decided to make their own movies, start their own schools, and vote for their own political candidates. Although they made few theological innovations, they significantly renovated conservative Christian culture.

When Pastor Larry refers to "the granola Christians . . . the fruits, flakes, and the nuts," he probably has "hyped-up" Jesus freaks in mind. In spite of his gentle ridicule, it is clear that the Jesus movement has influenced the Unchained Gang. The gang, for instance, promotes Christianity as a lifestyle that encompasses one's whole life. Chico's afterwork schedule of witnessing leaves little time for much else: "Monday nights I'm usually at the Monroe County Jail. Tuesday nights at the juvenile treatment center talking to the kids there. Every other Wednesday night I'll be at the Indiana State Farm. We have church services there." Although Protestants have always had a material culture, the distinctive Christian T-shirts, patches, and pins that the gang wears originated with the Christian counterculture. Jesus freaks made it acceptable to take the signs and "stuff" of American pop culture and transform them into religious sentiments. The slogan "100 Percent for Jesus" and the fact that the phrase was put on a patch illustrate the Unchained Gang's active participation in contemporary Christian subculture.

The Jesus movement drew heavily from the youth movements of the 1960s, just as the Unchained Gang continues to draw from their experiences as renegade motorcyclists. Jesus freaks wanted both a faith and a set of symbols that harmonized with the fashion and mood of the times. They wanted their Christianity to be relevant to their lives—either as hippies in the 1970s or as yuppies in the 1980s. Likewise, the Unchained Gang continues to ride Harleys, wear black T-shirts, and grow their hair long. Conversion does not necessitate embracing middle-class standards of grooming and fashion. The Jesus movement created a place for Christians who wanted to continue what they were—bikers, surfers, magicians, airline pilots—but still be "100 Percent for Jesus." Not only did Christians themselves gain a subculture complete with its own material culture, but within that Christian culture there was also a myriad of subcultures.

The Jesus movement is particularly important in American Protestantism because it carved out a space for lay men within the religious environment. Historically, women have dominated American Protestantism. They make up the majority of the people in the pews, fund missionary societies, and staff Sunday schools. Stereotypical female virtues—selflessness, humility, patience, and love—were considered Christian values. By developing a diverse Christian consumer culture, the reformers of the Jesus movement established ministries for men beyond those of preacher or teacher. Men could now start their own bookstores, manage their own Christian music companies, or organize their own Christian lobbying groups. As Christian men entered politics, they reclaimed the battle rhetoric used to describe the Last Days. They no longer had to become women—meek and mild—in order to follow Jesus. They could be Christian warriors where bravery and toughness were necessary and valued.

The Unchained Gang proudly asserts its Christian warrior masculinity. Sparky explains that there are times when after looking at a pretty woman, "I have to get down on my knees and fight like a man." He thought he was tough when he packed a .38 and carried knives, but if "you really want to be tough, you go to the Boogie and tell people about Jesus." Although they have become Christians, the members of the Unchained Gang continue to express their masculinity through violence—only now they fight Satan. In this Christian subculture, women also adopt a heroic stance toward their faith. Mary, for instance, wears a "Prayer Warrior" patch on her black leather jacket. Christianity may still be the religion of love, but it is a tough love. "Now Jesus has got a sword," Pastor Larry cautions his flock.

Rich Remsberg ends his story of the Unchained Gang by writing: "Christian bikers, for all of their controversial beliefs, dramatic worship, and uncommon aesthetics are searching for the most basic human needs: love, structure, and spirituality, the same as anyone else." Indeed, the religion practiced by these Christian bikers is much "the same as anyone else." The Unchained Gang shares many of the same beliefs with Protestants throughout the United States. Their dramatic worship is not substantially different from the Spirit-filled rituals of Pentecostal Christians, and their aesthetics are only a shade darker than those expressed by Jesus freaks of the 1970s. The Unchained Gang is one of the countless Christian subcultures thriving in contemporary America. "We're not just run-of-the-mill Christians," Randy aptly concludes, "whatever that is."

INDEX

Many listings reflect the fact that bikers and their friends and families are referred to by first names in the text. Surnames are included for some, however. The italicized numbers indicate photographs.

RICH REMSBERG is a documentary photographer who lives with his wife, Lisa Nilsson, in Bloomington, Indiana.

COLLEEN McDANNELL is the Sterling M. McMurrin Professor of Religious Studies and a professor of history at the University of Utah.

Typeset in 9.5/15 Galliard

with Gill Sans display

Designed by Copenhaver Cumpston

Composed by Jim Proefrock

at the University of Illinois Press

Printed by Friesens Corporation

on 100# Luna Matte

University of Illinois Press

1325 South Oak Street

Champaign, IL 61820-6903

www.press.uillinois.edu